PROLOGUE

Beginning Within

You know this story. Learned it as a child. Maybe even watched it up close.

But listen as I tell it again, from the inside.

It begins so quietly you cannot hear it and so small you can barely see it. Each monarch egg attached to the underside of a milkweed leaf is the size of a small white period—but that is misleading. This is not a sentence that has ended. Each of these periods marks a possible beginning.

The egg hatches into a larva born of hunger. Eating its way into the world, it devours the shell that held it and then moves on to eat the leaf beneath it. In a matter of days, the larva consumes more and more leaves, voraciously eating its way into visibility as a lengthened, wrinkled appetite, a striped caterpillar determined to grow.

From the beginning, it is accustomed to the losses that growth tallies. Four or five times, the caterpillar sheds its skin like an unwanted, too-small glove. Then, preparing to grow in ways that size cannot measure and skin cannot contain, the caterpillar develops a new shell under its final layer of skin. It turns upside down, practicing a radically new view and spinning from its backend a sturdy silken clasp from which its transformation will be suspended.

One more time, it wriggles and squirms, as the skin that no longer fits splits open and the shell beneath emerges in a different shape. Wide and curvaceous, taut and smooth, the chrysalis is camouflaged to hide the busy workshop inside where already the old is dissolving and the new has not yet taken form.

Here, on the inside, is where I call your attention. Like many mysteries, it happens out of sight. But listen—can you hear it humming?

Protected by the chrysalis, the caterpillar digests itself, releasing enzymes that break down all shape and form—caterpillar legs, eyes, mouth, its whole caterpillar way of being. It becomes a mass of goo, a thick soup cooking up something new. Only a few parts of the caterpillar will not be consumed: latent imaginal discs, a set of highly organized cells embedded from the beginning that contain everything needed for the change that lies ahead.

Imagine. The imaginal discs have been there all along, waiting. Designed to awaken in this breakdown and bring new shapes to the chaos: wing and eye and curled antennae. Like reverse fossils from the future, they are coded for metamorphosis, for emergence when all else has been dissolved and lost. But before they take on form, they begin with a thrumming.

Vibrating at frequencies unknown in the old caterpillar, the imaginal discs multiply rapidly. They cluster according to like resonance, communicating with each other until they grow into a shared knowledge of how to be something new. All have molted the identity of "caterpillar." One cluster becomes an eye, another a wing, another a leg, each tailored to a butterfly's ways, to the butterfly's needs. They take on shapes and functions while linking to one another, their own development dependent on the others', and in that interdependence, they become whole. They become one—a new organism unlike anything that preceded it, ready to emerge, orange and black to ward off attack, fantastically designed for flight and migration across multiple generations, for survival across distance and season.

Can you feel it—the humming in this story that calls to each of us now?
Are you listening to the ancient rhythms resounding in the between,
    old instructions for new arrangements
        beckoning us to ask: who are we becoming?
In the chaos of great change, what imaginal possibilities are waiting
    to awaken—
        in you,
            in me,
                in us,
                    in the world?
Are you willing
to let go of what you now know—
        to become something new?

INTRODUCTION

Living in a Time of Goo

Most likely, you know what it is to live through a time of goo. Quite possibly you have picked up this book because you are in such a time right now. You may be, like me, living in that gap in between, when old familiar ways are dissolving or already long gone but the new ones have not yet taken shape or name. Perhaps, like me, you know what it is to be awash in uncertainty and chaos in your personal life or in the world we share, alive with both fear and excitement, quaking on a cusp replete with endings and beginnings that do not always meet.

What does it mean, as humans, to be metaphorically in a state of goo? For some of us, it may be all we have ever known—having lived with so much at risk every day, year after year, that we know too well that nothing lasts, except perhaps change itself. In the dangerous journeys of immigration, or the exhaustion of chronic illness or the uncertainties of homelessness and poverty, or the daily toll taken by oppressive systems and relationships, we might experience all of life as a continuous state of goo, making it hard to find or to keep our footing. Or, if we have been lucky enough to know some stability and structure, at some point we too will discover that, whether suddenly or slowly, what we thought was solid and dependable can dissolve into a shapeless disarray like the goo inside a chrysalis. It might begin in disbelief as we stand with an unexpected pink slip in hand. Or we might feel it like the loss of solid ground beneath our feet when an important relationship comes to an end—or even when a new one begins. Or it could be a dizzying turn of perspective as an unfamiliar voice on the phone delivers heart-stopping news, maybe of cancer, maybe of cure, perhaps of a prized award we have long wanted or a failure we have long feared. Whether long-term or suddenly occurring, the experience of being awash in chaos, adrift in a state of goo, is more typical of every life than we might want to believe.

An experience of goo can also occur on a larger scale when an organization or congregation, a community or country we belong to pursues a new course. Even if it's a change we value—becoming more equitable and just, more multicultural and antiracist, more inclusive and welcoming—it can create turmoil in the community and in us as we let go of old ways of being often before we know what will replace them. And if the new direction is not one we agree with, the turmoil will be even greater. The tumult of change can rock our lives in many ways.

As I've been writing this book, I have frequently felt tremors of change that have harmed or endangered too many of us: pandemic and insurrection, hate crimes and gun violence, uprisings and crackdowns, climate change and border surveillance. The list is long, and the threats and the quaking they cause are real. Do you feel it too? On so many fronts—locally, organizationally, nationally, and globally—we are *all* living on the threshold of change. Together, we are experiencing great and necessary shifts that can amplify the changes reverberating in our personal lives. Similarly, any personal change we are living through will also increase the impact of the collective turmoil we share. In the reflections and exercises that follow in this book, I encourage you to notice how these different levels of change are related. I also invite you to use your experience of change on one level, whether it is the intimate, communal, or global, to participate in shaping transformations on other levels.

This book suggests that change, with all its gooeyness and trembling vibration, is what life is made of. That the world is meant to change and grow and move. We are being asked to change too. To grow and move with it, listening, learning, living by adapting. Not just being but also, always, becoming.

If only it were that easy. For humans, it is not. Who among us has not resisted change in any of the thousand ways available to us, even when the changes might be in our interest? The caterpillar doesn't question the chaos of the chrysalis. But we humans, with our gift of foresight and the burden of worry often bundled with it, approach change differently. We often try to manage it. We might plan for it and around it. We sometimes build dikes and dams to deny it and walls to fortify ourselves against it. Sometimes even when we want it or need it, we resist it. We balk at it.

"Balk," an old Norse word for a ridge left unplowed by mistake or intention, means a chance not taken that becomes an obstacle. What happens to the fertile, metaphorical land erroneously untilled in a time of great change? It is not just left unplanted, a missed opportunity. It becomes a ridge, a barrier, a hinderance. To balk is to hesitate, but the dictionary does not stop there. It tells us balking also means to thwart, to prevent someone from having something. Sometimes, I would add, it can be ourselves we thwart by balking.

With our uniquely human propensity for foresight and reason, we understand the world is meant to change. And *because* we understand that, in our fear of the unknown, we often do everything we can to deny it or prevent it. We miss the opportunities we are given to plow and plant the most fertile ridges beneath our feet—the holy ground of change.

This book is intended to help us not to balk but instead to *trust* change. To honor its place in the living world and our ability to participate in it, to plant its fertile ridges and work with others to sustainably harvest new possibilities both personal and shared. Not only to survive it but to engage its transformative power for ourselves and the wider world.

Do we really need another book about change, you might well wonder? Many resources already available, including a number listed in the appendices, offer sound advice. What makes *this* book unique and timely is its insistence on three particular principles of threshold living that shape its approach to change:

1. *Change echoes.* When we experience change on a personal level, its disturbances will bounce back from changes happening on shared community or global levels, amplifying any changes we encounter. And vice versa. Rather than becoming overwhelmed by these echoes or shutting them out, we can make use of change on one level to participate in shaping change occurring on other levels. Because the skills needed for healthy participation in global change are directly related to the skills needed for shaping changes in our intimate lives, and the other way around, we can move to the rhythms of change reverberating at any one level and they will support our participation in other levels.

2. *Participating in change is a shared task.* Whether we're talking about individual or collective change, we need the gifts of companioning on the threshold. Just as the imaginal cells in the chrysalis must re-assemble in a larger organism to complete their transformation and emerge as a butterfly, the most transformative changes we face as humans require realignment and relationships of interdependence with others. Many marginalized communities are well attuned to this truth, but dominant white culture has often undermined it. We need others' observations to widen our perspective, their gifts to supplement our

own abilities, and their assistance to help us cross those thresholds that will be too high, too terrifying, or too bewildering to traverse on our own. True interdependence is what makes it possible to trust change.

3. *Change is embodied.* Listening to our bodies' wisdom will unlock a vast storehouse of internal guidance for living well with change. This includes the body's messages of pain as well as its capacities for healing, joy, and resilience. This book's exercises and references to tuning in to our bodies and our dreams remind us to draw upon knowledge that travels with us across even the greatest of transformations. Not coincidentally, our bodies also often help to connect us to others.

In my own life and communities, and in the journeys of others, I have experienced and witnessed the power of engaging these three approaches to change. It is my hope that naming them in this book will issue an invitation not unlike the imaginal clusters' vibrations in the chrysalis, helping us to find our way through the goo toward something beautiful and new, into a larger tale we are all now co-authoring together.

Origins and Influences

This book began in community, while I was facilitating a group of seventeen "thresholders," each in a time of deep change in their own life. They had agreed to meet for two months to accompany and support one another on their thresholds. Among the participants' named passages were changes related to illness, disability, depression, and the death of a loved one. Other passages were more joyful but sometimes equally frightening, such as newly chosen vocations, relationships, habits, or housing. All were opportunities to turn toward change instead of away from it and to listen to their own deep questions without grasping for the quickest answers. Together, we were living in the between, and learning how to do it well.

Then, midway through the two months of our meetings, in the span of a single week my father went into hospice and I was diagnosed with breast cancer. My world turned upside down and the work I was facilitating among others became keenly personal to me.

In the wild emotional ride that followed, I learned my own lessons about threshold losses. How the pain they carry can come like a lightning strike or with a slow, spreading ache. How it travels across time, awakening old losses long past. How new injuries, including emotional ones, can be experienced in specific sites in the body, inflaming old wounds and confusing our search for the best balm to soothe our pain. When the call came from my sister two days after I'd said my own goodbyes to my father, I was expecting the news of his death, but I was not prepared for how it landed in my body. It came with a sharp blow to the exact spot in my breast that had been punched by a biopsy needle two weeks earlier, the pain specific, piercing, and real.

Over the next few weeks, I attended my father's memorial service and underwent a mastectomy and two emergency follow-up surgeries. While recovering, the news from world events added more layers of pain. In Baltimore, Freddie Gray died in the hands of the police. That same day, a ship carrying 850 migrants seeking safety in Europe sank in the Mediterranean, leaving most of its passengers dead at sea. I felt each news story as if it were one more incision, one more blow to my reverberating heart. Recuperating at home, I received a text from a friend: "Please let me know if you need company, rides, reading material, love, or world peace."

"All of the above," I texted back.

It was during my recovery that I decided to write a guide for living on thresholds both personal and shared. A book that would invite us to learn from our bodies, both their resiliency and the messages of pain they carry, and to listen for the wisdom within each one of us and the wisdom rising from our communities. To issue a plea for creativity and relationship as together we develop skills for trusting change and finding our way through transformative times.

Writing these pages has helped me to access and learn from my own wisdom and the wisdom of many others. I hope the book invites you to do the same, whether you do it with writing, conversation, painting, singing, walking, dancing, or sitting in silence—or any of the countless ways we humans have of pausing, listening, and participating in creation.

Many frames focus—and limit—my worldview. In addition to being a writer and retreat leader, I am an ordained Unitarian Universalist minister, a mother, wife, sister, daughter, and aunt, using she/her pronouns. As a lifelong upper Midwesterner living now on the homelands of the Dakota and Ojibwe people, the natural thresholds that have most shaped me include the shores and banks of Lake Michigan, Lake Superior, the Mississippi, and countless smaller lakes and rivers, as well as the less exacting borders where fields and forests meet. I am the youngest of four daughters born to two white German American Lutherans, and I grew up in a mostly white community of mostly Christian residents who mostly spoke English. It was not until I left home at seventeen that I realized how insulated my youth had been from the dynamic borders of cultural, religious, and racial difference that I now greatly value. In the decades since then, I have been working to notice and unlearn the dominant culture's messages about privilege and whiteness that shaped me and influence my life still today. It is a task I expect to last the rest of my life.

In adulthood, I have been significantly formed and fed by Unitarian Universalism, a religious tradition without creed that makes room for different understandings of the holy while building a more just and equitable world. We draw from a wide variety of wisdom sources, including scripture from many world religions, poetry, literature and history, nature, science, and personal experience, which is what this book does too. For me, when looking for trustworthy guidance in the midst of uncertainty, I especially depend on poetry, the teachings of Taoism, the practices of tai chi and qigong, and the wide varieties of wisdom offered by contemporaries and their forerunners working to end the grip of systemic racism on our world. Perhaps more basically than any of that, I turn to the natural world itself and the people, experiences, teachings, and other beings that help me live in right relationship with it.

While I have worked on this book, as with my first thresholding group, significant and overwhelming change arrived like a tidal wave, this time as invitations into collective transformation. If ever I had imagined that while I was writing this book about trusting change, the whole world would be turned upside down by a global pandemic and by worldwide outrage and uprisings over the murder of George Floyd and far too many Black Americans before him, I might not have been bold enough to write it. How could any words committed to the printed page remain relevant long enough to speak to a time when our personal lives and global realities are being rewritten nearly every day?

I had asked myself that question well before the pandemic and before George Floyd's murder. Several early readers I had asked for feedback on the book in progress pointed out places where its antioppressive lens still needed work. Since then, I have done my best to expand both the manuscript and my own understanding of these issues. I am enormously grateful for their input, and any mistakes that remain are my own.

Throughout this process of continuous revision, I have tried to follow the book's own advice, especially about letting go (of my attachment to early drafts and to the familiarity of my limited viewpoint);

pausing to learn, both from others and from my own heart; and moving on, widening what I trust to guide me going forward. It meant the book took a lot longer to complete, involved a lot more people, and along the way, changed both me and my creative process. I am deeply grateful for all of this. Skinner House was a committed and flexible thresholding partner in bringing this book to print. My early readers, including those named at the end of the book, were especially important. All of you—and the conversations that rose from your willingness to read, consider, and respond—created a book that more truthfully addresses the way change challenges us to learn and grow and stay in conversation with others, especially when it is hard.

So much is shifting today, and not just from the pandemic and from uprisings against racial violence and oppression. Thanks to the effort and persistence of many change agents around the world, we live in a time when the playbook of privilege is being rewritten. Though it will take generations to arrive in a place of right relationship across our differences, today we are witnessing dramatic if overdue shifts in language, narratives, paradigms, systems, and day-to-day life. For those of us longing to build and nurture the Beloved Community described by Martin Luther King Jr., these changes are welcome. Even so, they also mean that many labors of love are at risk of being outdated by the time they are finished.

I hope we—meaning all of us engaged in the effort to create a more just and equitable world—will not let the pace of change discourage us from creating. Let us instead offer our creative efforts in the spirit of thresholding conversation—an exchange not only between writer and reader but also between the past, present, and future. We can do our best today with the knowledge that those engaging our work in the future will do so with a thresholder's aim of sifting chaff from grain, letting the chaff be blown away while gathering up the nourishing germ that remains.

It is in this spirit that I send the book off to press now, knowing that in a time of rapid and significant change, we cannot afford to wait until we get it right. The threshold skills of letting go and seeking companions call us all into conversation to learn from one another, to keep moving even when we are uncertain, and to open our hearts and minds to the many ways a changing world is meant to change us too.

HOW TO USE THIS BOOK

No one knows better than you how this book might best serve you. You come to its pages with your own unique experiences of living on the threshold and your own resources for dealing with change. By resources, I mean your gifts and abilities, your own wisdom learned and inherited, and your relationships and communities of support.

In addition, each of us also comes with our own habits and challenges related to living through change. Sometimes, our instinctive responses to fear can cut us off from the very same skills and abilities we most need on the threshold. *Fight, flight, freeze, or fawn* are those impulses jump-started in the reptilian parts of our brains when we experience a threat, whether real or perceived. When we're in fight mode, we become defensive or aggressive. In flight mode, we turn and run, which can also look like denial. In freeze mode, we lose the ability to do either, instead becoming immobilized and incapable of making decisions, processing emotions or information, or moving, physically, mentally, or emotionally. And fawn mode is when we move closer to the source of the threat itself, by pleasing or appeasing the person causing it. Each of these instinctive responses is natural and instantaneous and can be critical to survival. All of them precede our rational thinking and create constriction in our bodies and our minds. Our vision literally narrows to focus in on the danger; our thoughts are limited to fewer options. Our blood vessels and muscles squeeze tight with tension. Our state of high alert positions us for aggression, rapid retreat, paralysis, or a submissive approach. But while they can be helpful in facing physical danger, the complex challenges of living with change in the twenty-first century and participating in change with creative agency often require something different.

To be sure, we need the information fear provides to warn us when we are in danger. But our human capacities for relationship, empathy and imagination offer useful options in responding to fear's warnings. It is no surprise that these capacities are often especially well developed in marginalized communities where danger can be frequent or constant. This book includes reflections and embodied practices for overcoming, redirecting, or channeling our instinctive responses to the threat of change itself, equipping us to make use of our times of change for creating greater safety in the long run.

This is an invitation into a fundamentally different relationship with change, personally and collectively. Just as the caterpillar's immune system initially attacks the imaginal cells and their coding for the new, winged form of the butterfly, the old patterns and authorities of the current dominant systems often work like an immune system trying to defeat any movement toward new, more equitable alignments with one another. It will take effort and intention to recognize and override the many messages, beliefs, and habits that protect the status quo with its underlying injustices intact.

When referring to these old authorities and ways of being, I use the word "Overculture," a name credited to Native studies educator Sarah Hutchinson and introduced to me by the poet Gregory Orr and poet and post-trauma specialist Clarissa Pinkola Estés. The Overculture is that dominant and oppressive story that explicitly and implicitly tells us how the world is supposed to be, including who *we* are supposed to be (and not to be). It works overtime, and often out of sight, to keep things just the way they've been before. Its messages preserve the underlying assumption that *It's just the way things are.* Because it does its best work when we don't even notice it is there, simply naming it reduces its influence. This is well known by those of us who have been oppressed by the Overculture, who have learned to recognize its false frames and know how to create and strengthen different narratives as a matter of survival and well-being. But even when we spot the Overculture's messages in the world around us, we might still struggle to be freed of its voice inside us, insidiously undermining our gifts, our wisdom, and even our identities.

Whether we are oppressed or privileged by the Overculture, learning to recognize its messages and influence will be necessary for opening our awareness to a wider range of options as we step into the unknowns of change, either personal or social. If we really wish to make use of threshold dynamics to create the life and world we long for, we need to welcome and foster some of these options that the Overculture tells us to discount:

- opportunities for collaboration and sharing power as alternatives to competition;
- the wide galaxy of identity beyond the binaries of male and female, gay and straight, Black and white, old and young, good and bad;
- the possibilities for a society without racism, patriarchy, able-bodied privilege, or gross income inequalities;
- the many effective nonviolent methods of resistance, social change, and power-sharing;
- our innate ability, personally and collectively, to create a future with a different trajectory from that of our past.

This book will not tell you which options to choose. But it does invite you to consider a wider range of possibilities by noticing the assumptions of the Overculture and reframing them, not as the way things must remain but as one of several options for how things *could* be. This is the gift of fully empowered participation in change: becoming aware of more choices.

It is also a significant challenge. Because it opens more possibilities, it raises the question of how to discern what to choose and what to trust. If this feels overwhelming, I offer some wisdom from my friend Kate Tucker, who learned it from barn owls. Barn owls, she tells me, find their food and prey in the dark, in part by listening in a unique way. One of their ears is positioned higher and tilted downward, while the other is lower and tilted upward, allowing them to correlate the sounds heard in each, in both volume and timing. When the owl's head is positioned so the sound level is equal in both ears, it can triangulate the signals to locate its prey in total darkness within one to two degrees of accuracy both vertically and horizontally.

This seems useful when considering the many unseen elements of threshold living. It is a reminder to get our bearings by metaphorically lifting our attention upward, toward God or Mystery or the higher truth that calls us, by whatever name we know it, while directing other aspects of our attention lower, toward the sacred earth beneath us and the many beings that share it. If we attune ourselves intentionally in this way, repositioning ourselves until the messages from multiple directions—above and below, within us and beyond us—are balanced, we will be facing in line with where we need to go.

Putting this into practice can be as basic as asking two questions. When in the midst of many options or uncertainty, ask yourself, which direction or choice will open me to a deeper relationship with what I regard as holy and true? Then ask, will this choice or direction connect me in a meaningful way to my own being and to the earth and other people and beings on it? The latter question raises different concerns if we are answering from a position of privilege or marginalization (and we all carry multiple identities, which means that many of us experience both privilege and oppression). If you are asking from a place of privilege whether your choice connects you in a meaningful way to others, it will be especially important to discern how your choices connect or disconnect you from those who do not share your privilege and who may be disadvantaged by your choices. But if you are or have been marginalized and oppressed, your discernment might first require *dis*connecting from those who have marginalized or oppressed you so you can notice your own voice and other marginalized voices around you.

When the answers to these questions confirm that your choice will deepen your connection to the holiness within you and beyond you, you are very likely positioned to cross your threshold in a way that will serve you—and the world—reliably and in true relationship with yourself and others.

Chrysalis Space: Checking In as You Go

This is not a book to race through. While reading these pages, do what you can to create "chrysalis space" for noticing your response to what you are reading. Take time regularly to pause and check in with your body, noticing, with curiosity and without judgment: What emotions rise and where? How is your body receiving what you're reading? Is there tension and resistance, or resonance and relief? All of these might be present when we are growing. Wherever possible, cultivate curiosity and kindness, *especially* toward your feelings and your body.

Some of our best guidance and assistance on the threshold comes from our bodies and our dreams, both discounted by the Overculture as less important and even invalid. To lift these sources up, every reflection in the book ends with questions or embodied practices under the heading "Chrysalis Space." These sections invite you to take a moment to reflect, noticing what you are experiencing, feeling, and thinking before you move on in the book.

You might want to start a new journal, recording your thoughts, insights, and responses along the way. Or maybe you prefer to sit with the questions silently or to engage them conversationally with one or more thresholding companions. Draw on whatever ways you most fruitfully turn your attention to particular topics or questions. If you reflect on the questions in writing, you will be able to return to your words in the future in a conversation with yourself over time—often a helpful exchange to have when living through great transitions.

Whatever your chosen methods, it will require intention to engage the reflections and practices in the book as you go along. For instance, if you are reading on the bus while commuting to or from work, don't just read until you arrive at your stop. Put the book down early to reflect while looking out the window for the last five minutes of your ride. Or if you're reading before bed, try to stop reading before you nod off to sleep. Give yourself five to ten minutes of quiet reflection time before turning your light off for the night.

Pausing means really pausing. Not just from all the activities begging for your time on the threshold but also from reading this book as you go along. Give yourself time and space to consider what each of these passages means in your own context, on your thresholds, in your life.

From Beginning to End

Thresholding is rarely a linear passage from the no longer to the not yet. More often, it loops around, weaving back and forth between letting go and moving on and making frequent pauses. In the circuitous journey across your own thresholds, you might wish to move back and forth in this book, reading and engaging with its practices in whatever sequence best meets your needs. But if there is a section you feel resistant to and are tempted to skip altogether, you might not want to leave it behind too quickly. They might be the very pages that will be most useful.

The book offers two important thresholding practices and ten thresholding skills. The following chapter, titled "Beginning Here," introduces the first practice of paying attention as perhaps the most important basis for trusting change. And the book closes with the powerful practice of blessing our passages. In between, it names ten thresholding skills, offering multiple reflections and practices for each skill, organized according to the passage from what is no longer, through a fertile time of pausing in the unknown, and toward what is not yet.

I suggest you start with "Beginning Here" and end with the final chapter, "Honoring the Journey." In between, the ten skills can be taken in the order presented or in any sequence of your choosing. Wherever the reflections and practices build on others that come before them, I have noted if it might be important to read a previous section first.

The opening and closing practices and the ten skills in between are:

BEGINNING HERE

NO LONGER
    1. Letting Go
    2. Grieving
    3. Practicing Equanimity

THE PAUSE
    4. Taking Part in Stillness

A Wider Horizon:
Considering Community and Global Thresholds

You can use this book as a companion on personal, organizational, or global thresholds. Or, better yet, all of the above; the different levels of change are more interrelated than we sometimes acknowledge. I can be so much more sensitive to events in my personal life when also experiencing seismic shifts occurring in my community, nationally, or in the world. Similarly, the upheavals and turmoil of the world or within my community or organization can pack a bigger emotional punch when my heart is already broken open by changes going on in my personal life.

This is not only a matter of sensitivity but also of agency. We can use the potency of a personal threshold to inspire and empower changes we wish to make real on a community or global level. And our work to support change on collective thresholds can similarly invigorate and support change in our personal lives.

The threshold practices and skills named here, and the questions for reflection that follow them, apply equally to our most personal experiences of transformation and the largest scale of changes we face together. It is my observation that opening ourselves to one level of change can be an invitation to participate more fully in other levels. In the midst of personal transformation, it can be helpful to metaphorically "lift our eyes," as the Chinese poet Lu Chi advised almost two millennia ago, to a wider horizon. If you are a person who instinctively or habitually connects your personal experiences to the larger story in which we all live, "lifting the eyes" might be a welcome affirmation that your own thresholds are nested in a wider continuum of change always in progress. If you are a person who more often processes your life's challenges in private, "lifting the eyes" can be a reminder that none of us is alone in dealing with change and an invitation to experience the support and camaraderie of sharing threshold living with others. Even when the particulars of our personal thresholds are entirely unique to us, we are always in the company of others who are also living through shared change on global or community levels.

It's also true that when our personal world is deeply shaken by core losses, we may feel too vulnerable to consider the wider span of global thresholds. To help you choose which levels of change you are ready to consider, the reflections with questions or activities most focused on global shifts are labeled "A Wider Horizon" and positioned as the closing passage in each threshold skill section. If you are reading this book on an especially difficult personal threshold, you might choose your own pace and sequencing for reflecting on personal and global thresholds. However, I do recommend engaging both. It will be important for tapping the transformative power of your personal threshold as well as finding your part in the shared thresholds we are navigating collectively.

THRESHOLDING TOGETHER:
Sharing the Journey

Whether it is personal or collective change that has brought you to this book, I also encourage you to share your thresholding journey and the book's practices with others. Learning to trust change begins with trusting others with the questions that arise on the threshold. It is not that anyone else has the answers you most need. But they may very well have additional questions that can guide you toward answers that may be hidden inside you. The questions and embodied practices offered here are meant for you to engage first on your own. Then, by sharing with others, you can uncover an even greater understanding.

To facilitate that sharing, each chapter ends with a section titled "Thresholding Together" that offers suggestions for starting conversations, or "imaginal clustering," with others. Maybe you pair up with a single thresholding buddy or gather a group of three to six others to meet on a regular basis. If you wish to form a thresholding group to use the book together, an appendix at the back offers suggested group practices and agreements to make that collective approach especially supportive and fruitful. The important thing is to remember that *we are not meant to move through change alone*. We humans have evolved in and for relationship, and the transformative possibilities of our current thresholds will depend on our ability to share the uncertainty and chaos of these times with one another.

BEGINNING HERE

The story of the caterpillar's goo might ring true for many of us meta-phorically, but the chrysalis as an architecture supporting change may be less familiar. A threshold, including the open doorway above it, has more typically served, literally and figuratively, to name our human experience of change and the site where it happens. A threshold is the meeting place between inside and outside, between here and there, between the familiar and the unknown. In my own life transitions, and in programs I lead for others in their times of change, I have followed the poetic tradition of naming these passages *thresholds*, and the ones crossing over them *"thresholders."*

In its most literal definition, a threshold is a strip of wood or stone at the base of a doorway. In many houses, it is a sill intended to keep the mud from washing into the home. In my cold, northern climate, it is also an important barrier to keeping the cold from sweeping into the house in the winter. In China, a threshold might be three or more inches high, keeping the rainwater outside but also encouraging attentiveness and an awareness of the honor of being invited into someone's home.

The word *threshold* also describes the doorway itself and the larger entrance into a building or home. It represents a contact point between interior safety and the outside world. Traditionally, it has been regarded as a site of encounter, risk, and danger. It can be a place of separation, requiring us to leave something, someone, or perhaps even some part of ourselves behind when crossing in either direc-tion. It is a locus of vulnerability where we face the possibilities of transformation, not only in our surroundings but often in identity.

1

On the other side of a threshold, we might be required to do things we've never done before, to face fears we have shunned for years, or to discover new gifts as well as limitations.

Honoring the risks and challenges present on the threshold, many cultures have stories, rituals, blessings and sometimes even deities offering protection and safe passage. In ancient Rome, the god Janus reigned over comings and goings. His image, carved over the gates of Roman cities, showed two faces connected at the back and pointed in opposite directions. With one face looking outward from the city gate and the other looking in, Janus provided protection while reminding those passing in either direction to notice what they were leaving and where they were going. Here, in the pages of this book, I hope you will find protected time for similarly noticing both what you are departing from and where you are headed, whatever the thresholds you are crossing.

Chrysalis Space

What thresholds are you on now that are especially resonant to you? How might you describe them—are they wide or high? Welcoming or frightening? Are you crossing them alone or with others? Are they personal or collective or even global? And are you more inclined to face behind you, toward what you are leaving or before you, toward the place where you're going?

As you begin reading, you might also begin reflecting, perhaps in a new notebook or journal devoted to your thresholds. Take a moment before reading on to name the thresholds, in your personal life, in your community, and in the world that caused you to pick up this book. Are there other thresholds that now occur to you as important in your life today? Name one wish you have as you begin or continue your passage through this time of change.

Paying Attention

The widest physical threshold I have ever crossed in an interior doorway was no simple sill, neatly concealed as the door swung closed over it. This was a beautifully finished piece of pippy oak stretching more than half a foot on either side of the doorway. A gift from the heart of a large tree that grew in England, the wood had been carefully chosen and crafted by artist Ross Peterson. He then sanded it smooth as a riverbed stone and varnished it like a sacred text preserved for reading across generations, a passage written in the cursive script of the tree's grain and punctuated by its large knots.

This threshold marked the entrance from a small hallway into the sanctuary of the Common Ground Meditation Center in Minneapolis, where I was working with a group from the sangha every Monday for ten weeks. For the first few weeks, every time I entered the sanctuary, I approached the threshold with reverent curiosity and took as big a step as my legs allowed to avoid treading on it, shoeless as I was in keeping with the sangha customs. Remembering ancient taboos against walking on a threshold, I thought how curious it was that this one was made so wide as to be almost impossible to straddle. Then I began watching the sangha members enter the room, and I noticed that every one of them stepped right on the threshold without worry, as if it were an arboreal doormat specifically meant for the soles of their stocking-clad feet.

When I asked Mark Nunberg, the founder of the sangha, about this, he smiled at my efforts to cross the sill without stepping on it. It was made wide to *require* that you step on it, he explained with a gleam in his eye. It is meant to make you notice, he said, a reminder to pay attention as you enter the sanctuary for meditation and as you leave after meditation is over.

"The journey of a thousand miles begins with the ground beneath your feet," wrote Lao Tzu two and a half millennia ago. By which I understand him to be saying (along with Mark Nunberg and Ross Peterson), take note of where you are, the first rule of navigation, if you want to know where you are going. And let your body inform you—the soles of your feet, the palms of your hands, your sense of touch, smell, taste, sight, hearing, and your body's ability to convey emotion. All of it can guide us if we stop to notice what our body is saying.

Most fundamentally, thresholds are a call to pause and notice the passage you are making. *Pay attention.* Use all your senses and every bit of intuition stretching beneath and beyond them—and your body's larger emotional wisdom, too. Engage as many sources of guidance as possible when encountering the unknown.

This can be overwhelming, like learning to drive a car and realizing it is not enough to look just one way. As a driver, you need to tend to multiple directions and many streams of information. Only with practice does this keen awareness become possible, manageable, even habitual when you slip behind the wheel to drive.

So, too, when learning to pay attention to our thresholds. It takes practice. We live in a world trying constantly to distract us with appeals to buy, to do, to desire, to improve. We are bombarded by so much information that we have become experts at shutting our senses down. We lather our bodies with scents that hover about us like individual weather systems we carry from one place to another. We wear ear buds that obliterate the sounds of our immediate surroundings. We sip lattes so strong it would be hard to taste the salt of a single tear running down our cheek to the corner of our mouth.

This is not a diatribe against the twenty-first century; it is an observation about contemporary obstacles to paying attention to who we are and where we are in any given moment. If we want to wake up our senses, we may have to begin by bursting the bubble we have carefully made to insulate them.

Perhaps you've experienced this when flying to a distant country. You board an aircraft that looks like any other plane you've been on, except bigger. Maybe the directions for seatbelts and air masks are delivered in an unfamiliar language, hinting that something new has just begun. Maybe the meal choices are more plentiful and varied. But as you make the long flight, hours and hours of it, in the familiar discomfort of that compact, sealed chamber, the triple-paned windows offer your only glimpse at the ground and the miles you are covering.

Then you land and disembark. First into the halls of an airport still possibly temperature controlled; but eventually, with bags in hand, you find yourself outside on the curb, where the exhaust assaults your nose and taxi horns blare and the breeze or the heat or a bracing subzero chill snaps your senses to high alert. It's as if a drill sergeant marched right through you, blowing their shrill whistle and snatching the cozy blankets of familiarity back from every nerve and receptor in your body and brain. You remember, suddenly, this is why you wanted to travel, even as it jolts you into questioning whether you really should have. But there you are: You are alive. You have arrived. You are awake, on the threshold of a new adventure.

Chrysalis Space

What do the soles of your feet tell you about the road that begins here, wherever you are now? What do they read in the ground that supports you, literally or metaphorically? What does your body have to say on this day—do you feel joy, trepidation, tension, caution, excitement, worry, anger, fear? And where do you feel what you feel? Note: we're just noticing without judgment. There are no wrong answers here. What you feel and where you feel it or whether you feel nothing at all—any answer is just something to notice and be curious about.

What do you smell and what does it evoke? Have your taste buds been especially attuned of late to the sweet or the sour, the salty or the bitter? Or do you taste nothing at all? And what do you hear—around you and within you—however you do your best listening? What words have piqued your interest recently, what signing or captions? What sounds or vibrations or sensations: The lilting birdsong announcing the dawn or the cacophony of car horns rebelling against grid lock? The oppressive heat or humidity blanketing you as you sit? The bowing and moaning of trees whipped by the wind or the shining descent of icicles falling from the eaves, shattering on the frozen ground below? If you are writing, list anything that comes to mind as you open your senses and your attention to this moment, and then pause to notice any commonalities—or the striking variety or contrasts—apparent in your list.

Learning to Listen

When I try to wake up my senses, I often begin with listening, not because it is a simple place to start but because it is such a critical one. Physically, we often associate listening with hearing, but I'm referring to listening as a form of attention that does not require the physical ability to hear. Rather, it refers to an attentiveness that does not blink or sleep but continuously gathers information from multiple directions and sources, both for our safety and for our delight.

Because we live in a noisy world, waking up our ability to hear, metaphorically or literally, is not easy. It requires sifting through the chatter all around us and turning *down* the volume on those voices that manipulate our fear and anger and make us defensive and small. Then we can turn *up* the volume on what we need to grow into a wiser way of being, whether it's the song of canaries in a metaphorical coal mine or the melodic music of our larger possibilities. In 1905, Nobel-prize-winning bacteriologist Robert Koch predicted, "The day will come when [people] will have to fight noise as inexorably as cholera and the plague." A century later, perhaps we are in that noisy day.

To become intentional about listening, we learn that it is less dependent on the ears than it is on opening the heart, sometimes to messages and voices we may not want to give our attention. In the thresholding groups I lead every year, we begin by reading these words from writer Brenda Ueland in her essay collection *Strength to Your Sword Arm*:

> *We should all know this: that listening, not talking, is the gifted and great role, and the imaginative role. . . . It will work a small miracle. And perhaps a great one.*
>
> *In order to listen, here are some suggestions: Try to learn tranquility, to live in the present a part of the time every day. Sometimes say to yourself: "Now. What is happening now? This friend is talking. I am quiet. There is endless time. I hear it, every word." Then suddenly you begin to hear not only what people are saying, but also what they are trying to say, and you sense the whole truth about them. And you sense existence, not piecemeal, not this object and that, but as a translucent whole.*
>
> *Then watch your self-assertiveness. And give it up. Remember, it is not enough just to will to listen to people. One must really listen. Only then does the magic begin.*

Some call this "active listening" because it involves actively paying attention to so much more than the spoken words—body language and gesture, tone and volume, emotion and pacing, and silence. It requires quieting our own noisy assumptions about what the person is saying, what we think they should be saying, or even how we might fix their problems or help them. We have to set aside our judgments about who they have been and who they are now to make room for who they are becoming. It depends on our ability to empathize. As the German word for empathy, *einfülung*, makes clear, this means "feeling into" another person so that their experience echoes inside us, allowing us to feel what they're trying to say.

No wonder truly active listening is rare. It's hard work. It requires setting our own egos and agendas aside and opening ourselves to others' feelings. This is also why it's powerful. If you've ever been listened to in this way, you likely won't forget it soon. It may have felt like someone lifted a heavy burden from your shoulders or opened a door into just the kind of room you've longed to linger in. It may have caused you to speak truths you didn't know you knew, but as soon as you heard yourself say them, you realized how much you needed to express them out loud.

Living on the threshold, this is also the kind of listening we need to offer ourselves to uncover the truth and wisdom buried inside us. But because it is so seldom experienced, it can be helpful to first practice offering it to others—and ideally, having them practice it with us—to discover how meaningful it can be and to learn how to go about doing it with ourselves.

Chrysalis Space

What habits do you have that shut your senses down and metaphorically lull them to sleep? What practices might you use to awaken your senses, to listen more carefully to yourself and the world around you, to increase your awareness of the joy and the pain you and others are experiencing? Maybe it's sitting in stillness or silence. Or being in conversation with a trusted friend or mentor.

It might be writing or painting or singing. Or for some, physical movement by vehicle or by body—walking, running, biking, dancing, tai chi— might help us listen to ourselves or others.

Experiment with one practice of awakening your senses. Listening to yourself without judgment or assumptions, what do you learn today? What old truth or new possibility is humming, waiting for your attention? What is sounding in the chambers of your heart now, beckoning you to listen not only for what your heart is saying but also what it is trying to say?

The Body of Love

Our first body knowledge, received in the womb, is one of complete connection. Even after birth, for years our physical, mental, and emotional growth is dependent on intimate connections with our caregivers. It is only when we learn to walk or talk or develop mentally and physically that independence becomes possible (and perhaps never entirely so). As humans, our bodies and brains have evolved over millennia for interdependence, and many cultures celebrate and value that. But for the past 500 years, the social structures and dominant culture in the Western world and the Overculture of whiteness that rules there have insisted that *in*dependence has the higher value. (I use the culture of "whiteness" here and elsewhere to refer to the dominant culture that breeds and preserves systemic racism. It should not be confused with white ethnic cultures, which may not be based on racial privilege or domination. The culture of whiteness is woven into systems, institutions, norms, and values in ways that may be invisible, especially to whites, but plays a continuing and important role in maintaining white privilege and the oppression of Black people, Indigenous people, and people of color.)

To manage the dissonance, many people adopt the perspective of the Overculture and stop heeding the signals and wisdom that come from the body and their body's need for the company of others. They emphasize self-sufficiency and distance themselves from others instead of trusting relationships, community, and even brief passing connections as important and necessary to their well-being. Or when they do enjoy associations with loved ones or strangers, they may dismiss what they learn emotionally and relationally as less important than more rational ways of knowing.

Nonetheless, the impact of others on our well-being is significant, as the isolation of pandemic quarantines and distancing has made clear in recent years. Our human brains are designed to be influenced by others. When we notice the postures, movements, and emotions of other people, the mirror neurons in our brains cause us to experience the same postures, movements, and emotions as if they were our own. If you've ever flinched when an actor on the screen receives a punch to the gut, you know how this works.

This means our own fear and suffering can be magnified by that of others, whether we recognize it or not. It also means that when we are with people who are calm, our mirror neurons will cause us to become more grounded, more aware of our own bodies and their signals and needs. This helps us tap resilience often lost in the midst of fear or trauma. (To learn more on this topic, see *The Body Keeps the Score* by Bessel Van der Kolk.)

I experienced this powerfully on a car trip through Utah and Arizona. I was already struggling with my fear of heights when we hired a Jeep driver to take us on a rugged ride into a steep canyon outside of Sedona. Thinking he was being funny, the driver pretended he was driving off the edge of the road—but it was no joke to me. I was terrified to re-experience old trauma I had not known I was still carrying in my body from a harrowing experience I'd had decades earlier in the Himalayas. That night, I awoke in a full-blown panic attack. Adrenaline surged through me, and the most primitive, fear-bearing parts of my brain took over my breath, my heartbeat, and my nervous system. Nothing I tried calmed me down until my husband David wrapped his arms around me from behind, enveloping my body in the warmth and support of his. His steady breathing and heartbeat gradually entrained mine into a similar, slower rhythm until I was again settled and calm.

Together, we all make up a collective body of beings, and we all have a part to play in the wellness and the breathing of that larger body. Each of us will, at times, provide a steady rhythm of breathing to support others. Each of us will also sometimes need the rhythms of someone else to ground us. Our bodies know instinctively how to give and get this support if we allow ourselves the comfort of connecting. It can happen through embracing or being embraced but also with singing or swaying, marching or dancing, leaning or touching, chanting or praying. The call and response of many African American churches on Sunday morning and other practices within communities of color and queer communities provide dependable embodied support for folks living with the daily experience of racialized trauma. The body of the earth also reliably grounds us when the trauma of change rocks our being. We can be soothed and comforted by the company of tall trees, the scent or sound of the ocean, or the warm touch of a beloved pet curled up at our side. The invitations to reconnect with our own bodies and the boundless body of love we all belong to are everywhere around us.

Chrysalis Space

What do you do to experience the embrace of the body of love? It might be the company of a single person—someone you live with or someone whose company you seek out. It might be a community of faith you join in person or online. It could be a group you join as needed for pleasure or protest or both, marching or dancing, singing or chanting. Or it might be a performance of music or dance, of rhythm or words that you attend, letting your body receive and respond to the energy of others.

Recall a recent experience of one of the above and notice the response it calls up in your body and your emotions. What feelings arise when you gather with others to move or to sing, to clap or to sway, to converse or embrace? How are your own feelings influenced, held, supported, fortified, or dissipated by others'? Place your hands on your heart and take in three deep breaths, breathing in through your nose and breathing out, more slowly, through your mouth. Consider your own hands' warmth as the touch of other loving and trusted companions on your threshold journey. What is made possible, in your life and on your threshold, by the company and support of others? How might you keep your body and your heart open to this loving companionship, even across physical distance?

To write your own reflection on this, you might begin with these words and follow wherever they lead:

"Held by this love, I . . ."

THRESHOLDING TOGETHER:
The First Gathering

With a thresholding buddy or a group of thresholders, including some you know well and maybe a few you don't, gather for a meal after each of you has read the introduction, "How to Use this Book," and this chapter, "Beginning Here." You might start by each sharing in turn, briefly but without interruption, the threshold(s) of greatest concern to you now and your answers to the questions below. (See the appendix for more detailed guidelines for forming a thresholding group.)

- Briefly describe a threshold you are most concerned about now, naming something you may be leaving behind, something (including the unknown) that lies ahead, and a question you may be carrying with you.
- What is a hope you have regarding your threshold?
- What is a fear or concern you have regarding your threshold?
- Name any particular kinds of listening, support, or feedback you do and do not want from the group.

Informed by your sharing of hopes, needs, concerns, and what you do and do not want from your group, adapt the proposed covenant in the appendices or write your own to guide your group's time together in future gatherings. Note that it will be a living covenant, open to revision as you go along. End by setting your next meeting date and what the focus of that gathering will be.

NO LONGER

The Moment I Heard the News

Though it would take years
    to learn what it meant,
    what it would bring,
    what it would claim,
the moment I heard the news,
I was no longer the same.

Already leaving
    what I knew,
    what I loved,
    what I had forgotten
    would not last,
letting go
—with nothing new
to grasp,

    just letting go,
    letting go,
    letting go
    of what was never mine
    to hold,

while the wind
brushed across
my open, cupped hands
and the soft moonlight
sifted down,
slipping through my fingers
to the ground below.

    Letting
    go.

Threshold Skill 1:

LETTING GO

It starts in our youngest days as we take our first uncertain steps and continues through the rest of our lives. We are encouraged and required, in words and nudges gentle or abrupt, to let go. Not only must we let go of what we no longer need, but astonishingly and painfully, we are repeatedly required to loosen our grip on what we love most.

The first threshold skill is learning to let go—of what we had or knew, of what had been before but now no longer is. Though some welcome this as adventure, each of us at some point encounters something we would rather hold onto—including those things, people or circumstances we depend on for our identity, well-being, and belonging. How to let go of touchstones like these?

The origins of the word *threshold* are disputed, but some say it comes from an old Germanic word meaning "to thresh." To separate the grain, or the nourishing part of a plant, from the inedible chaff. To take what feeds us and helps us grow and leave the rest behind. Notably, the act of threshing is not a gentle plucking or sorting, setting the grain to one side and the chaff to the other. It typically requires a fair amount of force and effort to loosen the grain from the plant's fierce grip. Threshing by hand is a laborious act of flailing the plants on a threshing floor, a flat, smooth surface made of earth, stone, or wood. When possible, animals have been enlisted to crush the plants by walking in circles on them, trampling the grain underfoot or sometimes dragging a board over it. By the nineteenth century, the threshing machine replaced this manual process, marking a significant advance for agriculture.

Whether by hand or machine, the task of threshing is followed by a second process called winnowing to sort the grain from the chaff. Winnowing is often done by letting the wind lift the lighter chaff and blow it away, while the heavier grain settles to the ground to be gathered up and stored. Old methods of winnowing used a shovel, a fan, or a basket to throw the broken pieces of plants into the air, allowing the wind to carry the chaff away. Some barns were built with small winnowing doors positioned to channel the wind inside, where it would assist this lifting and tossing and sorting. Often the work of threshing and winnowing was a community labor, a gathering of muscle and air strong enough to break down what had been cultivated and to recover the seeds and sustenance needed for the future.

No wonder the word *threshold* is so evocative, reminding us to separate what can be carried forward as nourishment from the chaff that sometimes hides it. No easy task, it can be full of grief. We are leaving behind more than the tough, dry husks we might not want, but also the plant as we knew it before, growing, blooming, and ripening its fruits and grain. The poet Rainer Maria Rilke described it poignantly, noting, "Every happiness is the child of a separation / it did not think it could survive."

If this seems difficult, think of it as the basis of every breath our lungs take, letting go with every exhalation to make room for the next inhalation. It is a rhythm we know, a give and take that cannot be done in the same instant and yet always done together. Breathing out. Then breathing in. Breathing out. Then breathing in. Each trusting the other to follow in a rhythm so reliable and constant we forget we know it, although our life depends on it.

When beginning our passage on any threshold, it can be helpful to develop a habit of returning our attention to our breath. With each breath out, notice the body's relief in this simple, repeated release, making room for the next breath taken in. At any time, when a threshold experience loosens our hold on something, we can pause, noticing our breath and learning from it again, remembering the life-giving practice of letting go, of release, of making room for the next breath in.

Chrysalis Space

What are you being asked to let go of now? Make a list. It might include people, relationships, things, or places; assumptions or expectations; conditions, circumstances, authority, abilities, or identities. Don't feel compelled to list it all, but try to be specific in what you name today. If you list health, name what capacities or wellness your illness or injury is taking from you. If you list wealth or belongings, name some of the particular losses you expect or are already experiencing in your activities, comfort, or identity. If your threshold is a desired one, your list will look different than if you did not freely choose it, but even chosen and desired change brings loss. In either case, include both things you'd rather keep and those you may be glad to be freed of. Honor your feelings of grief or relief as the list grows.

If your attention moves ahead toward what might replace these relinquishments (or, metaphorically, to the grain you will be keeping), bring it back to the experience of letting go without yet anticipating or gripping something new. Notice what that feels like, where you feel it, and how you feel it, even if it surprises you or brings conflicting emotions. Try to also let go of your assumptions about what you might feel or should feel, making room for what you actually feel.

After making your list, sit in a comfortable position, elbows bent at the waist, hands resting palm up on your lap and gently but firmly closed as if holding something. Notice what's supporting your body—a chair, the floor, the earth, or whatever you are sitting on. Notice how your body trusts it. Take a deep breath in through your nose, pause briefly, and then let the breath out through your mouth with a deep, audible sigh, releasing your fingers into an open cupped position. Repeat this three times, closing your hands with each breath in and opening them with each breath out. What does your body tell you about letting go?

Tapping into Courage

When I think of courage, I don't often begin with heroic acts responding to tragedy or war. I first call up a quote from jazz musician Benny Golson, who once said, "The creative person always walks two steps into the darkness. Everybody can see what's in the light. They can imitate it, they can underscore it, they can modify it, they can reshape it. The real heroes delve in darkness of the unknown. It's where you discover 'other things.'"

Living on the threshold requires the courage to "delve in the darkness of the unknown" and "discover 'other things.'"

In the house I grew up in, our basement was divided, one half paneled and furnished as a comfortable, pleasant rec room and the other half clean but unfinished, a place of cement floors and cinderblock walls and exposed rafters strung with cobwebs. The stairs descending into the basement opened into the rec room, but if you turned right at the bottom you faced an old, rough-hewn door offering passage into the unfinished area. The door looked like something from an old shed and had a big open knothole at an adult's eye level, behind which my father had taped a shiny photograph of a human eye as a joke. Though I was too short to see this eye without fetching a stool, just knowing it was there was no joke to me. Each time I needed to go into that room at night, I would pause at the door, first mustering my courage to open it and then facing the darkness behind it. A single lightbulb hung from the ceiling in the middle of the room, but the only way to turn it on was by pulling the string dangling from it at least eight feet from the doorway. I had to move fully into the darkness to reach it, reluctantly letting go of the door jamb as I did, feet stepping cautiously, arms flailing in front of me, sweeping the shadows to find the light's string.

This is the feeling I often get when embarking on any creative project. It is also the feeling I get on the threshold. Stepping into the shadows of the unknown, my whole body is alert to my surroundings, my senses flailing about for any thin string I can pull to light my way.

It's no accident that thresholding and creativity both require this kind of courage. Living through change *is* a process of great creativity. Moving away from what we have known to participate with unfamiliar circumstances and create a new way forward. Without creativity, we will not gain passage. When our old ways no longer work in new circumstances, we will shut down, break down, and stop moving, growing, and living if we don't discover new ways. How might we invite and nurture the new perspectives we now need? Creativity—and the adaptation it requires and cultivates—is the only way to truly participate with change. And that creativity begins when we courageously let go of the door jamb, step into the unknown, into the unfinished part of our lives, and open our whole selves to new awareness that will guide our way.

Chrysalis Space

When was a time in your life when you courageously stepped into the unknown? What new discoveries about yourself did you make?

What new possibilities were created—for yourself and maybe for others—by your courage? Can you remember what that courage felt like? Where did you notice it in your body? Was it in your feet as you stood or walked? Was it in your hands as they held something or someone, as they steadied you or maybe as they let go? Was it in your shoulders, your heart, your abdomen, your legs? If you can't remember, imagine where you might locate courage in your body now. If courage is still reserved there now, consider how you might draw from it. And if this pocket of courage seems diminished now, how might you begin to restore its supply? What small gestures, acts, or shifts might you use to remember and restore your supply of courage for the thresholds you are on now?

To write from a prompt, begin with these words and follow wherever they lead:

"What gives me courage . . ."

Clearing Open Space

In an old Buddhist story, a novitiate comes to a wise old monk, pounding impatiently at her door. He explains to the monk that he has studied long and hard and is well versed in Zen philosophy, but he's come just in case the old woman has something more to teach him.

The monk suggests they begin by having tea. She serves her visitor first, filling the cup and continuing to pour until the cup overflows, spilling across the table. The novitiate backs away with alarm and irritation, accusing the monk of a foolish lack of awareness. The monk shrugs and explains, "You are like this cup. You come saying you wish to learn, but you arrive with your mind full to the brim. Go home and empty your mind of its opinions and convictions. When you return with an empty mind, you will be ready to learn what you seek to know."

Like the novitiate in this story, we live in a time and place that values knowing more than it does learning. Many of us pack our minds full of convictions, opinions, and assumptions—including what we think we know about who we are and the way the world is, or about what the future holds. This knowledge fills us like heavy, oversized furniture, taking up so much room there is little, if any, possibility of rearranging it, much less adding something new. When change comes to us, as it inevitably does, we have no space to accommodate it.

Henri Nouwen, the twentieth century the theologian, said we do this unconsciously out of our deep fear of emptiness and change. "Our fears, uncertainties and hostilities," he said in *Reaching Out*, "make us fill our inner world with ideas, opinions, judgments and values to which we cling as to a precious property. Instead of facing the challenge of new worlds opening themselves for us, and struggling in the open field, we hide behind the walls of our concerns holding on to the familiar life items we have collected in the past." Crossing a threshold can feel like stepping into an open field, unsure of where we are or where we are headed.

A friend of mine grew up in a family that moved frequently for her father's work. Each time the family moved, they built a new house, always with the same floorplan. Inside, they enjoyed a sense of familiarity from one home to the next; but stepping outside the front door brought the disquieting surprise of a whole different neighborhood and community. As if somehow the world had spun beneath the foundations of the house overnight and they had landed on a new set of coordinates.

Most of us are unlikely to build a new home each time we move, but anyone who has moved into a home they've not lived in before can recognize the threshold dilemma of trying to fit old furniture into a new space. In our attachment to familiar ways, we convince ourselves we will not let the changes we are living through change us. We might even tell ourselves this is what integrity looks like. We keep the rooms and furniture inside us in the same configuration they've been in before, even when shifting circumstances all around us might be better handled by a whole different style or arrangement or quantity. Those heavy rugs, so welcome in cold northern climates, might just grow mold in the tropical heat. The tall breakfront in the dining room of a spacious Victorian might not even fit in the compact studio that will be our next home. This is true of furnishings and material belongings when we move from one place to another. But more important are the less physical rearrangements required of us when moving across a significant threshold. Our assumptions about the changes we're facing and how they will affect us can be as bulky and unwieldy as that large bureau you haven't been able to clean behind for years. Threshold times invite us not only to move the heavy expectations furnishing our hearts and minds but also to consider passing some of them on or leaving them behind.

The thresholding skill of letting go will become much easier if we can regard the space made when letting go as a welcoming clearing rather than a fearful emptiness haunted by what is no longer in it. I've heard many thresholders describe the dread they felt for the physical task of decluttering and clearing out belongings before making a move to a new home and phase of their life only to discover an unexpected glee and relief after the clearing was made.

Thich Nhat Hanh once noted how differently Eastern and Western cultures approach the concept of emptiness. Draw a circle in the air, he said in *The Heart of Understanding*, and a westerner might name it as a zero, representing nothing or a lack of value. A person from India, however, will more likely regard it as representing wholeness, totality, or completeness. What if we embrace *that* understanding as we cross our thresholds? Might it be easier, if we did, to clear our hearts and minds of old habits and expectations, assumptions and attachments, that leave no room for something new?

On our shared thresholds of climate change and environmental devastation, for instance, we know our current levels of consumption are not sustainable. And yet, we cling to old assumptions about what we need, what we want, and what we deserve. How might we clear out these assumptions to make way for new definitions of what a good life is and how many belongings and natural resources it requires?

Chrysalis Space

What assumptions do you have about a threshold you are crossing and what it will require of you? What "knowledge" is filling your inner space with old arrangements, even as circumstances are shifting all around you? Draw a circle on a piece of paper—the larger the better. Take a pad of small post-it notes, and on each one, write an assumption you have about what you need or want to keep (physically, emotionally, mentally) as you cross this threshold. Then, place them all inside the circle, filling it up and, if necessary, overlapping them on one another. Keep adding post-its until the circle feels crowded.

Now ask yourself which ones you might be able to clear out. Begin with whatever seems easiest. Move them, one at a time, to the outside of your circle, remembering that this clearing doesn't mean they won't return. It just makes room for you to choose what does return, how it's arranged, and whether it might be reworded or otherwise adjusted before it reclaims space inside the circle.

When you've cleared enough of them to make some space, notice what is still inside. How might the space around the remaining assumption(s) give you room to gain a new perspective on them, to arrange them differently, or to allow them to shift in some way on your threshold? If you wish to write about this, you might begin with the prompt:

"In the space I have cleared, . . ."

Shedding Old Skins

We might think that shedding skin is for caterpillars and snakes, but it is also what we humans do. We are continually letting go of the skin we wear, that largest of all our organs, protecting all other organs, constantly communicating between inner and outer realms and often a key player in how others perceive and respond to us.

The skin of an average sized adult weighs in at about eight pounds and covers, in total, 22 square feet. Its job, as the old jingle goes, is to "keep the inside in" and "the outside out," but it is neither as permanent nor as impermeable as that would suggest. The skin is an extraordinary switchboard facilitating a constant exchange, taking in information about our environment and its potential threats and pleasures, and releasing sweat, scent, and even anti-bacterial substances from the inside. This role as a two-way communicator is no less important than its function as protector, so the skin's ability to remain flexible and vital requires a continual replacement process, sloughing an estimated 600,000 particles of skin every hour. Our new skin cells last only four to five weeks before they migrate to the outer surface to be washed, scratched, or flaked off—in short, to be shed.

If we want to learn the threshold skill of letting go, we have no further to search than the rim of our own bodies, where in a most literal sense we are not wearing the same skin we were housed in just one month before.

Of course, this process of letting go often escapes our notice because it happens on a cellular level and not as a shedding of our whole skin at once. We can turn to other creatures for more obvious thresholding lessons. Caterpillars and snakes, for instance, need to shed because their skins do not grow with them. Molting their whole skin, as if pulling off a sock at the end of long day, is necessary whenever their growth makes their skin too tight and too small.

Snakes do this two to four times per year, or as often as every two weeks when a snake is young and growing rapidly. Caterpillars, with a total lifespan of ten to fourteen days entirely devoted to eating and growth, will shed their skin four to five times, or almost every other day. In both cases, the shedding begins with a small breach in the old skin near the head. Caterpillars' growth itself will split the skin, whereas snakes may have to make the breach by rubbing on a rock or log, often after swimming to first loosen the old skin. Then, for both, the wriggling begins. It is an almost rhythmic rolling of the body, undulating as it loosens all attachment to the old skin and allows the body to pass through the sheath like a new shoot emerging from a stem. The old skin piles up behind it. For the snake, it is a soft, translucent artifact to be left behind. For the caterpillar, it is a heap of nourishment it will turn around and eat, leaving no trail for predators to track.

On the threshold, where the ingredients for growth are plentiful, we may have many skins to shed: ideas too small or rigid for what lies ahead; habits, practices, or roles no longer possible or practical; identities, appearances, names, or relationships that do not fit who we are becoming; reliance on old networks of awareness not attuned to the new conditions, opportunities, and threats of our changing environments. It is a molting that can be either terrifying or exhilarating. Often it is both. Always, it is a natural requirement of growth.

For the caterpillar, each new developmental phase between moltings is beautifully named an *instar*. Poetically, it calls to mind the stardust of which each one of us is made and with which we are continually finding new ways to let the ancient light shine. Etymologically, the word *instar*, derives from a Latin root meaning "form" or "likeness." Either way, we are reminded of the memory that remains when old skins are shed.

What a caterpillar learns about its environment will be carried over across several instars. Even through its greatest change, from caterpillar to butterfly, the memory of dangers to avoid and environmental mapping survives. We too can trust that when we let go of whatever has become too small in the changing conditions of our lives, we will retain the knowledge we need on a cellular level. On the global thresholds we now face, one significant shedding we are all (especially white people) asked to undertake is to wriggle free of the too-tight skin of the Overculture's message of self-reliance, instead affirming the interdependence practiced by many other cultures today, and to recall what previous instars knew about the necessity and givenness of relationship and belonging.

Chrysalis Space

Where in your life or in the world today do you feel constriction that might indicate a skin—a belief or identity or opinion—too small for who you are or who you are becoming? Is there a breach already opening, or will you need to make one? What are you already doing or what might you do now to loosen the old skin from the new skin already grown beneath it? How are you now doing, or might you do in the future, the wriggling that will draw you through the old, allowing a new skin to meet the light of day? And what will it feel like when you finally do?

If you enjoy stretching, with yoga or other exercises, take a few minutes to do so. Or if you like jiggling, do that in small or big ways, letting it loosen your muscles and your skin. Or stretch your arms out on either side, then raise them above your head as high as you can. Lower them back down at your side and roll your shoulders back and down, stretching your chest open. Stretch your lungs, taking a deep breath in and then releasing it again.

"If I keep stretching and growing . . ."

Inner and Outer Identities

Letting go of old skins is a reminder of what remains when we do—
the deep reservoirs of identity we carry inside, out of sight to the rest
of the world but intricately woven through our being.

For the caterpillar, each skin it sheds is replaced from the inside,
already formed out of sight. Even in the last shedding, the chrysalis
needed for the caterpillar's biggest transformation is already created
before the last skin splits. We humans do this too. In our dreams,
our intuitions, and our inner ways of being and knowing, we often
develop and grow the identities we need when living through change.
Predictably, when I am working on a new book or big creative project,
I have repeated dreams about babies being born and the support they
need, the vulnerability they carry, and the delight they promise. Each
dream is my own new skin growing inside me, reminding me of both
my intention and my ability to nurture this new being, this creation
that is partly me—and something more.

Other times, dreams have prepared me to let go. In the later years
of my father's life, after my mother died and he suffered a stroke, my
sisters and I were responsible for his care and affairs. It took me a
while after his death to realize I no longer had to worry about him and
tend to his needs. One night I dreamt he moved to a new home, and
I realized I didn't know where he was or how to reach him. Having
managed several of his earlier moves into and out of different care
facilities near the end of his life, I'd grown accustomed to my role,
moving him and his furniture, setting up his accounts, lining up caregivers, and transferring his phone service so he could call us. But in the
dream, I couldn't do any of this for him because he'd moved without
telling me where he was going and without taking his phone. I marveled that he'd been able to make this move without my help, but I
was concerned about how to fulfill my duties for him. Upon waking,

I laughed, understanding what the dream was saying—my responsibilities for him were over. He didn't need me now to do any more than live out my own days, to turn my full attention back to my own life and to other loved ones around me. This might have been obvious given his death, but it wasn't truly part of my own awareness until the inside world of my dreams incorporated it into my inner identity and consciousness.

It can also be true that our inner identities are what we need to shed as we cross a threshold. Old trauma or messages of diminishment can be embedded in our inner identities, where they may be triggered or reinforced by oppressive systems and relationships that still limit or traumatize us daily. Or for those of us privileged by the dominant culture, we might (even unconsciously) be unwilling to shed an identity that has advantaged us, often without our acknowledgment. It can be especially challenging to shed these deeper, sometimes unnamed identities that no longer fit who we are becoming or who we wish to be. It can be a lifelong project. There is no single or simple approach, but community support of some kind is imperative. We need the voices of others to mirror back to us who we are becoming, to affirm our strengths, value, and beauty—and to re-establish our confidence *and* our belonging to and with others.

My husband David is often part of an annual retreat with high school students where they use a group exercise called "If you really knew me." They begin by telling one another something about who they are—their name, relationships, roles, skills, favorite activities. Then, with each round of sharing, they begin peeling back those outer identities to reveal more of who they are on the inside. Beginning with the words "If you really knew me, you'd know that I . . . ," they take turns completing the sentence in new ways. What often starts with superficial information ("If you really knew me, you'd know that I can't stand pickles"), quickly goes deeper. When one member of the group risks telling others about a fear or vulnerability, an experience that has left them wounded, a dream they haven't dared say out loud before, trust builds. Soon others share their hidden identities too. There are tears. There is laughter. Eventually, a great weight is lifted as they receive one another's inner identities with support and care and as each of them experiences the repair that comes when our inner truths are given passage to surface in the outer world.

Certainly, we are wise not to bring our most vulnerable identities out into the light of day with just anyone or in any place. For some of us, it may be far too dangerous to express our true identities in a time or place determined to invalidate or harm us because of who we are. But this underscores the importance of seeking out people or communities where we can be our whole selves, vulnerabilities and all. For while identity emerges from within, it deepens and grows in encounters with others who appreciate, nurture, and support it .

Globally, one of the identities many people have is that of being "masters" of the earth and other beings. Even many environmentalists consider humans to be in charge of nature, an identity that prevents us from fully appreciating the gifts and the demands of true ecological interdependence. While we may feel vulnerable in a more mutual relationship with the earth, some say that given the changing conditions of our planet, letting go of our role as "masters" may in fact be our best hope. It doesn't mean we're off the hook. As the species most responsible for causing climate change, we are also most responsible for changing our ways in the effort to reduce it. But if we can shed the egotism that created our identity as "masters," we will be much more effective in changing our old destructive habits, because we'll more likely understand that the well-being of the planet and other species is one and the same as our own.

Chrysalis Space

What are your outer identities—the appearances and roles and relationships that you can readily name, that others notice and know, that define who you are? Make a list of these identities. Circle any that are significantly shifting on your thresholds.

Now, consider other inner identities lingering beneath the surface. Perhaps they're identities you can name easily, though you may not often share them with others. Or they may be carried so deeply they are hidden from you too. Imagine yourself with a trusted companion—someone you know or someone you wish into being. (If you are thinking of someone you know, you might also consider doing this exercise in person with them.) As you settle in with this person, imagined or present, you know they want nothing more than your growth, self-discovery, and well-being. Addressing them, complete the sentence, **"If you really knew me, you would know I . . ."**

Keep repeating this phrase, completing it differently each time. Challenge yourself to name at least one identity of vulnerability or need, but also name identities of strength and hope that might support you in the challenges ahead. It could be your faith or your resilience; your ability to laugh or cry, to sing or dance. It might be a memory or a dream; a skill or a habit; a connection to ancestors or children, to animals or nature, to stories or poetry, to music or art. Each time you complete the phrase, try to ask what is the deeper identity beneath the one you've just named. For instance, if you write about your identity as a person who dances, what is the inner identity beneath that—one that is not dependent on your body's ability to dance, but is rather an openness and response to rhythm and music and to the shared heartbeat each can create? Or if your faith is an identity, look beyond and beneath the specifics of religious institutions, practices, and creeds. Is it your faith in a particular religion or in the wider web of life and love that holds you? Or if you identify as a writer, for instance, what is the deeper passion, perhaps for stories or history or imagination, on which that identity depends?

You can also write this as a dialogue, with both you and your trusted companion taking turns completing the phrase "If you really knew me . . . ," each of you revealing new layers to the other.

Then, having named several facets of your identity, outer and inner, choose one of the identities with strength or wisdom to provide on your threshold but perhaps one not often visible to yourself or others. Ask yourself, what might help this identity to grow? And what would it be like if it did?

A WIDER HORIZON:
When (Climate) Change Comes Slowly

A common misconception of the letting go required on the threshold is that it is marked by a single line, a hard and fast border between what was and what will be. But when we are looking for dramatic shifts or a specific point at which everything changes, we can easily miss the larger change that requires letting go over time. The simple practice of watching a pot of water come to a boil can bring us back to the fact that change seldom comes in a precise instant, even when we measure it with a thermometer in hand.

At 212 degrees Fahrenheit or 100 degrees Celsius, at sea level, we know that water will boil. But those who are familiar with the finer points of steeping tea will point out that boiling really begins 50 degrees Fahrenheit sooner and includes five distinct stages. It begins with a *shrimp eye* boil, moves on to the *crab eye* and continues to a *fish eye* stage. At shrimp eye stage, the first pinhead-sized bubbles appear, and the water is about 160 degrees. At crab eye stage, when the temperature reaches 175, the bubbles have grown, and a few wisps of steam will rise from the surface. At fish eye stage, about 180 degrees, the bubbles swell to the size of fish eyes or pearls, the steam increases, and your teapot might begin to hiss.

It's after this that things really start happening. At 205 degrees, in the *rope of pearls* stage, the pearl-sized bubbles queue up on their way to the surface, and before you know it, mayhem breaks out in the *raging torrent* stage at a full-tilt 212, the threshold scientifically named as the boiling point of water. In this last, fifth stage, the water's surface roils like the rapids of a river, bubbles all elbowing their way up, breaking open wherever they can in an urgent and mass attempt to escape one another.

It's true. All those water molecules that had been comfortably swimming together at lower temperatures lose their attraction to one another as the heat rises. Like teenagers leaving home to rent their first apartment or head off to school, they do what they can to go their own way. In the opposite direction, on water's freezing point, the molecules' attraction to each other grows stronger, bonding them to a greater number of other molecules and locking them solidly into ice form. Like kindergartners on a field trip, the freezing molecules follow instructions and grip one another's hands fiercely, refusing to let go. In between, I like to think of water molecules moving in and out of their bonds with each other like people at a square dance, each slosh of the pail just another watery do-si-do.

Threshold living is sometimes like these watery variables. The temperature of new events can heat up or cool down, changing the way one part of our life relates to another. A friend once told me that in the final stage of her failing marriage, long before I met her, she woke up one day realizing she had been living in a deep freeze for some time. It took years after that for her heart to thaw again. Other big changes, personal or shared, come like the stages of a slow boil, awareness growing as our inner eyes widen, from shrimp to crab to fish-size and pearls. Something whistles a tea kettle's warning and suddenly all hell breaks out on the surface we've worked so hard to keep smooth and undisturbed, little parts of ourselves lifting off and going their own way.

Remember the old tale of a frog dying in a pot of water that was brought to a boil so slowly the frog never tried to escape? It turns out that the lesson of this story is not what I always took it to be. A healthy frog in a pot of water being slowly heated up will *not* linger to its death as the myth tells us. In fact, it will do everything it can to jump out. This is not only because frogs rarely hold still but also because they pay attention, as evolution has taught them to do. The poor oblivious frog posthumously famous for not jumping out as the water slowly rose to a boil was the subject of an 1869 experiment by German physiologist Friedrich Goltz, who had first removed part of the frog's brain before turning up the heat. The real lesson proven by the experiment is how much we need our full capacities of attention and warning, especially when danger mounts slowly.

Learning the full story, I can't help but wonder about our collective well-being today as the earth and our climate are slowly growing warmer. Have we effectively shut down the part of our human brains that listens to our bodies and the messages of pain they deliver from our own experiences and those of others, displaced by rising floodwaters or raging wildfires or threatened by drought and famine? Have we removed from our collective awareness the alert system that warns us as the earth's temperature rises and countless species lose their habitat and die off? How might we recover evolution's lessons about how to protect and preserve the environment and let go of old habits that are turning up the heat beyond livable levels?

Chrysalis Space

Consider the global threshold of climate change that has already warmed the planet by one degree Celsius. We can name numerous indicators warning us of the dire consequences: the flooding of coastal shorelines; increasing intensity and duration of heatwaves, droughts, and wildfires; the bleaching of ocean coral reefs, threatening a quarter of the world's marine species; the extinction of species losing habitat and the spread of disease-carrying species no longer checked by winter freezing. The evidence is accumulating, but unless we have experienced these impacts personally, it might be hard for us to receive and heed their warnings.

How have you already responded to the warnings sounding all around you? What next steps might you take, letting go of old habits and patterns of consumption while supporting the necessary legislative, corporate, and collective action needed to significantly slow climate change before it is too late? Might your attention to the losses already being tallied motivate you to a new level of commitment or action? List any changes that have already occurred or changes expected to occur in your lifetime that have had or will have a personal impact on you or on someone, something or some place that you know or love. Be specific. Maybe it's a wilderness area you cherish that is no longer healthy or accessible. Maybe it's a species you care about that is going extinct. Maybe it's a place destroyed by wildfire, or drought, or flooding or other disaster. Or maybe it's a person you care about who has suffered these or other losses.

As you let yourself feel the impact of these changes, ask yourself, are there choices available to you that will engage you in meaningful action while also further reducing your ecological footprint?

If you let yourself feel the slowly rising heat in our shared world, what action are you willing to take in response? What complacency and familiarity will you let go of, as you sharpen your awareness of the slowly mounting dangers of the warming of our world?

THRESHOLDING TOGETHER

With a thresholding buddy or a group of thresholders, gather for a meal after each of you has read the reflections on letting go. You might begin by together experiencing the exercise on page 19, following the first Letting Go reflection. Then choose any of the following questions to start your conversation:

- What are you being asked to let go of now, on your personal or global thresholds? And does that stir grief or relief? How do the norms and responsibilities of the Overculture affect your ability to let go? What does your culture teach you about releasing and letting go? Might your ancestors support you in this process? Who or what else might help you to let go?

- Share an experience you have had in the past where you mustered courage to step into the unknown. Where did you find that courage? How might it be available to you now, on the thresholds you are currently living on?

- What assumptions do you have about your personal or shared thresholds that might be freeing to let go of? What possibilities open up if you let go of those assumptions?

- Is there a "skin" you wear that no longer fits who you are or who you are becoming? How might you wriggle free of that skin, letting yourself grow into your new possibilities? What is a stretch you might welcome, living on the threshold?

- Do you have an outer or inner identity you might need to let go of on your personal or global thresholds? What is an identity that might carry over through the change? Will that identity need to adapt or adjust to this time of change, and if so, who or what might support that adjustment?

- When you consider the global threshold of climate change, how have you personally experienced the losses we are already accruing? What old ways are you ready to let go of in response to those losses?

Threshold Skill 2:

GRIEVING

If it seems odd to think of grieving as a skill, then it may just be a threshold skill especially worth your time and attention. Threshold living is made of losses, and grief is the heart's reflexive response to loss. The more we learn to welcome grief instead of shutting it out, the more adept we'll be as thresholders, personally and globally. As many environmental activists have pointed out, without the ability to feel true sorrow for the loss of habitat and species caused by climate change and other ecological devastations, we will likely be unwilling to change our personal and collective habits sufficiently to interrupt the environmental crises we now face.

Grief is all the more important as a thresholding skill because it is something many of us are not practiced at. Not that we've been lacking in opportunities. But the Overculture can be quick to regard grief as a malady, at best a signal that something's gone wrong. Or in a twisted turn of judgment that blames the victim, it suggests grief may be a sign of the bereaved's own inability to accept life's losses and move on. The message being that the best way to move on is by getting over our grief, by leaving it behind.

To the contrary, the medical sciences tell us that grieving is a normal and necessary human experience, as natural a response to loss as exhaling is to our inhaling. The grief we don't express doesn't just evaporate; it becomes packed into our bodies and our psyches in tight knots of pain and distress that will cause us trouble, whether we recognize their origins or not. We might carry these compacted pockets of unexpressed sorrow for a lifetime without naming their source, knowing their presence only as an inexplicable pain or discomfort or unease that we work hard to ignore or blame on other causes.

In her book *Getting Our Bodies Back*, psychologist Christine Caldwell writes about a client who continually rubbed her face when talking about loss. As her therapy progressed, the woman told a story about her mother's funeral when she was four years old, and how her father caught sight of her face distorted by sorrow and demanded, no doubt in an effort to keep his own grief at bay, that she "wipe that look" from her face. Only after sharing this memory out loud did she realize how literally she had taken that comment by developing a physical habit of rubbing her face when experiencing or thinking about loss.

Each of us has our own methods of wiping grief away. We might rub our eyes or tense our muscles or blink away tears or even force a smile, tentative or stony. Some of us choose to numb our pain with drinking or drugs, with busyness or buying, with distractions or obsessions. Or we might expunge all references to our loss with an almost surgical extraction. A friend whose own mother died in her childhood some years after her parents' divorce, remembers her father telling his children of their mother's death and then instructing them to never speak of her again. Not only was grief exiled but also the one whose death caused it.

The problem with these approaches to grief—either numbing it or eradicating it—is that they leave us with dead spots, places in our memory, awareness and body that are no longer alive with feeling. Trauma, addiction, and avoidance each have this capacity to deaden the physical nerves and emotional sensitivities that we may need on our thresholds. Often, they affect not only the place of injury and pain, but other areas as well. When we become numb to pain, for instance, we also lose some capacity for feeling joy. When we carve out all memory of a loved one who has left us, we are also carving out the love they once gave us. When we defend ourselves from the pain of loss, the armor we put on will restrict our movement as well as our sensations, damaging our ability to receive comfort and love from others.

These defenses against grief also rob us of its transformative gifts, or what therapist and author Miriam Greenspan calls grief's alchemy. "The gift that grief offers us," Greenspan says in *Healing Through the Dark Emotions*, "is the capacity to see deeply into the way things are. Life is limited. We are here for a short time. Grief asks us to know this, not only in a disembodied, cerebral way, but in the marrow of our bones—to look into the reality of death and loss without our usual egoic blinders on." Or without numbing ourselves in one way or another, I would add. The capacity to give and receive love is just one of the gifts that, Greenspan says, come "from looking into the face of death, not from turning away."

The curious thing about these gifts is that they can only be received with our willing participation. Often, they are offered to us but passed over unopened if we are unable to accept their wrappings in tears and emotions. This—the opening of sorrow to receive the transformation it carries—is why grieving is a primary skill on the threshold. In order to fully engage in the dynamic change available on a threshold, we must open our hearts to grief and the radical reorganization it makes possible.

Grief is also connective across time. One experience of grief will call up other sorrows we have had before. A minor loss might cause disproportionate tears because it opens a door inside us, behind which we have stored earlier sorrows. They may be neatly packed away in boxes on shelves or randomly stuffed into place in a small closet, waiting to tumble back out as soon as the door is opened. If we're uncomfortable with grief, this storehouse of old losses and unprocessed sorrow will make us even more uneasy about experiencing new losses on the threshold. We might even add another padlock to that door inside us just thinking about what's packed in behind it.

Instead of locking these feelings away, imagine the transformative power they might offer if we kept the door open or even invited them to come sit with us, to help us rejoin or remember who we really are. How might we make use of the natural gifts of grief to dissolve our attachments to the way things were and no longer are? To wash our eyes with tears, making new vision possible. To open our hearts to a different way of being that neither denies who we have been nor resists who we're becoming.

We are living at the outset of the world's sixth mass extinction, the first ever to be witnessed by humans. Every 20 minutes, another species goes extinct. Every year, more forests are cut down, more wilderness paved over. We don't often cry over these losses, but on some level our bodies and hearts know that the dead zones in the larger web of life are growing—and knowing this without feeling its impact emotionally will create dead zones inside us. How can we *not* feel, express, and be changed by the grief this can stir? How much more can be stored behind the closed door inside us?

Chrysalis Space

The poet Denise Levertov wrote about grief as a stray dog seeking a home and a name, a bowl of food, a bed of its own. The Sufi poet Rumi described it as an unwanted guest on our doorstep waiting to come in. If you imagine grief waiting on your doorstep, what form might it take? Is it a stray dog, begging for a place to rest? Is it a wanderer wanting a drink of water? Is it someone you know, with wisdom to offer as well as a need for your shelter? What might happen if you opened the door and invited them in? What will you offer them, and what might they teach you in exchange?

Imagine a dialogue or interaction you might have with your grief, and how it might change you if you give it a home and let it live with you for a while. If you want a prompt to begin, let your grief address you first, saying to you,

"Thank you for answering the door. I have been wanting to tell you . . ."

Taking Time for Sorrow

While poets' imagery asks us to make room for grief and welcome it in, it may be time that grief requires more than space. A transformative experience of grief takes time—sometimes a lot of it. And yet, in the twenty-first-century United States, the Overculture tries its best to convince us to ferociously guard our time and not to "squander" it on things like emotions. Notice how many English idioms equate time and money, referring to how we "spend" or "waste" or "save" time, as if it were held somewhere in an account that might grow interest. This is problematic in the face of sorrow because the time it takes to fully grieve a loss is neither paid time nor is it likely to add up as material wealth. It is, however, often directly correlated with emotional wealth and the richness of being fully aware and open to the gifts and losses woven into every life.

If your threshold is one that began with a precipitous loss— whether sudden or stretched out over years—taking time for grief will be especially important. The death of a loved one, the loss of health or strength or ability, the foreclosure of a home or a firing from a job. Each of these carries a special load of grief, along with society's expectations (and your own) of how long your bereavement should last. Personnel policies typically give us a few days to plan or attend a funeral. Friends, we hope, will lend their support longer, but even with them we might feel their patience wearing thin long before our sorrow has passed.

The *Diagnostic and Statistical Manual of Psychiatric Disorders* used by mental health professionals to name and treat their patients' suffering recently extended the duration of a "normal" grief process from two to six months. But who's to say six months is enough? Just when you think your grief has subsided, the anniversary of loss comes around and pulls the emotional rug out from under you again. This "anniversary effect" is real and not necessarily a sign that we are stuck in our grief. Rather, it underscores how grief continues to speak to us, sometimes with new things to say, across many years.

A common practice that does better at honoring how much time grief requires is the Jewish tradition of sitting *shiva*. For the first week after a death, those mourning a loved one's death will stay at home, receiving visitors and remembering the one who has died. Mirrors are draped in black cloth to avoid concern over appearances. For the following month, the mourners follow a less restricted practice, and then for eleven more months, they return to previous activities while continuing to say the mourner's prayer two times each day. After that, the dead are remembered each year on the anniversary of their death by lighting a candle that burns all day long.

A true practice of grieving is like any healing of the body. It requires attention and patience. It takes its own time. It will be uniquely ours, perhaps similar to others' but never identical—and sometimes wholly unlike the experience of anyone else.

When recovering from my mastectomy, I dutifully showed up for the six-month follow-up appointment my surgeon had suggested. Before my surgery, I'd expected this appointment to be rote, a check-in that would primarily check off every category of recovery. But many factors had been unexpected, from the two emergency surgeries that followed within forty-eight hours of the first to the resulting anemia and the frozen shoulder I developed later. At six months out, I outwardly appeared to have fully recovered, but I was discouraged that I was still sleeping more than ever before and in many invisible ways I was still seeking the surefootedness of my pre-surgery days. When I expressed surprise over this with my surgeon, she sat back on her stool and smiled at me compassionately. Do you remember, she asked, how much you've been through in a short amount of time? Then she cataloged for me not only the half-dozen medical procedures and surprises I'd experienced, the blood lost in two hematomas, the general anesthetics administered almost back-to-back in three surgeries in less than three days, but also listing my father's death and the settling of his estate as physical and emotional losses just as significant to my recovery as the removal of my cancer. Six months, she said, is nothing when processing losses as multiple and deep as those.

A fellow breast cancer survivor, Sally, had also advised me to be patient with the length of time it could take for the anesthesia to completely leave the body. She told me she could still remember the moment, months after her own mastectomy, when she felt, with a kind of whooshing relief, that her body was finally clear of the last remnants of anesthesia. Perhaps it was the power of suggestion, but many months after my own surgeries, while camping with a friend and gazing at the stars shining in the clear night sky, my pupils widened in the darkness and I felt my whole body opening like an aperture, awakening my senses and sensations, insisting in a strong and beautiful voice, "Yes, I am alive!" As I reported back to Sally, it was my experience of an exuberant whoosh, the last flushing of anesthesia from my cells.

If our healing on unwanted thresholds often lasts longer than we'd like, it can be even harder to take enough time to recover from sorrow on a threshold we have chosen. We might be surprised or even feel guilty that we experience grief when moving toward a change we desired. But grieving what or whom we are leaving behind does not diminish the value of what we're moving toward. The decision to move into a new home or a new community doesn't have to render the one we're leaving as wholly undesirable, nor does a new marriage, even to one who has fully claimed our heart, mean we will not miss some parts of our single life or some aspects of a previous partner or spouse. Our ability to name these as losses and sorrows need not weaken our attachment to the new life we are choosing. It may actually enrich it, because naming our losses is a first and important step in naming our needs as we go forward. The honesty that opens us to the bittersweet nature of all change will also open us to a wider range of possibilities and choices as we move forward.

Chrysalis Space

How much time have you cleared for sorrow on your threshold? Given all the demands on your time right now, what might you do on a daily or weekly basis to open up a set amount of time with no purpose other than making way for feelings, especially those related to your threshold? Perhaps it's a daily practice of fifteen minutes to write in your journal, or to visit a natural setting. Or a weekly phone call or meeting with a trusted friend who will ask, "How are you feeling?" and with whom you are likely to answer honestly.

These are useful practices in any circumstances, and even more so on the threshold. Choose any way of making time for feeling that you haven't done with regularity before and make a habit of it for three to four weeks. After regularly doing it for a week or more, ask yourself, what feelings have you named that you might not have noticed before and what have you learned from them? Has this allowed time for your grief to speak? Is this a practice you might wish to continue?

Alternately, if you are experiencing significant grief that causes you to tear up frequently throughout the day, sometimes without warning, you might want to specifically make time for crying. Try giving yourself fifteen to twenty minutes each day to cry, for several days in a row. At the end of your twenty minutes, wipe your tears and promise yourself you'll take time to do it again the next day. Do this for as many days as the tears come, journaling for five minutes after each time if you choose. After a number of days, when you're ready, use the allotted time to write instead, letting yourself wonder what your grief is telling you now that it knows you will listen.

Decentering

Life is always moving us off balance. Each time we restore our balance, we know we will lose it again. This is the nature of time and growth.

When change happens, whether as unwanted loss or in new circumstances that we desire, we are required to shift our center of gravity to keep our balance. Consider the arrival of a new child or a new lover. When we give our heart to another person—or to a cause, a community, or a commitment—we experience the tug of living off-center as our heart opens to an awareness and balance extended beyond our individual self.

One of grief's more surprising gifts is that, like love and commitment, it shifts us off balance. If you, like many, place a high value on keeping your balance, this might not seem desirable. But just as shifting our posture in yoga or tai chi will require a different set of muscles and awareness to recover or maintain our balance, the metaphorical shifting of weight in our hearts when living on the threshold can similarly awaken new strengths and consciousness. Sometimes called the decentering effect of loss, it can unseat the ego long enough to make new movement and spiritual growth possible if we let it.

Most full-bodied movement—such as walking, dancing, or tai chi—is based on a repeated experience of shifting balance, or giving up our static balance. If we are ambulatory, we sometimes forget this, but watching a toddler learn to walk is a delightful demonstration of how much imbalance is involved in a single step. Consider how much weight shifting is required for the simple alternation of left-foot-right mobility. Or, for those who move in a wheelchair, the transfer into and out of the chair, with or without assistance, might be an analogous experience of shifting weight from one center of gravity to another and the unsteadiness it can bring.

For many people who have walked easily without assistance throughout their lives, this can be a common loss when crossing thresholds in the aging process. As balance becomes more challenging and strength more compromised, we are reminded more often than we'd like how much walking decenters us, which is why canes and walkers come in handy—and even lessons in safe falling from physical therapists. These aids to balancing can teach us in our grieving on the threshold. By opening ourselves to grief's emotional shifts and using support when it is needed to regain our balance, we can begin to move not just into grief but through it. We can create momentum not only for healing, but for spiritual and emotional growth. "The truth is that you learn the most about yourself and about life on earth from falling off balance, then finding your way back to balance again," notes José Stevens in *Tao to Earth*. "Healing, then, is the balance or the neutral position of acceptance."

In the thresholding groups I lead, participants are encouraged to connect with one another when we meet together and, if they wish, between our gatherings. During our meetings, we pledge to be present with one another as nonjudgmental listeners and witnesses, without investment in analyzing or fixing what others share. We also acknowledge that each of us is living with heightened sensitivity and must prioritize our own needs. If someone from the group contacts us between sessions, we encourage each other to be honest with ourselves and one another, especially if we need to decline that invitation. And if we are the ones reaching out to others between sessions, we name an intention not to take it personally if our overtures are not reciprocated. We practice staying with our own feelings and needs as we alternately step into and out of a wider awareness and relationship with others. It is a rhythm akin to breathing, and just as vital.

For some of us, grief will cause us immediately or quickly to turn to others for support and comfort. Or, conversely, we might need solitude to absorb or even name our loss before we can share it or be available to others in their own grief, related or not. Whenever we are ready, though, opening ourselves to others during our sorrow offers an important invitation. It brings the relief of knowing we are not alone, allowing us to receive support while reminding us that life is made of loss and that we are not the only ones suffering. That experience of kinship and belonging gives us an expanded, more trustworthy sense of balance for even the most difficult times.

An old Buddhist teaching story tells of a woman, devastated by her son's death, who visits a local monk and asks him to restore her son to life. The monk tells her that in order to do this, he will need a mustard seed from the home of someone who has not suffered their own personal loss. So the woman sets out, going door to door, asking at each home whether they have lost a loved one. Repeatedly, she is told sorrowful stories of losses experienced by her fellow villagers. Unable to find a single household without its own losses to provide her with the necessary seed, she returns to the monk but is no longer distraught. In the process of her search, she has joined the great family of mourners whose shared sorrow makes way for greater compassion and the lovingkindness that will help her heal.

Moving into relationship with others who are grieving may at times increase our pain. But as we learn to be present for others' grief without trying to hasten their healing, we will also be learning how to do the same with our own grief. It is also important in this grief work to continually reconnect to internal and external sources of support and grounding—first regaining our balance, returning to our own experience, and then back into our exchanges with others. With practice, this can make us more available to our own feelings, including joy as well as grief. It will also give us greater access to the support of others and of community. As we develop our capacity to be with others' sorrow and to feel the shared grief evoked by thresholds we are crossing together, we will find new opportunities for healing and growth, both personally and with others.

Chrysalis Space

When was a time that you shared grief (yours and theirs) with someone else in a way that was helpful to your own healing? How did it help you? Did the other person tell you if it was helpful to them? What do you remember about how it felt? If it decentered you or caused discomfort, what did that mean for you then and now? Consider a threshold you are on now, personal or global, and ask yourself if it is inclining you toward others and shifting you to a new center of gravity. What movement might occur, what new awareness might arise, as you recover your balance in this in-between place?

Remembering and Forgetting

It's called the "doorway effect." *Destinesia*, we call it in my house. I get up from my desk and walk into the hallway and no longer remember why I left the room in the first place—food, beverage, a book, a newspaper, a pen?—before going back empty-handed and sitting down again.

I forget a lot of things, but this one is apparently wired into the human brain and how it handles memory. Researchers from the University of Notre Dame studied the doorway effect by asking their subjects to pick up an object from a table in one room, place it in a shoebox where they couldn't see it, and carry it to another table where they exchanged it for an object they found there. Some passed through a doorway en route to the second table; others did not, and along the way they were all quizzed about what was in the box. The study found that after passing through the doorway, many of the participants could not recall what was in the box nor what they were to do with it, while those who did not pass through a doorway were more successful in remembering. Even passing back into the original room did not have a significant impact on restoring their memory. The doorway itself seemed to function as a reset button, clearing out information held in one context and making room for new information in the second context.

Of course, many memories, stored more deeply, survive the passage—not only when crossing physical thresholds but also the larger emotional ones as well. But if the passage is a significant one, our memory of the other side might seem much farther away than it actually is. When our son Cat was young and learning to ride a two-wheeled bike, we tried training wheels and many methods over a long summer to no effect. Then one day, my husband David took Cat to an empty parking lot and ran along behind, steadying the bike with his hand until Cat got enough speed to experience the necessary balance. When David finally let go, Cat rode off on their own, going round and round the parking lot in delight, at last returning to David and dismounting the bike to proclaim confidently, "You know, I remember the first time I ever enjoyed riding a bike. . . ."

Memory is a mysterious gift. It can help us or hinder us. What we remember from the far side of life's many doorways can guide us as we step into the unfamiliar frontiers of the future. But it can also weigh us down with information and frameworks that no longer apply, or some that never did serve us well to begin with. Perhaps the gift of the doorway effect is to remind us we don't need to carry it *all* forward. With practice, attention, and intention, we can choose what we want and need to keep and what might be best left behind. We can also choose how we carry forward what we decide not to leave behind.

Which memories will we bring with us? And which will we put down? Good grieving can help us answer this question. If we're feeling grief because someone never quite gave us what we wanted or needed to receive, naming that sorrow can be a way of setting the memory down and moving on. If we are grieving a person or place or time we loved so much we do not want to let it go, then grief can be a way of transforming that memory into one that will survive the test of time and continue to support us through the changes that lie ahead. And in any kind of grief, we can call up our own wisdom by remembering other times of loss and what we depended on to get us through them.

Counselors, therapists, and spiritual directors will ask us, "Have you ever suffered a different, earlier loss and found a way to keep your footing? What helped you then?" From the deep storage of our own experience, we can often call up wisdom that will guide us through a current passage of loss and sorrow. As we do, we will be weaving our past into our future and creating a design that reflects the larger wholeness of our life.

Admittedly, this is not easy. Our brains are not only wired to reset themselves when we pass through doorways. Many cultures are inclined toward the future, encouraging us to let go of the past quickly and not to look back. In the dominant English-speaking culture of the United States, our language and gestures both tell us the past is behind us, orienting us instead toward the future that lies ahead of us. Other cultures gesture behind them when talking about the future to indicate they can't perceive it, and when talking about yesterday, which they know all about, they point in front of them. Neither perspective is right or wrong. Taken together, they honor the hinge in time of every moment, linking past and future. They remind us that the present moment is a door that swings both ways and that we are wise to keep our hinges oiled.

Chrysalis Space

What are some of your significant memories from before you started crossing this threshold that are no longer the same for you today? They might be memories of things you wish were still happening today or things you're grateful to have left behind. You might call them up by repeatedly writing or reflecting from the prompt, **"I remember when . . . ,"** each time completing the prompt with a different memory.

After naming as many as you can in about ten minutes of reflecting or writing, look back over what you've written. Considering the gift of the doorway effect, ask yourself what your grief teaches you about which of these memories to set down and which to carry forward, perhaps in a different form.

You might also ask what you remember about a different threshold you've crossed before that involved significant loss. What helped you express and move through your grief over that loss? How might a similar approach help you now?

What We Carry Forward

One of the most common myths about grief is that it means we're too attached to what we've lost and that our grief will keep us from moving on. To the contrary, good grieving allows us to open a path to what we have lost and to keep it open in a way that creates a new relationship with whatever or whomever we've had to leave. Honoring both the old and new relationships, we can move on without the denial or severance that cause such deep fracturing for many on the threshold.

Many cultures recognize the importance of maintaining our connection to ancestors and others who die before us with rituals and celebrations that intentionally offer the dead an open invitation to our hearts. The Mexican celebration of Días de los Muertos, or Days of the Dead, is one example. Based on Mexican–Indian traditions that are over 2,000 years old, the Days of the Dead are celebrated October 31 to November 2 as an annual remembrance of loved ones who have died. Coinciding with the migrating monarchs' arrival in Mexico for their winter stay, the waves of a million or more orange wings fluttering overhead are sometimes regarded as the returning souls of loved ones. For several days, the festive and colorful celebration continues with elaborate ofrendas or altars prepared graveside or in the home, with photos and mementos of the ones who have died as well as their favorite foods, lovingly prepared and laid out to entice their return. These are joyful invitations to the dead, featuring skulls made of sugar and miniature skeletons often depicted dancing and playing music. My friend Juanita Garcia Godoy, a scholar of this celebration and now herself on the other side of the divide she studied and wrote about, once put it this way: "Días de los Muertos is a great family reunion that especially honors those who no longer have bodies." It provides, she said in Digging the Days of the Dead, a kind of solidarity across a longer arc of time for a people facing tremendous forces of disintegration.

On the threshold, one could say we are all facing forces of disintegration as whatever is no longer dissolves and passes away. We experience some of our biggest threshold losses when loved ones have died or left our lives in other ways. But other losses—of health or abilities, of workplace or home, of freedom or safety or potential—can create an absence just as palpable as the gap left by a loved one. Because these losses aren't always acknowledged as reasons to grieve, they are sometimes called "disenfranchised grief," or what grief researcher Tashel Bordere calls "suffocated grief"—when someone's grief is punished for being inappropriate, which happens more often for people of marginalized identities. Being able to feel and express our grief, especially when it is not honored by ritual or recognized as legitimate, is an important step in our passage through loss. It can be a way of letting go of the way things were while inviting what we have lost to take a different form that we can carry forward in new relationship.

This is not just about being comforted by our memories, although it can include that. More fundamentally, when we let ourselves feel sorrow for what we have lost, we gain access to what we received from it when it was ours. Grief loosens our grip, helping us bow to the impermanence of the living world. Then our awareness of the living world—of ourselves and others in it—can become more spacious, connecting us in surprising new ways to what we have left behind as well as to the possibilities that lie ahead, as yet unseen.

Chrysalis Space

Sitting in a chair comfortably, notice where the chair and floor support you. Scan your body for points of discomfort or sorrow and turn your attention toward them, rather than away. Notice if you experience grief or loss in a particular place in your body, and if so, breathe deeply into that place. What do you feel there? Maybe a tingling, or a knot. Perhaps an absence, or numbness, a cold spot, or a hot ember of emotion. Without judgment, let yourself be curious about whatever you feel and where. If no place in your body rises to your consciousness as you scan it for pockets of grief and loss, let yourself be curious about that. Have you tamped grief down or turned it away? Have messages from other people or from the Overculture caused you to suffocate or ignore your grief? Remembering that no observation is bad or wrong; simply invite curiosity about whatever you feel or do not feel.

If your scan brings your attention to a particular place in your body, use your breath to open that place and consider what new understanding or energy might grow there now and how might it help you in crossing your threshold.

A WIDER HORIZON:
The Power of a Broken Heart

Guarding ourselves from grief can be a dangerous thing. In our personal lives and in a world full of injustices and suffering, the shields we use to prevent our hearts from breaking can be the very thing keeping in place the conditions that cause the suffering and injustices in the first place.

"The broken heart," notes adrienne maree brown, "can cover more territory." In her "Spell for Grief or Letting Go" she says, "Grief is the growing up of the heart that bursts boundaries like an old skin or a finished life." Overcoming injustice requires our hearts to grow beyond the boundaries created by oppression. Simply put, we cannot engage in social change without heartbreak.

Some of the most transformative, heartbreaking grief I have experienced in group settings has occurred in antiracism study dialogue circles I have participated in. These interracial circles meet weekly for several months to learn and better understand the history and current manifestations of racism in our systems and lives. We share countless moments of deep grief throughout our time together, but usually around week three, the emotional weight of the work takes our conversations into new and challenging terrain. It is different for each person in the circle, depending on our race and social location, the work we have done before or have not done, and the circumstances of our lives in that moment. Often there are tears, with each of us responsible for tending to and learning from our own broken hearts and, especially, for discovering how we will transform our grief into a commitment to undo the racism that has caused it. This is the challenging work of letting our hearts break open and holding them open in ways that keep us in relationship with one another and with the long struggle itself.

It is tempting to avoid the heartbreak. I have many ways of guarding against it myself, and I suspect I am not alone in this. There is good old-fashioned denial or the often-favored variation of just looking the other way. But there are many other methods that appear less resistant or clueless. There's the "what difference can one person make?" claim of powerlessness sometimes masked as humility, and its seasoned but sinister cousin, cynicism. There's the plea of being too sensitive for the hard truths or the sometimes bruising battles, this response being especially and unfortunately common among whites avoiding the important role of the privileged in calling out and ending systemic racism. There's the myth of busyness—not only being occupied with competing obligations but even with our commitments to the cause of challenging systemic racism, which can ironically become a barrier to the deeper and necessary heart work of seeing and routing out the internalized impacts of racism on our thinking, our emotions, our bodies, and our lives.

Our study dialogue circles end with each person naming action steps we will take to undo systemic racism after the circle stops meeting. For some, this might be as basic as continuing to learn and grow in understanding. For others, it will include specific strategies to address racism in their workplace, community, or educational or criminal justice systems. I know these action plans are important. But, for me, the first and necessary step preceding any strategies I name is to figure out how to keep my heart engaged and vulnerable, which is to say broken open and getting bigger.

Oppressive systems gain and hold their power by causing hearts to shut down. Because we humans have evolved for relationship and community, any system that brutishly divides us one from another also severs us from our own compassion, for others and ourselves. Where in your life is compassion most needed to keep your heart open to the work of ending the oppression of racism? This question will necessarily sit differently for people of color and indigenous people than it does for white people; but for all of us, it is important to return to the question over time, noticing how our answers shift due to changing circumstances and understanding. Do you have habits that keep grief at bay? How do you distinguish between the habits needed to keep your heart safe and those that make your heart small and too tightly confined? Learning to feel grief and transform it into open-hearted engagement will be necessary for dismantling the racism that persists by shutting our hearts down.

Chrysalis Space

Notice what has been happening in your body as you have been reading the reflection above. Pause for a moment to breathe deeply and attend to any sensations you notice without judgment. What do you feel and where do you feel it? It might be grief, or some other emotion—anger, shame, guilt, resentment, despair, or denial. Grief itself can wear any of these faces, and these are all emotions that can surface, especially for white people, in discussions of race and racism. They create tension that we experience physically or mentally—with a guarding of the heart, a shortening of breath, or restriction of muscles or thinking. Let the circulatory power of your breath, in and out, in and out, create movement within you, dispersing any tension and dislodging any feelings that are stuck. Let the space you create with your breathing be your own invitation to move on.

When you are ready, consider how your heart typically receives the lived experience and hard truths of racism or other forms of systemic oppression. What do you do with the grief these can stir? If you turn from this grief, notice how you experience that turning. What might it mean to turn toward it instead? If you feel this grief, does it empower you to take action or does it cause your retreat into silence? Can you feel this grief without expecting others to alleviate it?

What do you learn by listening to your broken heart in the work of social change? How might your broken heart burst the boundaries of old ways, creating a wider territory for your compassion—for yourself and others? And what could that mean for how you respond to racism or other forms of oppression? Begin writing with the prompt below and follow wherever it leads, writing a few sentences or paragraphs. Then repeat it again, each time exploring another question about what your broken heart teaches you and what that means for your perceptions, your understandings, and your actions in everyday living.

"If I let this broken heart be my teacher . . ."

THRESHOLDING TOGETHER

With a thresholding buddy or a group of thresholders, gather for a meal after each of you has read the reflections on grieving. Then choose any of the following questions to start your conversation:

- If you imagine grief waiting on your doorstep, what form might it take and what conversation will unfold if you welcome it in?
- Name one daily or weekly practice you have tried in the past few weeks to get in touch with your feelings on the threshold. What feelings have you named that you might not have noticed before and what have you learned from them? Has this allowed time for your grief to speak?
- Describe a time when you shared grief with someone else in a way that was helpful to your own healing. How did it feel? Naming a threshold you are on now, personal or global, describe how it connects you with others. What might that mean for you and them?
- What does your current grief tell you about memories you might choose to set down or change the way you carry them with you?
- What do you remember about a previous threshold you crossed that involved significant loss? What helped you express and move through your grief? How might something similar help you now?
- Where in your body do you experience grief or loss and what do you feel there? How might your awareness of this help you while living on the threshold? Do you have habits or practices that will keep this grief from getting stuck there?
- What do you learn when listening to your broken heart in the work of social change? How might your broken heart grow

bigger to increase your compassion, both for yourself and others? And what does that mean in how you respond to racism and other forms of oppression?

Threshold Skill 3:
PRACTICING EQUANIMITY

In the early stages of any threshold, telling the story of our passage and its losses is one of the ways we begin to let go. But as we tell it over time, it is a good idea to let the story change and advance. Ironically, it is not uncommon to get attached to a story about letting go. We can become so accustomed to a particular way of telling it that we get stuck in it, or fail to leave room for the story to develop in new directions. Perhaps we've been victimized by people or fate. Maybe we feel cheated—out of a job or a relationship or long life or robust health. Or, alternatively, we may be so blessed by a turn of events that there is no room in the way we tell the story to acknowledge even the best fortune can have its downside. These may each be accurate elements of our story. Indeed, for any of us living in the margins, we will likely have daily evidence of being victimized by systems set up to do just that. It is important to name this. But if we unwittingly become too attached to a single part of our story, it doesn't leave sufficient room for the many ways it can make a turn.

Buddhist teacher and writer Pema Chödrön says there is no "true story," meaning not that our stories are false but that they are incomplete. They are only true to the degree that we let them keep changing as long as we are still living them.

The third threshold skill, equanimity, is about not becoming attached to one particular telling of our story—which is especially important when naming what is "no longer." We are advised to notice and name our threshold gifts and losses—and our responses to them—without assuming they will lead in one direction or another. We keep the story open.

Emotions can be greatly heightened on the threshold, which can overwhelm our awareness of options and invite premature conclusions about where our story will lead. By suspending our judgment of both our circumstances and our responses, we open space for honestly noticing what we're experiencing and feeling and how that is shaping our participation in the story. The goal is to open our senses wide and with curiosity, naming what we experience and feel without the certainty that we know what will come next. Equanimity, as Buddhists name this practice, is the first step in cultivating the open-hearted self-awareness that will give us more choices in how we respond.

It also makes us more receptive to the wisdom of our intuition, which can be easily pinched off by either/or judgments about things being right or wrong, good or bad, desirable or undesirable. When we stand on the edge of the unknown, we can foster a more nuanced awareness by resisting the urge to tame or conquer it with simple judgments. As Clarissa Pinkola Estés points out in *Women Who Run with the Wolves*, our intuition will always offer us at least four options: "the two opposites, and then the middle ground, and 'taken under further contemplation.'" She writes:

> *If you're not vested in the intuitive, you may think you have only one choice, and often that it is an undesirable one. And you feel that you should suffer about it. And submit. And force yourself to do it. No, there's a better way. Listen to the inner hearing, the inner seeing, the inner being. Follow it. It knows what to do next.*

This act of inner listening requires that we first let our inner voice speak, which can be harder than you'd think. There's nothing, in my experience, that so quickly and effectively silences my inner voice as my own inner critic. *That's just crazy,* I say to myself. *Impossible. How could you do that, Karen? Why would you feel, or say, that? Who are you to suggest that? Do you know how much trouble that would cause if you really said, believed, or pursued that? No, don't even go there. Then you'd have to change. Other people might have to change too. It would be a lot of work. And likely costly. People might think you're crazy. (Maybe they'd be right.) Better to not say it or even think it.*

This inner critic can be activated without my awareness because it is a voice that is amplified by the Overculture and its valuation of certainty and control, of intellect over intuition, of mind over body, of resisting change to the ways things are. All we need is a small whisper of our own personal doubt and criticism and, encouraged by the Overculture, the whisper quickly gains volume. The inner voice of our intuition is silenced before we've received a word of what it has to say. The truth budding in our heart gets snipped off before it has a chance to open.

In the uncertainty on the threshold, it is important to keep our judgments at bay long enough to become aware of even the most unlikely possibilities and to become conscious of what we might learn from even the least pleasant of our emotional responses. Call it making room for intuition. Or taking a cue from a physics lesson involving Schrodinger's cat in the box, dead or alive. Or strengthening our powers of imagination (explored in more detail in threshold skill #9). Threshold living asks us to make no assumptions about the possibilities waiting out of sight so that we might discover and embrace them.

The old story from China says it well. A farmer tells his neighbor that one of his horses has run off, to which the neighbor replies, "How unfortunate. What bad luck." The farmer shrugs and says, "We'll see." A few days later, the farmer updates the neighbor, reporting that the stray horse has returned with a whole pack of wild horses, which the farmer is now keeping. "Marvelous," exclaims the neighbor. "What good luck!" And the farmer shrugs and says, "We'll see." A week later, the farmer tells the neighbor his son was breaking the wild horses in and was thrown from the horse and broke his leg. "That's terrible," the neighbor replies. "What bad luck!" And the farmer shrugs and says, "We'll see."

The next month, a war is declared, and all able-bodied young men are required to report for military service, whether they are needed at home or not. The farmer's son, still recuperating from his broken leg, stays home. "How fortunate," says the neighbor, whose own son must leave for battle. To which, the farmer predictably shrugs and says, "We'll see."

What would it take to say "we'll see" upon every new development on our thresholds? To remember that the story's never complete while we are still living it. To remember history is still unfolding and its dialectics can surprise us. Saying "we'll see" is not denying the realities of our circumstances or our world; nor does it ask us to step back when we are called to speak out when we or others have been wronged. Rather, it equips us to step forward because when the future is not already decided, it can still be influenced by our own response to the present. Saying "we'll see" is an antidote to both complacency and despair, a call to wake up and be aware that *anything* can happen and that we have a part to play in determining what that *anything* will be. The threshold skill of practicing equanimity means this kind of wakeful living, without certitude, judgment, or inertia. It challenges the assumption that "It's just the way things are."

Chrysalis Space

What is the story you've been telling about a threshold you are on personally or the threshold times we now share? Is it a time of despair and decline? Or one of new hope? Can it be a story of both? Choose one threshold development of concern to you and consider how your perspective on it might change if you say "we'll see" as you wait for or cause new developments to occur. How might saying "we'll see" affect how you talk about this threshold and with whom, and what you are motivated and empowered to do?

Cultivating Curiosity

When my mother was first diagnosed with ALS, she was as shocked and terrified as anyone might be, given the horrific losses of strength, mobility, and independence that this terminal illness brings. But about two and a half years later, and half a year before she died, I asked her what she could tell me about her experience. By that time, she had lost her ability to use her legs, arms, and hands and was only able to eat through a feeding tube. She was unable to speak more than a few words unless she used a computer that she directed with her eyes. As a minister, I said to her, I wanted to know what it was like to live through so much loss. And what she told me couldn't have surprised me more.

It didn't feel like she'd lost that much, she said. Mostly, she explained, what it felt like was being surrounded by an abundance of love.

I knew—and I suspect she did too—this was not a denial of the ways she suffered because of her illness. They were too many, too deep, and too ever-present to disregard. But in that moment, what she most wanted me to know was how her awareness of love had been expanded.

I want to be clear; this is different from the dismissive proverbs about making lemonade when life gives you lemons or the insistence that "when God closes a door, God opens a window." I still wince when these words are spoken in response to my own losses or those of others. Practicing equanimity is about the importance of making room for contradictory experiences, such as tragedy that also brings an abundance of love or a blessing that also brings acute loss. It challenges our assumptions that we know just what is coming and how we will feel about it when it does. If we expect our experience to be either consistently desirable or undesirable, we might be wholly unaware of the wider range of emotions co-existing in the midst of change. We might miss the emergence of an unexpected outcome.

David and I once shared an evening with a sound healer and about a dozen other folks, mostly strangers to each other, many of us suffering from our own pain or that of the troubled world we shared. We gathered in a circle for an hour of meditative silence guided by Kristin Fischer's vocals and instrumental music. Afterwards, many of us described our experience as a waking dream state as mysterious as it was creative and healing. David noted it felt similar to a free jazz performance with wide-ranging and unpredictable musical riffs, to which Kristin nodded. She explained that as a classically trained musician, she had transitioned to her new vocation as a sound healer in part because of her desire for more musical surprise. That surprise, she added, was a key element of what made her music especially healing.

How do you generally receive surprises in your life, whether they are unpredicted personal experiences or unexpected events in the world around you? For many of us, a surprise is just packaging around one more thing we do not control, raising our hackles on the threshold. Cultivating curiosity as a first response to surprises will not only help us when living on the threshold; it will greatly increase our quotient of delight even when change is not in the air.

Chrysalis Space

Consider any of your body's typical responses to surprises of any kind, large or small. Do you tense up? Pull back? Cover your eyes? Clench your jaw? Or do you reach out a hand to explore it by touch, or cock your head to the side like a dog listening to a new sound, adjusting its ears to better hear it? If you notice constriction or repulsion or attraction in response to a surprise, it isn't either bad or good. It's just an observation. Imagine your observed response as if it were a package you've been given that you are setting aside for later. You can get back to opening it and actually feeling it later. But by pausing to observe it without judgment for a few moments, you can experiment with curiosity and simply explore it instead.

Now think of a surprise that has come to you as you live on the threshold. The surprise might be an unexpected turn of events, or it could be a response rising in you that you hadn't seen coming. Recall how the surprise affected you when it happened or still affects you now in thinking about it. Does it stir fear, delight, anxiety, or a blank state of shock? There is no right or wrong response. Whatever you feel, send your attention to the part of your body where you feel it most, guided by a gentle curiosity. If you often rely on your vision, try closing your eyes to awaken other ways of knowing. What do you notice about your body and your feelings? What do you discover as you notice them?

Then, setting those feelings aside, ask a few questions about the surprise. What does it involve that you didn't notice or know right away? What are some possible choices it offers, including some that might seem absurd? What do you learn by naming these options side by side? What might be your next response, one that perhaps has been lying in wait, ready to emerge if given a chance?

Doors Opening and Closing

Threshold living begs the question of where we open doors over our thresholds and where we close them. Practicing equanimity asks us to notice both options without judging one as better than the other.

In Rome, in an ordinary year, an interior brick wall covered by cement conceals and seals what is called the "Holy Door" of St. Peter's Basilica. The door is only opened in a Jubilee Year, announced by papal decree every fifteen to one hundred years with the promise of mercy and forgiveness for those who pass through it. The week before the door is opened, a crew of masons begins chinking away at a rectangle beneath the large bronze cross hanging on the interior cement wall. Brick by brick, a small area in the wall is opened, giving access to a zinc box filled with documents from the last time the Holy Door was closed as well as a ring of large keys to reopen it.

"A Holy Door," said Pope John Paul II in declaring the Jubilee Year of Grace in 2000, ". . . is a visual symbol of internal renewal, which begins with the willing desire to make peace with God, reconcile with your neighbors, restore in yourself everything that has been damaged in the past, and reshape your heart through conversion." John Paul II marked the end of the year in January of 2001, solemnly closing the tall brass-paneled doors and kneeling in silent prayer before them.

Fifteen years later, Pope Francis opened the doors again, announcing the Jubilee Year of Mercy. "The Holy Door," he declared, "will become a Door of Mercy through which anyone who enters will experience the love of God who consoles, pardons, and instills hope." Pushing the double doors inward on December 8, 2015, Francis paused prayerfully, alone on the threshold, attendants and media gathered at a distance in the courtyard behind him, a few others waiting inside. His robes billowed gently from a soft wind already moving through as if it had been there all those years, leaning against the bricked doors, waiting patiently for the quiet nudge of Mercy's hands to open them.

It is the nature of a door to be closed as well as opened. Sometimes our most important task on the threshold will be to close a door that has been open too long or one that can no longer stay open. Closing it might turn our attention in a new direction. But when living through change, we also want to notice the doors that have been long closed. What is the task of the lock and the hinge when the mortar has dried and the bricks are settled in? In ancient Armenia, when bad fortune had fallen upon a household, its door would be permanently bricked off and another new one opened. Is a door still a door when its doorknob is hidden? Is a door still a door when concealed or forgotten?

In ancient Rome, the doors of the temple to Janus were almost always kept open. Not only was Janus the god of arrivals and departures, he was also the god of beginnings and endings, honored at the start of the year, the first day of every month, and the beginning of each season. People sought his favor at the start of activities with ceremonial entrances and exits through freestanding gateways located throughout the republic. He was considered key to every new conflict on the battlefield. Soldiers departing for war were careful to leave properly through the brass doors of Janus' temple, which then remained open as long as the warfare continued. Only peacetime allowed the doors to be closed again. According to the Roman historian Livy, the doors were closed only twice during the five centuries before the start of the Common Era.

Chrysalis Space

Where on your threshold are you encountering doors that are open and doors that are closed? Are there doors you might wish to close or open as part of your passage through change? What might help you to do that and what might it mean if you did?

Are there doors within you that are currently concealed? If so, where might they lead? What possibilities are leaning against the closed doors of your heart, waiting to be let out or let in? What is blocking the doors of mercy on your threshold? When those doors open, offering grace, extending hope, who will you become? Where will it be possible for you to go? What practices might help to keep them open?

Opening Toward Forgiveness

Equanimity is not always accompanied by forgiveness, but it can be an orientation that makes forgiveness possible. Other writers and teachers have explored the complexities of forgiveness with the attention it requires. My task here, regarding threshold dynamics, is to note that forgiveness can sometimes aid our passage, given the right circumstances. It is not mine to say whether or not any of us should forgive particular wrongs we have suffered. When it comes to the ongoing and life-threatening injuries inflicted by systemic racism, for instance, it may not even be fitting. I do believe, however, that when we are in the upheavals of change, we are often well served by cultivating the openness of heart and mind that makes way for forgiveness, *when* we need it and *if* we choose it. That openness is created by the threshold skill of equanimity.

In its true and healing form, forgiveness is neither a denial of an injury inflicted nor a deliberate effort to erase its impact. The old admonishment to "forgive and forget" is simply wrong. The amnesia this saying encourages misses the point of both the power and the requirements of forgiveness, and the necessity of truth telling that names the injury and the responsibility of those who inflicted it. True forgiveness changes neither the wrong that was committed nor the consequences of it. As the saying goes, "Forgiveness means giving up all hope for a better past." If anything, it is an honest acknowledgment of what was done and the impact it had. What forgiveness does is to add what Quaker writer Douglas Steere calls a "fresh act" to the events of the past, specifically one that opens the way for a different future, especially for the one who does the forgiving.

On some thresholds, we might need to name those who have wronged us or caused our losses. It may be important to hold them accountable, directly or indirectly. On other thresholds, when no one is directly responsible, it is common to look for someone to blame. Or we might blame ourselves, rightly or wrongly. The point of cultivating an opening toward forgiveness is not to deny our own responsibility or others', but to notice how our assessment of blame affects our ability to move across the threshold.

Notice, if you name those responsible for your situation on the threshold, does that naming lighten your load or make it heavier? Does it open you to more possibilities or keep you in a role or a pattern longer than is helpful to you? If you name yourself as responsible, does that blame help you grow and change, or does it weigh you down with shame? How you answer these questions might help you consider whether forgiveness might be important or helpful to you on your threshold.

Sit quietly for a moment, noticing where the word "blame" lands in your body and how you experience it. Gently bring your attention to that place, observing what is happening there without judgment. If you feel nothing from reading the word "blame," let yourself be curious about that. Then take a few breaths, focusing on the air moving in and out, replenishing what you need, exhaling what you don't. When you are ready, continue reading.

Blame can be a charged word. Some of us automatically turn it outward at others or at the larger world for being such a brutal and punishing place. Some of us automatically turn it inward, counting ourselves responsible for everything that has gone wrong, even when the evidence points elsewhere. Practicing equanimity asks us to turn off our automatic responses, whatever they are, and to wonder open-endedly about the many ways in which change comes and responsibility is carried and choices are revealed. It means interrupting the patterns that have gone before, including patterns of judgment, guilt, blame, or shame, and shaking off their hold on us so that we can grow, discover new choices, and create new patterns.

As a threshold skill, equanimity means we can name those responsible for past events while unhitching them from the rest of our thresholding story. If we hold ourselves responsible, equanimity honors our ability to change and choose differently in the future. It is the skill of turning the page and writing a new chapter, fully aware of what has gone before and creatively open to what might follow. It is an invitation to wield the wild, imaginative, and redemptive power of authorship in writing what comes next.

Chrysalis Space

What is a pattern of blame or forgiveness you have experienced on the threshold? Is it a closed or open pattern? Does it leave room for shifting to a new pattern? If you hold yourself or others responsible for changes occurring on your threshold, does that increase or decrease the possibilities you allow yourself as you cross this threshold?

On a sheet of plain, unlined paper, let yourself doodle, drawing a repeated pattern that might represent your threshold and how you experience the question of responsibility for your threshold changes. After drawing this pattern across half of your page, interrupt it, opening it up in any way. Continue your doodling, intentionally choosing shapes and patterns that are open and changing. What do you notice in your doodling and how you feel as you do it?

360-Degree Living

The dominant culture in the United States is forward leaning, often failing to even notice what is not squarely in front of us in space or time. My tai chi teacher, Chungliang Al Huang, grew up in China but has lived in the US for six decades. Pointing out that not all cultures share this forward proclivity, he leads an exercise to remind us that true awareness and presence is an invitation to orient ourselves in *all* directions, forward, back, and side to side. First, he says, stand facing whatever direction represents your "personal south" at that moment, south being the direction of greatest sunlight. One's "personal south" is whatever direction connects you to the light and energy you need. In a room, it might be a window with a view. Outside, it might be east in the morning, west in the afternoon, or at any time in the direction pointing you toward a shoreline or vista. Doing this in a group, you might form a circle facing your teacher or one another as a source of light.

Having chosen our "personal south" in that moment, we then pivot 90 degrees to our left, taking one step toward that direction with our left foot and, with our opposite hand up and arm bent at the elbow, lowering the hand while straightening the arm as a simple gesture of acknowledgment. This is a "wind-up" direction. Turning back to the right (and facing our personal south again), we then repeat the single step with our right foot and the alternating arm gesture. Then we continue pivoting to the right with another 90-degree turn each time, moving in a full circle to end up back at our personal south. For good balance, we then complete the same sequence in the opposite direction.

I find this exercise especially useful when living on the threshold, where change is rarely linear. A threshold passage might circle around many times before we have finished, and it will often include multiple turns of direction we had not seen coming. To really pay attention in between the no longer and the not yet, we might need to orient ourselves in a full 360 degrees, as well as above and below us. As we do, it will be helpful to note which direction offers us the most energy while also acknowledging that guidance, wisdom, and opportunity can come from anywhere around us, regardless of the direction we are facing.

Parker Palmer notes this truth as being hidden in the Quaker saying, "Way will open." In his book *Let Your Life Speak*, he describes a difficult time in his mid-life years, when he waited faithfully but became frustrated that way was not opening. He turned to a Quaker elder and asked her why way seemed to open for others and not for him. To his surprise, she assured him that way had not opened in front of her either. But, she added, "a lot of way has closed behind me, and that's had the same guiding effect."

When a door closes in front of you, what do you do? Keep knocking on it, maybe pounding harder? Do you sit down in despair? Or do you turn in a new direction to discover whether another way may be opening for you there? As the Buddhist teaching puts it, just when you think you know where you're headed, the universe will roll boulders into your path. Walking around them will either confirm your commitment to the path you are on or open your awareness to a new path you might otherwise never have found. Neither will be possible if you just stand there cursing the rocks.

We think we know where we're headed. But how can we possibly make a wise choice if we are only looking in one direction? Chungliang also likes to say, if you feel like you're lost, first get centered. Then explore your options.

In another exercise, we stand still and ask this set of questions to open our awareness not just 360 degrees, but above and below, and within and without as well.

Is the energy in front of me equal to the energy behind me?
Is the energy to my left equal to the energy to my right?
Is the energy above me equal to the energy below me?
And is the energy within me equal to the energy all around me?

As we ask the questions, we open our awareness in these multiple directions and begin to calibrate and equalize the flow of energy around and through us. Like a flower opening to the sun, we receive what we need while offering whatever we have to give. This balance centers us in the present moment, where we pause to experience what is happening now, profoundly open to the many possibilities waiting within and around us.

Chrysalis Space

Are you typically oriented in one direction more than others— ahead of you or behind you or any other direction? What new options might you discover by pivoting and exploring a wider sphere?

Pause for a moment to take inventory of the energy described above, noticing where you are open or closed to the energy before you and behind you, to your right and your left, above and below, and within and outside. Then follow the "personal south" exercise also described above. Where is your personal south today, physically as well as metaphorically? As you open your awareness in a full 360 degrees, what do you notice? Where do you currently experience the greatest sources of support and energy, both within and around you? Where might you discover new sources as yet untapped? How might you regularly connect with these resources for guidance or support as you step into the unknown?

If you want to write about this from a prompt, start here and follow wherever it leads:

"When I turn in a new direction . . ."

A Wider Horizon: Border Dwelling

On the border between Mexico and the United States, not far from the reach of the Pacific Ocean at high tide, is a small international park established during President Richard Nixon's administration named "Friendship Circle." It was a modest undertaking, a circular plaza created around an historic border-marking monument and intended as a meeting place for people from the two nations on either side. In 1971, First Lady Pat Nixon inaugurated the park by planting a tree, having her security people symbolically cut through the barbed wire running along the border and reportedly saying, "May there never be a wall between these two great nations. Only friendship."

By the time I visited Friendship Circle from the United States side, some forty-five years later, it was a different scene entirely. A twenty-foot wall of corrugated steel, built by the United States, scored the border, running inland as far as the eye could see and stretching out into the ocean well beyond low tide. An equally tall and formidable fence cut through the small park itself, leaving the obelisk on the Mexican side and the remaining portion of the circular plaza on the US side, penned in and resembling a small prison yard of dirt and cement with a few scrub trees under twenty-four-hour surveillance.

Next to the secured gate on the US side, two yellow warning signs, one in English, one in Spanish, read, "CAUTION: ENTER AT YOUR OWN RISK"—"PRECAUCIÓN: ENTRAR BAJO SU PROPIO RIESGO." The US side of the "park" was only open Saturdays and Sundays, from 10 a.m. to 2 p.m. During those hours, under the careful screening and watchful eye of the US Border Patrol, ten people from the US were permitted to enter the locked area at a time. From there, they could speak to people on the Mexican side through a fence so tightly woven the only touch possible was by pinky fingers small enough to reach through.

At the time of my visit, the Mexican side of the park was a vibrant and less guarded scene. The southern side of the fencing around Friendship Circle was colorfully painted and the area leading up to it was planted in small, tended gardens. On the beach nearby, families were laughing and playing and periodically stepping up to the slatted metal wall to look through it toward San Diego. By contrast, on the US beach, only the birds were allowed that close to the wall, where a row of orange cones and the constant watch of Homeland Security officers preserved an empty, silent zone about sixty feet deep.

It was, and still is, more than a division of land and people. The wall and other US policies and measures enforcing this border have long been part of a complex and intentional system of power and control specifically designed to limit the movement, choices, and treatment of Mexican and Latinx people coming into the US. On the summer day of my visit to Friendship Circle, I was not allowed near the US side of the wall. But had I shown up at the border crossing a few miles inland, as a white US citizen speaking English in a midwestern accent, I would likely have been granted easy passage from north to south *and* back again. To the contrary, anyone brown-skinned and fluent in Spanish crossing from south to north, no matter what papers they present or where they call home, can expect to be regularly detained for hours in an often disrespectful review by the US border patrol. It is not the simple math of division, but an exponential multiplication of power repeatedly used against particular people. As poet Alberto Ríos put it, "The border is an equation in search of an equals sign."

Who knows what the border looks like now as you read this, and from whichever side you are on as you do? On the day David and I were there, we stood for a long time on the US sand, watching the waves rolling in along the formidable wall. Maybe it was the ridiculous sight of a wall trying to divide an ocean. Or maybe it was all the water in my body responding to the water in which the wall was submerged. Or maybe it was the sounds of the families playing on the beach in Mexico or the birds flying freely overhead from one side to the other. All I know is that in that moment I felt the wall inside me, as if it cleaved through my own being. How much more painful must that incision be for those traveling to the border from the south seeking asylum on the northern side and instead, being regarded as a dangerous threat and turned away? Or how much more cellular the fracture might be for the many local residents north and south whose families, friends, and work lives straddle both sides of the border and whose reunions and crossings are interrogated and regularly denied by the US national policies of othering?

What is the price we *all* pay when one group of people has the power—and wields it—to cut itself off from another group of people? Carl Jung insisted that the people we name as "other" represent parts of ourselves we are not yet willing to encounter. Which is another way of saying that every exiled "other" leaves a wound on both sides of a border drawn and defended to keep them out.

Practicing equanimity can be a powerful exercise in reconciling ourselves with anyone we have labeled and shunned as "other" and in reclaiming the disowned parts of ourselves. Equanimity does not erase true differences—between nations and identities, between you and me, or between the parts of myself that I welcome and those I don't. Difference itself is real and often important. But equanimity refutes the declaration that everything and everyone on one side of any line is good, acceptable, and safe, and that all on the other side is not. It opens us to relationship, not only with people who are different from us but also with parts of ourselves we wittingly or unconsciously try to deny or exclude. Equanimity is a posture of heart and mind that makes the borders of our worldview and our psyche both more visible and more porous.

Lillian Smith, a writer and white southerner devoted to antiracism work in the mid-twentieth century, described a childhood experience that first alerted her to how racism had shaped and divided her from others and from herself. "Without words," she said, "it comes. And suddenly, sharply, one is aware of being separated from every person on one's earth and every object, and from the beginning of things and from the future and even a little, from one's self."

To willingly encounter not only the ones we label as other, but also the unwelcomed parts of ourselves, is difficult but healing work on a deep and personal level. It also serves as an inoculation, equipping us to resist injustice—not only around immigration but also other faces of racism, sexism, ablism, heterosexism, transphobia, and classism, to name a few. Oppression in any form requires a violent separation of the self from others and from our own conscience. It depends on a disruption and denial of the natural relatedness and interdependence of all life. When we heal these schisms, we tear down the walls within us that abide and support the false premises of oppression and the separation on which it is built.

On the Mexican-US border, long after the steel barrier was constructed into the ocean and Friendship Circle was fenced in and guarded, people on both sides of the border have jointly organized many events to defy the wall and the divisions it tries to enforce.

Poetry readings, yoga gatherings, and concerts have all insisted on connection through the barricades and across the border. Bird-shaped kites have been lifted by the wind to traverse the schism. And the waves keep rolling along and through the steel wall, sounding their question: how will we find our way back to the goal of befriending ourselves and one another without fences and othering judgement?

Chrysalis Space

Where do you draw the line that marks off the "other"? Is it a line or a fence or a wall or some other form of gated separation? An opinion, a stereotype, a judgment? Does it run through a plaza where you meet others for encounter and exchange in your work for social change and community healing?

The global refugee crisis of the twenty-first century is a worldwide threshold we all play a part in, whether we have immigrated or not. Whom do you regard as the other when considering immigration and how does that affect your engagement in the many related issues and concerns? What power dynamic is created by the lines you draw defining the "other?" Challenge yourself to name different kinds of "others." When I ask myself this question, I am often quickest to name "opponents," people with different opinions than my own about what should be done. But it is possible to label someone as "other" out of sympathy, too, holding their suffering at arm's length and sometimes creating an unhealthy model of charity or service based on a distanced, one-way relationship. Uruguayan writer Eduardo Galeano made a helpful distinction between charity and solidarity, saying, "I don't believe in charity. I believe in solidarity. Charity is so vertical. It goes from the top to the bottom.

Solidarity is horizontal. It respects the other person. I have a lot to learn from other people."

Now recall a situation in your own experience, related to immigration or not, when you shared an open-hearted encounter with someone you had regarded as "other." It might have been just a brief exchange or something that turned into a lasting relationship. Maybe it was a person from a different country or culture, of a different race, age or gender identity, or someone from a different religion, political party, or perspective. As you remember this encounter, notice how it felt to let your guard down and meet the person just as they were without trying to make them more like you. As you recall it now, do you feel your defenses rise? Or does any part of yourself become more curious, present, or alive? How might you connect with that undefended part of yourself? Or if your defenses have risen, how might you cultivate a greater curiosity? What creative acts of relationship, small or large, might you engage and what might that mean in your understanding of or involvement in the humanitarian crisis on borders around the world? What might it mean in your relationship to the "other" within you?

If you like, begin with the prompt below and follow wherever it leads:

"Reaching through the fence toward another . . ."

THRESHOLDING TOGETHER

With a thresholding buddy or a group of thresholders, gather for a meal after each of you has read the reflections on practicing equanimity. Then choose any of the following questions to start your conversation:

- What is the story you've been telling about a threshold you are on personally or the threshold times we now share? How might your perspective on it change if you say "We'll see" as you wait for new developments and watch for new possibilities?
- What are your typical responses to surprise? Do you tense up? Pull back? Clench your jaw? Feel delight? Approach it with curiosity? Talk about a time when your curiosity helped you keep an open mind in the face of change.
- Describe an experience you have had when forgiving someone, or being forgiven, interrupted the story you were in. What impact did it have on the way the story continued or might have continued?
- What would you name as your "personal south" today—a direction you turn toward for light and energy? In this threshold time, what other sources of support and energy might be available to you as you turn in new directions and open your awareness in all directions?
- Share a time when you open-heartedly encountered someone you considered to be the "other." Did they make the first move to bridge the gap between you or did you? What did the encounter mean to you? How did it make you feel? What part of yourself did you experience or engage in the exchange?

THE PAUSE

A Primer in Pausing

He learned it
listening,
watching his newborn sleeping.
Her pause

between breaths
causing his concern,
testing his assumption
that another breath
would follow.

Spiritual teachers
call it the gap—
                a space
between this and that,
a second split and
stretched, making room
for options.
This is how patterns
break open.
How choice happens.

Slow
down.
Make
room.

Remember this rhythm
carried within—
an expectant pause
between inhale
and exhale.

Fertile
  waiting,
    bearing
      an emergence
    wanted,
needed,
not yet
revealed.

Threshold Skill 4:
TAKING PART IN STILLNESS

Imagine that first moment in the chrysalis. The caterpillar's last skin has been shed, its last meal consumed, its attention turned within as the chrysalis shell changes color to mask its existence and its task from the outer world. Certainly, there is a stillness in that sheltered place, but not a barren one. It is a stillness alive with transformation about to begin.

The caterpillar has entered a state no longer guided by appetite and consumption. From the outside, it would appear to be inert. Inside, though, the deconstruction has already begun, in a state perhaps more accurately dubbed an alert participation in a creative stillness teeming with potential.

To say that living on the threshold requires us to pause is not quite adequate, for it requires reimagining what a transformative pause means. We know *pause* as a word born of cessation. Its Greek and Latin roots make that clear. But a brief wandering through the dictionary brings us to another definition. As a verb without object, to pause is to wait or hesitate; to dwell or linger. Which is precisely what all threshold skills come back to—our ability to linger and dwell in between, to perch in the unknown long enough for entirely new possibilities to emerge.

This is not just for people inclined toward spiritual practices. It is especially important for those of us who most readily choose strategic action over sitting still. Executive coach Jennifer Porter notes that in her work with organizational and corporate leaders, the biggest challenge she faces is with those executives who are unable to pause long enough to reflect on themselves. "Reflection," she explains in a *Harvard Business Review* article, "gives the brain an opportunity to pause amidst the chaos, untangle and sort through observations and experiences, consider multiple possible interpretations, and create meaning. This meaning becomes learning, which can then inform future mindsets and actions. For leaders, this 'meaning making' is crucial to their ongoing growth and development."

Pausing in the between is about stopping. Ceasing our efforts to control and determine future outcomes based on what we've known in the past and what we've expected for the future. Braking the forward momentum that preceded our arrival on the threshold and projected us in a particular direction. It is *caesura* in prosody, *fermata* in melody, *lacuna* in botany, *hiatus* in history. Each a stoppage that is not final but fertile, an opening toward something new, a participation in the mysteries of what might yet be but is not now known.

This is the stillness of the chrysalis. This is the pause on the threshold. A lifted foot in the march of time that might come down in an entirely new direction. It is stillness preparing to spring into action, a pause that is not powerless but a gift of temporary suspension in which any number of futures are possible.

Chrysalis Space

What are your practices of pausing, and which of them create a stillness of heart and mind that makes way for something new? Consider your daily habits and list those that allow you to pause. Maybe it's a cup of tea or coffee in the morning. Or a moment of meditation or prayer. A practice of yoga or tai chi. A walk with your dog or time with your cat. (Sometimes we experience stillness in our thoughts or spirit by keeping our body moving.) A hug shared with your child or a loved one of any age or species. An entry in your journal. A daily reading. An evening prayer. Make a list as long and inclusive as you can.

Then go back and review your list. Ask yourself of each item: on the threshold I am now crossing, does this practice reinforce the way things have been? Or does it make a small clearing for the way things might be, as yet unnamed and unknown? Does it open space in my life, my heart, my ways of being, for new understandings, habits, or possibilities? Circle those that make such a clearing.

If you have several practices circled, choose one and do it now. If you have only one or maybe none circled, consider what new practices might open such space and offer you room to dwell creatively on your threshold. Or ask yourself how you might modify an existing practice to make it more spacious and welcoming of new ways of being and living. For example, if you have a practice of daily walking that is now physically more difficult or impossible to do, how might you move differently—with a walker or a wheelchair, or on paths through your imagination? Or is there another form of movement altogether, like cycling or swimming, that might be possible instead? Take time to try that new or modified practice now or in the next day. Notice, as you end your practice of participating in stillness and the unknown, what does it feel like in your body, in your spirit, in your mind? What desires and fears, what emotions and hopes arise in the clearing you have made?

Spiritual Practices

Habits and activities that make space for personal growth, for love, and for connecting with the sacred and with others are often considered to be spiritual practices. The list you just made might include examples of some of your own spiritual practices.

Is everything on your list a spiritual practice? Possibly, but probably not. Only you can say for sure. The definition of what makes a practice spiritual is hardly set in stone. I like to say that spiritual practices are known by their fruits—activities and postures that awaken us to the ground of our being and to the pulse of life within us and around us. A spiritual practice will deepen our relationship with the sacred source of life, by whatever name we know it—Enlightenment, God, Allah, Spirit of Life, or Truth itself. But it doesn't stop there. It also calls us into a more salutary relationship with ourselves and others, alerting us to the connectedness of life and our role within that expanded kinship.

One might say that spiritual practices, in their infinite variety, are simply different ways of attentively pausing. They involve stepping back from doing and directing ourselves into a heightened awareness of what is going on right now, inside us and all around us. Can this be done while washing dishes, as the Buddhist teacher Thich Nhat Hanh claims? Probably. But it depends on *how* you do the dishes. Can it be done while you are skiing, as the title of a book on spiritual practices suggests? Maybe. But perhaps only if your skiing connects you to more than the moguls you are maneuvering.

Wisdom teachers from different religious traditions have noted that spiritual practices can be especially important in their ability to create a gap between the past and the future, an opening in our thinking, feeling, and acting that releases us from the unchallenged tyranny of cause and effect. Simply put, it is an opening that makes room for choice. The Buddhist writer Pema Chödrön says we can engage the fruits of these practices in the middle of our daily lives. "Pausing," she writes in *Taking the Leap*, ". . . creates a momentary contrast between being completely self-absorbed and being awake and present. You just stop for a few seconds, breathe deeply, and move on."

"You don't want to make it into a project. . . ." she adds. "You [just] pause and allow there to be a gap in whatever you're doing."

Living through significant change insists on that gap. As a comma between the no longer and the not yet, a threshold, whether personal or collective, requires us to let go of our past before we know what the future will bring. It opens a space in which we can experience both the terror and the promise of change. Acknowledging this simultaneous threat and thrill, we turn to spiritual practices, writ large or small, to steady us and to intentionally make choices. They can slow us down enough to avoid running away in fear or leaping ahead heedlessly, led by assumptions of what the next day will bring. Spiritual practices help us make good use of the gaps that significant change necessarily entails.

In retreats led by Thich Nhat Hanh, Chödrön writes, participants often learned to pause throughout each day as a practice of mindfulness. Periodically, their activities would be interrupted by a bell rung at unpredicted intervals. At the sound of the bell, they were instructed to pause and breathe deeply and mindfully. The idea was to practice pausing on retreat so that one might remember to do so at home during everyday life, interrupting the stagnant chatter most of us carry on within.

Significantly, engaging our spiritual practices on the threshold is more than a path to inner peace. It is an interruption of the ego's insistence that it must know (and control) where we're going. It also disrupts the notion that our passage can only be made alone—a notion sometimes eagerly advanced by the ego.

On the most challenging personal thresholds, the details will be specific to our individual circumstances. But who could possibly be equipped to self-sufficiently face all those challenges alone? On the global thresholds we are crossing now, it is even more obvious that we need one another. Many of the threats we face collectively today—from environmental devastation to gun violence to systemic racism—were established on a foundational myth of individualism and a distrust of community, especially a wariness of people and beings we regard as the other. Pausing on the threshold often invites and fosters a sense of belonging in a kinship that spans time and space and species. When that happens, it challenges the individuality our ego so cherishes.

Pausing does not have to be elaborate or even contemplative. It can be a common activity if it is done with regularity and openness to its fruits. In my early twenties, I served as the communications director for a district of a liberal Christian denomination. Like so many jobs, there was more work to be done than there were hours in the workday, and the temptation was to burrow in at our desks, working without breaks to get more done. But the bishop who led our district had a daily requirement that each one of us on staff, including himself, would pause from our work at 10 a.m. and convene in the kitchen for conversation and coffee. Phone calls were redirected to voicemail. Our appointments were scheduled around that gap in the day, or if we were meeting with a visitor, they too were invited to the kitchen for coffee. And for fifteen to thirty minutes each day, we sat around the kitchen table sharing bits of our work and our personal lives.

We did not call it a spiritual practice. We did not pray, at least explicitly. But we did a lot of storytelling and laughing, some head shaking, and occasionally shared a few tears. We sometimes complained about having to break our workflow. But mostly, we made use of that opening in the day to shift gears, to refresh and remember we were all part of a community larger than any of our offices or work calendars could hold. Like a little Sabbath each morning that required us to park our agendas and commune with others, it was a practice more spiritual than it might have appeared, an interruption more radical than it seemed, and a pause more productive than you might think.

Today, looking back on it, I would call it a spiritual practice, a daily disruption of the notion that we were each individually responsible for completing what, in truth, could only be accomplished in relationship with others.

This kind of interruption becomes more important as the Over-culture and new technology together encourage a relationship with time that is increasingly individualized and guarded. As smartphones and personal devices align our schedules with clocks that never stop, we are continually told not only what time it is but what we are sup-posed to be doing and where we are supposed to be going. How differ-ent it must have been before the invention of the wristwatch.

In ancient Beijing, the *gulou* or drum tower built in 1272 housed twenty-four massive drums installed in its top story for musical per-formances that could be heard for miles around. Not long after, how-ever, the tower was repurposed as the city's timekeeper, tracking the hours with bronze clepsydras, or water clocks, in a lower level of the tower, all connected to a large bronze gong that sounded every quarter hour. In the evenings, at 7 p.m., the drums were struck 13 times in a daily practice called "setting the watch" and marking the end of the workday. Thereafter, the drums were struck just once every two hours throughout the night.

Around the world, chimes and drums and music have been used to govern time among the masses, mostly telling us when to show up for work or worship. Bell towers, drum towers, and clock towers all interrupted an older sense of time found in relationship with the sun itself. Today, when our time is governed by devices most of us carry wherever we go, what would it mean to set these with a bell or a drum that would sound periodically as a reminder not to work but to pause? If you are a practicing Muslim, you know how this works—how the call to prayer orients each day with five pauses for stopping all activ-ities to turn with others toward the holy, bowing down to remember

Allah, to seek guidance and forgiveness. What might be possible if everyone shared a practice of pausing like this, using the gap in the day's business to contemplate and invite something holy and connective to guide and restore us? This was the intention, during World War II, of the war-weary British who created the "Silent Minute" observed nightly at 9 p.m., when the nation paused for a full moment to silently pray for peace. It was also practiced in a prayer tent in north Minneapolis after George Floyd's murder; every day, from morning to late afternoon, people gathered in the open-air tent to share silence for the length of time that the police officer held his knee on George Floyd's neck, killing him. To share that same length of time with people working and longing for peace was a powerful practice inviting us to pause and consider how much can happen in less than ten minutes and how we might each use the time we have to turn our city toward a different, more just future.

Chrysalis Space

Imagine a bell ringing or a sensation gently calling you to pause. If you have a chime or bell or a singing bowl on hand, let it sound. Sitting comfortably, for just a few minutes, turn your attention to your breath. Whatever thoughts arise, let them go on the out breath. Release anything but your attention to your breath and your body and the opening in time you are creating with this pause. Then, slowly, attentively, draw in a new breath. Continue this intentional breathing for at least one full minute, more if you can and if it is fruitful. Whenever you're ready, take one more deep breath, stretching your arms wide on either side on the in breath. On the out breath, raise them above your head and, with palms together, bring them down to rest in front of your heart. When it feels right, continue with the reflection questions below.

What spiritual practices do you engage that remind you to pause? What practices do you already have, or might you develop, to disrupt your attachment to action and instead make space for you to be? If you are quick to connect with your communities of support, what practices do your communities have, or might you develop, for pausing together? If you are more likely to pull into your shell when facing change, how might you more regularly interrupt your isolation and re-member yourself as part of larger community? What do you do regularly to open a gap between your old habits of thinking and doing and new or different options for the future? In that gap, what new choices on the threshold might become visible, audible, and possible?

The Gifts of Stillness

One of the useful modifications of traffic lights and crosswalk signals in recent years has been the addition of spoken messages to supplement the flashing lights with repetitions of the word "Wait." Not only does it make the warnings more accessible to pedestrians with visual impairments, it's also a simple command that can apply to any place of high traffic. "Wait!" Which is to say, be still before you proceed. Pay attention.

Living on the threshold, we know that change is underway, like traffic flowing all around us. Structures, identities, and givens are all shifting. When we pause and wait to pay attention, it may feel like we are going nowhere, but our future is being created in that stillness.

The tradition of keeping Sabbath is one of many lessons teaching us that repose is as necessary to creation as any action. The biblical creation story that takes place over seven days says that on the seventh day, God rested. One rabbinic interpretation, writes Wayne Muller in his book *Sabbath*, makes it clear this resting was not without purpose. Rather, it was *in* God's resting that creation was completed. Stillness makes room for creative movement and completion that might not be possible in the hustle and bustle and noisy clamor of our daily lives.

During a national election that was particularly cantankerous and cacophonous, I had become especially anxious and overwhelmed. I knew I needed to step out of that argumentative atmosphere to better understand the turning point we were collectively experiencing in the United States. So, I made an appointment at the Orfield Sound Lab in Minneapolis, where I had long wanted to experience a yin-yang pair of rooms, one full of sound and the other a space of total silence. I was hoping to learn something about stillness and about paying attention—to sound *and* silence, to origin *and* echo, to the pulsing within me and the pulsing all around me.

First, I visited the reverb room, which was carefully hung with reflective surfaces designed to bounce any sound in all directions so quickly and completely, the sound is instantly and equally distributed. Every tone produced there will reverberate a full six seconds from all four corners of the room, obliterating the trail from where it began and making you wonder if it will ever end. Words strung together there—in a sentence, a question, a promise, a plea—will quickly make a caucus, speaking with and over one another, in dissonance or in harmony.

Standing in a corner of the reverb room, I sang a few notes which were immediately offered back from every direction, my own voice becoming a small choir containing several sections. Steve Orfield, who accompanied me, instructed me to close my eyes while he crossed the room. When he spoke again, I lost any idea of where he was as his voice surrounded me, refracted from every surface in every direction.

Does it matter that we know the difference between origin and echo? Or is it enough to hear what we hear? This is not a literal question. I'm asking philosophically. Metaphorically. Poets and theologians alike have described humans as echoes of the divine. How do we open our attention to that? Is it possible to trace our way back from echo to origin, especially in a world as noisy as ours, reverberating with so much hatred and greed, selfishness and injustice?

Next I moved on to the anechoic chamber, a 15′ x 15′ room insulated by a soundproof shell and encased in two-foot-thick corrugated baffles that constituted its walls, floor, and ceiling. The baffles absorb 99.9 percent of all sound made within the chamber, swallowing up every last decibel with voracious appetite, giving back nothing but a silence so muffled it's like stepping into a head cold. Inside the room, I settled into its only piece of furniture, a straight-backed, cloth-covered chair, where Steve left me for a half-hour of solitude with the doors closed and lights out. I sat in the silence and the darkness and waited.

It was not completely quiet, but the only sounds in the room were ones I made myself. The thrum of my voice as I experimentally spoke and hummed, then sang. The rustling of my cotton jacket. The bellows of my breath and my pulse's muted vascular footsteps slowly marching, going nowhere. I was the sound, the sound was me. And every tone I emitted was immediately stolen without echo, erased so quickly I asked myself if I had really heard it or had even made it in the first place.

As a person who has been able to hear my whole life, this was a new experience. I felt profoundly alone in a most peaceful way. I had no fear. Nor any elation. Just a calm emptiness I wanted to lie down in. Will it be like this after I die, I wondered? Was it like this when I was stardust? My fingers tingled as if alerted to increase their awareness now that my ears and eyes had so little to tell me. After a time, I felt myself tipping backward as if floating, though I knew I was still rooted in the chair. Is this what a caterpillar experiences in the chrysalis? What were my cells saying in the muffled silence? What old cellular memory or imagination was being stirred by the absence of new information?

If I had silence like this in my daily life, I told myself, maybe I would notice what I really needed to know. I thought of the biblical prophet Elijah running for his life in the wilderness. Called out of the cave he had been hiding in overnight and told to stand in the presence of God. A fierce wind howled and split the rocks in two, but God was not in the wind. An earthquake shattered the ground, but God was not in the quaking. A fire roared, but God was not in the flames. Then came a still, small voice. A whisper. Some translators have called it "a thin silence," and the stillness itself was what Elijah needed to know what to do next.

Silence, Florence Nightingale said, is as essential to health and recovery as medication and sanitation. Long after Nightingale's day, neuroscientists have explained that experiencing a new silence lights up the auditory cortex of the brain. As the silence continues and the brain adjusts to it, it doesn't put the brain to sleep but rather opens a conscious workspace within it—a place where we can integrate the outer world with our inner realms of imagination and reflection. Perhaps something like a chrysalis.

In the anechoic chamber, I breathed deeply, comforted by the rhythm of my own inhaling and exhaling. Breathing in, breathing out. Everything around me was designed to receive. Like a towel wicking up the panic of the times, the room's wide baffles absorbed my worries and left me peacefully waiting, listening to the thin silence within and around me.

Chrysalis Space

Where do you go to experience stillness? Maybe it is a place in nature or a daily practice of silent meditation or prayer. Perhaps it is the brief time you linger in bed before sleep at night or before morning rising. Or maybe it is the fresh, private time of your shower. Wherever and however you experience stillness, for the next few days, offer it your deepest attention. In the stillness, whether brief or lasting, practice letting its "thin silence" widen the aperture of your heart's ear. What do you notice when you do?

To write about this from a prompt, begin with the words below and follow wherever they lead:

"In the stillness, I notice . . ."

Getting Comfortable with Ambiguity

The human brain craves order. The more chaos we experience, the more we reach for structure, clarity, and answers. It is entirely natural to become anxious in the metaphorical chrysalis of change when what we've known breaks down into a state that feels like the caterpillar's goo. Jamie Holmes, in his book *Nonsense: The Power of Not Knowing*, calls uncertainty "an emotional amplifier," turning up the volume on all of our feelings, but especially our anxiety.

One definition of *ambiguous* is something that is "unclear or inexact because a choice between alternatives has not been made." Its roots can be traced back to the Latin *ambigere*, or to go around, from *ambi*, meaning both ways, together with *agere*, or to drive. In the Buddhist saying about the universe rolling boulders in our path, we are reminded that when the way is blocked or unclear, we are called to pay attention. We must stop operating on autopilot and be present not only to the path we thought we were following, but also to its many branches and to new paths waiting to be made by our own feet. We are advised to wake up to our choices.

If this sounds like a recipe for heightened anxiety or what some call "decision fatigue," it's worth noting that it may also increase our joy. When Holmes describes uncertainty as an emotional amplifier, he adds that it can also magnify our pleasure.

We can gain appreciation for the power and amplification of ambiguity from Chinese philosophy and Taoist teachings, which describe the state of *wu ji* as the origin of yin-yang and of all being. While yin-yang teaches us that opposites cannot exist without each other, wu ji describes the chaos out of which opposites emerge. Represented by a circle of alternating black and white spiraling out from the center, wu ji is the swirling chaos of potential that not only gives way to opposites but also gives birth to being itself and to all creativity.

Translated literally, *wu ji* means "without ridgepole," which is to say without that horizontal beam in a roofline that holds the rafters up. Like a body without a backbone, a roofline without a ridgepole is hard to trust. But Taoist sages tell us that this state of chaos is teeming with prospects. It is the proleptic energy of an idea, a relationship, or an  experience about to emerge. It is the waiting in the stillness that comes before any judgments of good or bad are made. It is the moment experienced briefly in our hearts before attachment and aversion position themselves for their customary emotional tug of war.

If we can suspend our aversion to uncertainty and open ourselves to the power of wu ji, we will enter a creative state often described as "the zone." It might look like nothing. It might feel like goo. It might terrify us with its lack of shape and order. But it contains an exhilarating overspill of possibility. It is precisely the kind of generative abundance that allows the multiplying imaginal cells in the chrysalis to overwhelm the caterpillar's immune system as it tries to attack them as something foreign and new.

How do you court the power of wu ji? Or do you perhaps avoid it at all costs, understandably preferring the ridgepole, as I sometimes do? Holmes says one common way to get comfortable with ambiguity, and the power it holds, is to do puzzles or brainteasers that "fight against the mind's natural tendency to quick closure. They ask us to battle our reflexive assumptions." In other words, it's one more invitation to let go, especially of the ego's need to control where we're going.

It's not that the ego is bad. There are plenty of times when we need it, just as more often than not, we appreciate or depend on having a ridgepole in place. The problem with the ego and its insistence on control is that it pinches off our access to the vast store of knowledge carried in our unconscious and in our bodies. When we pause on a threshold and set aside our need to control what comes next, we are opening the door in our awareness to the wisdom of our emotions, our bodies, and our unconscious. It's the kind of wisdom we access when we "live the questions," as Rainer Maria Rilke advised in *Letter to a Young Poet*:

> ... be patient toward all that is unsolved in your heart and ... try to love the questions themselves like locked rooms and like books that are written in a very foreign tongue. Do not now seek the answers, which cannot be given you because you would not be able to live them. ... Live the questions now. Perhaps you will then gradually, without noticing it, live along some distant day into the answer.

Chrysalis Space

What might happen if you loved the questions surfacing in your life now without trying to seek quick answers? What if you took time to live those questions for a while instead of answering them? Maybe you already do, in which case this exercise will come easily.

Find a supply of index cards or small pieces of paper and a container, such as a ceramic jar or a small box, that you will enjoy having out in plain view and of a size that will hold a good number of cards or papers. On each piece of paper, write a question related to your threshold to which you do not know the answer. Fold them to fit in your container and leave them there for several weeks, months, or longer. If the container has a lid, put it in place. Knowing the questions are there and will not be lost, let go of the need to answer them for a while. As other unanswered questions occur to you in the future, go ahead and write them down too, each on a different piece of paper that you then add to your container.

Some weeks or months in the future, after you no longer remember what all the questions are, take a few of them out randomly and read them, choosing one that resonates with you on that day. Without trying to answer it, carry it in your thoughts (or your pocket) for a day or a few days, just living it. Loving it without answering it. Explore it like a book written in a foreign tongue, appreciating its heft and its cover, and maybe flipping through its pages, knowing you're not yet ready or able to read it. After a few days, try writing about it or reflecting on it (still without necessarily answering it), beginning with the prompt below and following wherever it leads:

"If I live this question now . . ."

A WIDER HORIZON:
Beyond the Binary

David and I are the proud parents of a single child, now beautifully grown into adulthood. Sometimes when making small talk with new acquaintances, I am asked if I have children. *Yes*, I reply. *Just one.* It surprises me how often the next question is, *boy or girl?* To which occasionally I have paused and said, *both*.

More than anyone else in our family, our child Cat has taught us to hold questions open. As parents, we noticed early on that, even as a toddler, Cat was rejecting the small boxes of gendered stereotypes, instead cautiously and creatively expressing an identity that either enlarged or defied those boxes. It was the early 1990s. David and I knew almost nothing about gender identity as more than the male/female options we'd been given. We did know something about love, though, and tried our best to accept and support our child for who they really were. It just wasn't always easy to know how.

We sought out information and professional counsel and learned about questions we had not even known to ask. Though no one early on in our search told us about gender-neutral pronouns, we were taught the difference between sexual orientation and gender identity and advised not to jump to any assumptions, but instead to pause, keeping many options open for Cat to claim in their own time. We were often confused and made mistakes and now, years later, could name numerous things we might do differently. But we did our best with what we understood to be our primary assignment—to make it clear we would love and support our child however their identity emerged and bloomed.

It was no simple task, especially for Cat. It was painful to discover how ubiquitous and rigid the two-gender system was, and how deeply it is scored not only in our culture but in our own brains that are shaped by that culture. We were surprised and often discouraged by how much effort—and equanimity—it takes to break free of boxed-in binaries of male/female thinking and being. My longstanding feminist philosophies, which I assumed would be helpful in dismantling gender stereotypes, quivered to consider that the mantle of womanhood that had shaped my own coming of age in the women's movement might not be broad or flexible enough for the job. I would have to loosen my grip on that too. What would it mean to open my awareness *beyond* gender or into a more multi-dimensional and fluid understanding of it? Could I let gender be a galaxy, or a many-partnered dance, instead of two polar stars endlessly, dizzily locked in a spin around each other? These, I am coming to believe, are deeply feminist questions, but it was hard for me to understand that until I first let go of what I thought I knew about being a woman and a feminist identity based on that understanding. I needed to pause for a while in a state of not knowing to make room for a different, wider perspective.

Today, around the world, we are witnessing a growing openness to gender's extraordinary diversity and fluidity. Tragically, as with other significant shifts, especially those related to identity and power, these are not straight-line winds of change moving in just one direction. We have also experienced a terrible backlash against transgender and nonbinary people and the policies and laws that acknowledge, welcome, and support them. All of this confirms that we are living on the threshold between old understandings of gender identity already changed and new understandings still emerging. Who knows where it will lead? Any time we break free of either/or thinking, whether it's about gender or something else, we might also be making room for other new ways of thinking and being that haven't even occurred to us yet. There are so many questions we could be living now. I have noticed that using they/them pronouns for any individual person serves to remind me of how many identities we all carry within us and how few of them can really be adequately described with either/ or propositions. When we upend the categorical thinking of gender binaries and other boxed opposites, we are creating chrysalis space where any number of new ways of being might yet emerge.

Chrysalis Space

How and when does binary thinking play a role in your life? And how might a practice of pausing help you notice it long enough to choose a more nuanced or multidimensional understanding?

If you're already living beyond the gender binary in your own identity and understandings, you might choose to skip the following exercise. Or you can use it to reflect on another form of either/ or thinking that is at play in your life—for example, the distinction between self and other. Adapt the exercise or bypass it as you like. But if your understanding of gender, unconsciously or explicitly, tends to divide the world according to masculine and feminine categories, try this exercise as an invitation to pause from this sorting and consider what might be discovered beneath and beyond these two categories.

Find or create a strip of paper about eighteen inches long and an inch tall. (If you only have shorter paper, cut two or three one-inch strips and tape them together.) Then take a moment to pause and consider: what positive traits come to mind when you think about masculinity versus femininity? On one side of this strip, write down some positive traits you associate with masculinity or men. Write them large enough to read easily and so that they create a single line of a few words that fills the strip from left to right. Then turn the paper strip over and, on the other side, do the same thing with positive traits you associate with femininity and women.

Bring the two ends of the strip together, flip one end over, and tape them together, forming a Möbius strip—a closed loop with a single twist in it. Notice what happens to the formerly separate sides. Gently run the looped paper through your fingers, reading the words as they move from associations with one gender to the other and back again. Looking at the strip as you hold it still and flatten it a bit, what do you observe about the layering of these associations? What does the Möbius strip suggest about the assumptions built into binary thinking? How might pausing be a useful practice for disrupting these or other assumptions?

THRESHOLDING TOGETHER

With a thresholding buddy or a group of thresholders, gather for a meal after each of you has read the reflections on taking part in stillness. Then choose any of the following questions to start your conversation:

- Describe one way to pause you have recently practiced that makes way for new thinking and ways of being in this time of in-between. Is it a new practice or one you have done for a long time? Do you need to modify it to be helpful in the changes you are now experiencing? How does it help you participate in the stillness of your current threshold(s)?
- Tell about a time when a spiritual practice you were doing disrupted your old ways of thinking or being, making possible a new direction or choice. Is that a spiritual practice that could be helpful to you now?
- Describe something you do to find and enjoy stillness or silence. What happened when you did this recently with heightened attention to what you noticed?
- Share one question you are living with now that has no answer yet. What might it mean to love this question without trying to answer it?
- Recall a time when your assumptions about another person's identity were disrupted, opening a new space for you to encounter them in greater dimension and wholeness. What did that space make possible?

Threshold Skill 5:
NAVIGATING THE UNKNOWN

Inside the chrysalis, when the caterpillar's form has broken down, it would be difficult to recognize anything in that goo as a blueprint for a butterfly. For the caterpillar, having never witnessed or experienced it before, it feels like destruction without any new form apparent, which is why the caterpillar's immune system takes aim at the imaginal cells as they begin to vibrate. The humming cells appear to be something foreign. They bring the threat of the unknown. In truth, they are carriers of a new code and map, a necessary guidance toward the caterpillar's next life.

The inclination to attack the unknown showing up on our doorstep (or inside us) is a human trait as well. In the human psyche, Jung called this our shadow—those unwanted aspects of ourselves that we deny or repel at great cost to our wholeness and our relationships with others. Writ large, it is a tendency tragically played out in systemic racism and in the plight of refugees around the world turned away at borders in the name of national defense. Fearful instincts often cause a pulling back, withdrawing from relationship with others and repelling the unknown itself. We seek to conquer and control, to limit our exposure to what we name as foreign, and to tame the unknown by developing a mastery so intent on control it often pinches off the greatest promise waiting on the threshold.

In the chrysalis, metamorphosis is only made possible by the profligacy of the imaginal cells. Multiplying faster than the caterpillar's immune system can contain, they overwhelm all efforts to control and conquer. Like a cancer—but one that leads to life—the imaginal cells take over. They grow in number. They vibrate. They cluster. And the invisible maps encoded in them begin to take shape and provide exactly what is needed for the butterfly's form to appear.

The thresholding skill we find here is the skill of remaining in relationship with the unknown, greeting it, letting it change us instead of trying to change it. This skill is about naming our fears without getting attached to them. Remembering that wherever fear is present, we also find an invitation to muster courage. We are asked to companion our fears so that we can companion the unknown and the future itself. Evoking a spirit of curiosity and exploration while rejecting the impulse to conquer, we will call this threshold skill Navigating the Unknown.

In an era of Google Earth, it can be hard to imagine the mindset of explorers who purposely set out with a destination entirely off the map. *Terra incognita*, some European mapmakers of old labeled the uncharted regions, or *Parts Unknown*, as English-speaking mapmakers sometimes called them. *Here Be Dragons*, said one ancient globe (the Hunt-Lenox globe, now in the collection of the New York Public Library), projecting a monstruous shape on territories they had never visited.

By definition, threshold living occurs in *terra incognita*. Though we might turn to maps prepared by others who have crossed similar thresholds for guidance, no one's experience will be quite like ours. Their maps might offer useful information, but they will never be complete, and they might also be biased. On any threshold, personal or collective, we will encounter areas that have not been fully charted. Our challenge, in entering and naming these regions, is to cultivate an explorer's curiosity strong enough to replace the battle stance triggered by speculation of dragons or other mythical hazards.

We might begin by noting that dragons do not always need to be slayed. In some Chinese teachings, the appearance of a dragon is an invitation to encounter our own sources of personal strength. Before any attempt to conquer or slay a dragon (or any other perceived threat), we might first ask whether it could be embraced and befriended, enlisted as a guide or teacher. During the early months of the Covid-19 pandemic, Eula Biss, author of *On Immunity*, observed numerous problems with framing our global struggle with the virus in terms of war. In an interview with New York Public Radio's *On the Media* podcast, she suggested that a better metaphor for disease, based on language used by immunologists, might be education. Just as immunologists describe pathogens as "tutoring" our immune systems, Biss proposed that we ask ourselves how we are being "schooled" by our illnesses and to notice how they might change our relationship to our bodies and our health, as well as our engagement with the "teachable moments" illnesses bring to us.

Metaphors matter. To describe our thresholds as scenarios of battle requiring the conquest of external beasts and forces hardly does justice to the inner dimensions of passage and their many teachable moments. Honoring the double nature, internal and external, of every significant threshold, we might gain access to more wisdom by framing our passage as a journey rather than a battle. "The art of life is more like navigation than warfare," writes Alan Watts in *The Watercourse Way*, "for what is important is to understand the winds, the tides, the currents, the seasons, and the principles of growth and decay, so that one's actions may use them and not fight them."

How do we recover the sensibilities required to understand the winds and the seasons, the laws of growth and decay, so we might better navigate the unknown terrain on our thresholds? In an era when many of us often find our way by satellite guidance rather than activating our own senses or drawing upon our knowledge of nature and our inner winds and seasons, we might have to brush up on skills that have atrophied or perhaps were never fully developed in the first place. The revival of wayfinding, an ancient Polynesian art of long-distance navigation, offers some clues about what is required.

In the late twentieth century, Nainoa Thompson became the first Hawaiian since the fourteenth century to practice this art. President of the Polynesian Voyager Society, he trained for decades with one of the last master navigators, Mau Piailug from the island of Satawal in Micronesia, and in 2007 was himself named a master navigator by Piailug just three years before Piailug died. Thompson has made countless trips in the Pacific, crossing thousands of miles in a traditional double-hulled canoe to land at his named destination without so much as a compass. He describes this art of wayfinding as a challenging discipline of attention, requiring constant observation and memorization. You must note and remember, he says, where you are at all times, based on many factors, including the position of the sun and its path on the water; the position of the wind and the character of the waves, seen and felt; the formation and position of clouds, their type and their movement; the stars—about 220 in particular—and where they rise and set; the appearance and flight patterns and species of birds; and even the appearance and condition of natural flotsam: if a leaf floating on the water is still green, how far away is the land where it grew, calculated by the speed of wind and waves?

Clearly, it would take tremendous time and effort to learn to read and interpret all of this. But Thompson says it is more than a training of the mind and senses. It is also a condition of the heart, a caring for canoe and crew, nature and culture. "Our ancestors," he is known to say to his crew, "learned that if they took care of their canoe and each other, and if they marshaled their resources of food and water, they would arrive safely at their destination." It is no surprise then, that his message posted online in the early months of the pandemic offered similar wisdom to his fellow voyagers and others for navigating the unknowns of a threshold time:

"I want to thank you for the way you treat each other, always with kindness and respect, and for bringing the best out of each one of us when we're united. Because we're going to need it. In the upcoming months and years, we're going to need that unity as a message and a symbol of what powerful good can come out of communities when they're unified around the right sail plan."

How do the rest of us, who are not master navigators, know what the right sail plan is and how to follow it? We each have the capacity to pause attentively in the unknown, to orient ourselves to polestars and currents, to landmarks and coordinates, in ways that will help us chart our way across terrain we have never before traveled. It is attention turned outward *and* inward, to the emotional instruments we have all been given for this navigation. Taking time to notice and understand our emotions on the threshold is a key tool that will help us respond to the uncharted waters we are crossing.

"Our emotions are our human radar or lookouts," writes Susan David in *Emotional Agility*, "a neurochemical system that evolved to help us navigate life's complex currents. Emotions, from blinding rage to wide-eyed love, are the body's immediate physical responses to important signals from the outside world."

Unfortunately, instead of checking our emotional radar for guidance, many of us put our emotions on lockdown when living on the cusp of change. Every time I lead a group of thresholders, in our first gathering when participants describe their thresholds to one another, some are surprised by their own tears in the telling. Participants who are on thresholds they have wanted and chosen may be especially confused about why they are crying; others, telling stories of obvious and deep loss, often do not expect the strong emotions that come as they share with the group. A good number will apologize and try to stop their tears. But tears, we remind each other, can be a sign that truth is being told and that trust is forming. So we pass the box of tissues and try together to welcome tears, honoring the truth and the trust they may signal.

How often, when making a decision about an unknown future, do some of us insist on not letting our emotions get in the way? We might consult experts. Make lists of pros and cons. Tally expenses and revenues. This is not true for everyone or in every culture, but the Overculture's emphasis on reason as more reliable than emotion teaches us to especially value information that is measurable, suggesting that numbers are more truthful than the uneasiness churning in our stomach or the joy dancing in our heart or the tension knotting in our shoulders. What if, as many cultures teach, these emotions themselves are important instruments meant to help us navigate the decisions and uncharted terrain opening before us?

The poet Jorie Graham once said this is the work of poetry: to connect us to our feelings. More particularly, she explained that her own poetry about the devastation of the earth is meant to make herself and her readers "not only understand—we all seem to 'understand'—but to actually 'feel' (and thus physically believe) what we have and what we are losing—and . . . devastatingly [how] much more of creation we are going to be losing." What might change on the environmental thresholds we're on together—and our ability to make our uncharted way across them—if we really felt our grief over the losses in the natural world? Or, on thresholds related to any system of oppression, how long would that oppression last if those benefitting from it personally and emotionally felt the painful reality and impact it has on the ones being oppressed? When the video of George Floyd's murder spread across the world, millions of white people who had previously ignored the racial violence of the police joined in protest because they grieved his death under the officer's knee. Now the challenge for them is to not become numb to the toll that violence continues to take, in addition to the toll it took long before George Floyd died.

On your threshold(s), personal or shared, what guidance might you receive by tuning in to your feelings and letting them continue to offer their wisdom?

Chrysalis Space

What emotions have you been experiencing on your threshold? Without needing to understand the reason for those emotions, take a moment to name them. Make a list, if words come to you. If it's hard to name them, take out your smartphone or other electronic device and open a screen of emoji options. Which ones express your feelings about the threshold you are on? Send yourself a message with all of the emoji that seem relevant to your threshold experience. Print it out and over the next week, make notes on it with words that name those emotions. Or give your own expression to the emotions in music, art, dance, or any other form. Notice especially if any of these emotions surprises you or if there are any you have been ignoring or denying until now. Sometimes on a threshold marked by loss, for instance, there may be mixed in with our grief feelings of relief or even joy that we don't give expression to because we deem those emotions inappropriate to our loss.

After listing as many feelings as possible, choose one and ask yourself, what signal are your emotions giving you on your threshold? What knowledge do they offer for your navigation? How do they advise you to chart or to change your course, considering where you have been and where you are going?

Reading the Signs

At the Pipestone National Monument in southwestern Minnesota, a small wooden sign on the Circle Trail says simply, "Look Here to See the Oracle." The words are carved into the sign directly above a one-inch peephole. The first time I encountered this sign, I looked around. Where was the Oracle? I studied the scenery behind it. Any oracle with a sign pointing to it must be stationary enough to find with my own eyes, I thought, but all I could see was an expanse of the Sioux quartzite outcropping that bordered the path we were walking.

I dropped down on my knees to look through the hole in the sign, and sure enough, there it was. Clear as could be in that circular view: a large angular face chiseled into the outcropping by nature's hand. The steep, bony forehead sloped back over a sharp-edged nose and cold, stone lips. Perhaps tribal shamans could read those lips and decipher their messages for others. As a twenty-first-century white visitor new to the site and its history and its stories, I struggled to hear the oracle's voice, peering through that hole pointed like a telescope through time. But I did not doubt there was truth spoken and found there.

Standing up again, I could find the oracle without the sign's assistance. Grateful for the sign's frame that trained my attention to find the right spot, I noticed it also trained my heart to take note of my surroundings in a new way. In that moment, I found wisdom speaking all around me: *Look here to see the oracle. And here. And here.* I spun around, acknowledging the place, its contours and voices, its messages and wisdom. *Here and here and here.* Truth and wisdom spoken everywhere, if only we will pay attention. If only we will stop and bend a knee.

We live in a world teeming with signs, guides, landmarks, and symbols, so many more than I sometimes notice as I trudge along with my sights set on a distant destination or preoccupied by other thoughts. Learning to pause on the threshold develops the skill of seeking, finding, and receiving guidance available to us wherever we are along the way. Anything can serve as a guiding sign as we move through the unknown if it helps us notice where we are in the moment and offers new options for moving on. It might be an animal or natural object that has long been present, either symbolically or physically, in your life, or it could be something showing up for the first time, alerting you to particular strengths and perceptions you now need. Carl Jung called these "hints," or clues to the unconscious knowledge we all carry within but often do not access in our conscious thinking. The knowledge will still be there if we do not seek to understand it, Jung said. But without understanding it, we will not be able to participate in it and, instead, will be "dragged along" by it.

Learning from signs and oracles does not require turning away from science and reason. But it may be necessary to pause and let nature—and our own creative unconscious, activated by nature—speak first. Think of the wisdom and guidance lost by the early industrialists puzzling over how to power their factories and cities even while standing in the sunlight or the blowing wind, never noticing the renewable energy abundantly present around them. We may need to become still long enough to receive the wordless missives of wind and water, of fire and earth—and our own inklings within. Then, having listened in curiosity, we might be surprised by the new paths our reasoning takes, as we wonder anew with an awareness stretched larger and an aperture opened wider.

Chrysalis Space

What images and words or phrases are capturing your attention as you live in the between? Start a collection of poems or sayings, photographs or drawings, symbols or emblems that you're drawn to now. It can be especially fruitful to begin collecting these when you're not trying or looking. Try pausing after meditating or walking or roaming; after playing with a child or a pet; while singing or chanting or humming; first thing in the morning after sleeping and before coffee; or when waking in the middle of the night, still lingering in the creative theta brainwaves of dreaming. These are all good states for gathering images and words, signs and symbols that can offer you guidance or wisdom. The content of your dreams is an especially good place to look.

After you have gathered some visual symbols or images, make a collage, assembling them in an arrangement that you find satisfying, whether you know why or not. Add any important words or phrases that come to mind. Keep the collage on hand while living on the threshold, revisiting it from time to time and asking yourself what these symbols, images, words, and phrases might mean to you on any given day. Consider it as you would a dream. Just as the meaning of a dream can sometimes be revealed by consulting guides of common archetypes and symbolism, you can research the significance of the symbols you've chosen, while remembering the real meaning (of dreams as well as any symbols you have gathered) can only be determined by your own inner knowing. When a suggested symbolism resonates with you (or if you fiercely resist it!), it is likely true. If it carries no weight when you consider it, it is best to dismiss it. You are the authority on what any symbol means—and your authority comes from noticing your intuition about its meaning.

If a particular image or item gives you courage and hope in the changes you are living with, consider how you might keep it with you when you need it. If it is an image, can you keep it on your cell phone? If it is a small object, can you carry it or a piece of it in your pocket? As you move through this time of great change, be on the lookout for new signs and symbols that might speak to you through the unknowns that lie ahead.

Making a Map

One of the first tasks many of us turn to when preparing to travel to places we've never visited before is to consult a map. Whether on paper or on Google, we might measure the distance from here to there, the different routes by which to go, and the variables we can expect to encounter on the way and when we arrive: differences in climate and terrain as well as any barriers such as borders or language or geographical formations. A good map can show you all of these and more.

In *Sylvie and Bruno Concluded*, an expanded fairy tale written for adult readers, Lewis Carroll offered an unusual exchange about maps between the narrator and a mysterious old man from a foreign place.

"What a useful thing a pocket-map is!" I remarked.

"That's another thing we've learned from your *Nation," said Mein Herr, "map-making. But we've carried it much further than you. What do you consider the* largest *map that would be really useful?" he asked.*

"About six inches to the mile," [I answered.]

"Only six *inches!" exclaimed Mein Herr. "We very soon got to six* yards *to the mile. Then we tried a* hundred *yards to the mile. And then came the grandest idea of all! We actually made a map of the country, on the scale of* a mile to the mile!"

"Have you used it much?" I enquired.

"It has never been spread out, yet," said Mein Herr. "The farmers objected: they said it would cover the whole country and shut out the sunlight! So we now use the country itself as its own map, and I assure you it does nearly as well. . . ."

When living on the threshold, the most important map is the one spread out beneath our feet. The place where we stand now and what we might surmise, from this vantage point, about the terrain ahead. But you can also benefit from making your own map of your journey. As a creative charting exercise, it will engage your memory of where you have been before and your imagination about where you are headed. Teaming these two human faculties together can reveal surprising glimpses of your own inner knowing.

The Atlas of Experience by Louise Van Swaaij and Jean Klare is an extraordinary book of evocative maps to spark your imagination. The atlas maps places such as the "Sea of Possibilities" and "Frozen Wasteland;" "Mountains of Work" and "Plains of Solitude;" the "Slough of Despond" and "Swamps of Boredom." There is a lighthouse on the tip of the Island of "Clarity," where the biggest settlement is called "Vision." A rocky peninsula labeled "Adventure" is marked off as unknown territory that includes landmarks labeled "Challenge" and "Surprise" and the "Point of No Return." There is the city of "Change" and its adjacent suburbs, "Evolution" and "Revolution." And there is the town of "Belief," halfway between the villages of "Wish" and "Hope" and a little farther on from "Fantasy" but not so far from "Superstition."

Pausing on your threshold, ask yourself how you imagine the terrain ahead and how you might name it. Is it a Stormy Coast, a Sea of Plenty, or an Ocean of Peace? Is it crossed by a Stream of Ideas or a river of Blood, Sweat and Tears? You can map the terrain as a flattened cartographic chart or as an imaginary landscape populated by beings. In a recent threshold group, one participant began mapping her threshold with a tree that was full of birds of different kinds, including bluebirds of happiness and a woodpecker of self-criticism. Another person, coloring in a region of her map, discovered the letters she'd taped to the cover of her thresholding journal, which was beneath her map as she colored, came through like a ghostly image of a name on her map. Another participant, approaching retirement, drew a map she described as moving from "BusyBusyBusy Land" (very familiar territory) to "The Land of Quiet." Several of the towns in BusyBusyBusy Land, she noted, were named "Goal," and she realized when writing that on the map how close that spelling was to Gaol, the old-fashioned word for Jail. "Huh!" she exclaimed, gaining a new appreciation for the freedom she was about to experience. "I have my eye on that Quiet Land," she said, "where I can write more, spend more time in my lovely study."

The point of this exercise is not its accuracy of distance or terrain or its artistry of drawing. Rather, its wisdom (often shared with curiosity and humor) is typically found in the names given to places and challenges mapped and to the relationship between one part of the map and another. It is perhaps more a map of our expectations, including some we are aware of and more interestingly, others hiding in deeper pockets of our consciousness. Knowing more about the emotions and assumptions we carry internally about the unknowns we are encountering externally can help us claim greater balance as we move on.

Chrysalis Space

To make a map of your own threshold, begin with where you are and what you know. First brainstorm different kinds of terrain— mountains and valleys, deserts and oceans, gorges and swamps, prairies and forests, islands and cities. Make a long list of any kinds of geography that come to mind. Which of these might lie ahead as you cross your threshold, and how might you name them?

Take a blank sheet of paper and some colored pencils or markers or crayons and, with colors in hand, ask yourself, what is the frontier that awaits you? What is its geography and how might you name it and draw it? Engage your imagination. It can be a wilderness or a metropolitan area, fantastical, or based on familiar reality. When you're done drawing, if you wish to write about your map or reflect on it, consider what it tells you about where you are headed and what you are feeling. What will you need to cross this terrain and what will be best left behind? What tools and supplies, nourishment and protection, knowledge and abilities, guides and advice? Begin with the prompt below and follow wherever it leads: **"Crossing this frontier, I will need: . . ."**

Finding True North

Living in the north, as I do, I know how quickly a big snowstorm can obscure even the most traveled highway. When the snow falls heavily, it shrinks the distance one can see to almost nothing. At the same time, its accumulation will rapidly obscure the edges of the road, the curves, and the ditches. Those living in the country with animals in the barn will tie a long rope between the house and barn to guide their way at milking and feeding time. And those in the city might do best to weather the storm in place.

The lack of visibility in a snowstorm is not unlike the conditions on the threshold, so I am fascinated to learn how animals navigate and hunt or forage in a world covered by deep snow. One winter's day, I watched a squirrel leaping lightly across the surface of the snow outside my window until it arrived about ten inches away from the base of a small oak sapling. Immediately, as if it knew the spot precisely, it began to dig with its front paws. The snow flew and the hole grew until the only part of the squirrel still visible was its bushy gray tail. It paused, out of sight, and then emerged, sitting upright on its haunches, front paws holding a small prize the size of an acorn. Lifting it to its mouth, it nibbled nervously and then, having verified its fruit, the squirrel tucked the nut into its cheek and scampered up to a high tree branch to eat.

How did it know the nut was there? Some nuts may be found by scent, I've read, but squirrels also create spatial maps in their memory when burying their cache of nuts in the fall. Then they use landmarks, like a nearby tree, to orient those maps. I think of the forests of old that once grew near my home, and the way even the loggers who ruinously practiced clearcutting often left standing a single "landmark tree" to later help them navigate the flattened terrain of their destruction. In the middle of forests that have since grown back, you can still find a few of these old landmark trees surviving, recognized by their girth and strength, their height and age. They now provide another kind of landmark, too, as milestones in time, old ones testifying to what was lost under the loggers' slaughter; memorials to what might have been, under a lighter touch of axe and saw. They also represent a promise of what might one day still be if we change our habits of harmful harvesting.

Watching a fox hunt in the winter is even more instructive for navigating thresholds where the terrain is invisible or deeply buried. When a fox hunts a mouse tunneling out of sight beneath several feet of snow, it can make a kill with a single leaping lunge almost three of every four attempts—but only if the fox is facing northeast. About 20 degrees off magnetic north, to be precise. Scientists don't yet know *how* foxes do it, but they have observed that when the foxes tune in to the earth's magnetic pole, using it to triangulate what they hear, they are able to set their aim more accurately, much the same as missiles do to find a target not visible to the eye.

What is your magnetic north, and are you tuning into it on the threshold, as you navigate unknown and unseen terrain? Opening our whole being to the vibrations within and around us and learning to correlate them with whatever we claim as our magnetic north is less dependent on our ears and auditory nerves than it is on our ability to listen with our hearts. Your magnetic north might be God, Allah, or the spirit of life, by these or other names. It might be the universe, known by science or spirit, or your communities, your ancestors, and your stories of history or myth. Any of these will provide a magnetic field we can home in on, correlating it with what we learn from our own heart and from the world around us.

What the fox knows, hunting in the winter, is not so different from any of us consulting our own instincts as well as science and the wisdom teachings of old stories. When these sources and the ley lines they draw for us intersect, we might experience a pull in a particular direction, a vibration or energy resonating deep within, or a surprising sense of certainty in the midst of great unknowns. We may have no words or names or explanations for this, but it can be as key to our survival as a hungry fox's catch on frozen winter's day.

Chrysalis Space

What is something you have trusted as your magnetic north? How do you align with it? What daily practices keep you attuned to it? When you engage those practices regularly, what do you notice about how your magnetic north helps you get and keep your bearings in the midst of a storm? Remembering a time when it guided you reliably in the past, what might you learn if you let it guide you today?

A WIDER HORIZON:
Mapping Unity and Bridging Religious Diversity

Human beings may be the only species that draws maps, but we are far from being the only ones to use them. Using tools of orientation scientists are still working to understand, insects, animals, and birds find their way with magnetic field detection, by counting their paces, or by making complex calculations of the position of the sun and the latitude, time of day, and season. These navigational methods create cognitive maps of their surroundings that allow them to know and remember where they are in relation to other parts of their habitat, whether they are on lengthy migrations or crossing the shorter distances between food and home.

The human brain also uses cognitive mapping by creating a matrix of triangles overlaid on our brain's image of our surroundings. As we move through physical space to the tip of each triangle, the grid in our hippocampus is activated, orienting us to our position within the larger mapped area. These cognitive maps of physical space, in turn, affect our understanding of and response to our social space and the people in it. As early as 1948, psychologist Edward Tolman suggested that a narrower cognitive map of physical space could result in more closed attitudes toward, or downright hatred of and violence against, others not like us.

How, then, do we expand these cognitive maps—not only our own but also the narrow maps guiding the growing number of people forming or supporting hate groups within the US and elsewhere, including those targeting members of non-Christian faiths? A project in Omaha, Nebraska, called the Tri-Faith Initiative offers one promising example of changing the physical landscape to create a new map of relationship. Started in 2006, the Tri-Faith Initiative was formed by members of three Abrahamic faith communities—Jewish, Muslim, and Christian—who joined together to purchase, plan, and build a joint campus they call the Tri-Faith Commons.

Since then, each community has constructed their own place of worship on the campus according to a plan developed together. A fourth building, the Tri-Faith Center, provides a space for members of all faiths to share, along with a circular bridge at the center of the Commons connecting all of the buildings and faith groups while offering passage over Hell's Creek below. Imagine the cognitive map of relationship this campus is creating in the minds of those who worked through years of challenges to make it possible and real. Then consider the cognitive maps its buildings and grounds and circular bridge will draw in the minds of all who inhabit and visit it for years to come. Just reading about it is likely already laying a few new gridlines in your cognitive map, as writing about it has done in mine.

"Coming together in one neighborhood addresses the topic of fear directly," said Tri-Faith board member Wendy Goldberg. "We could never build walls high enough to protect ourselves. But if we were to build bridges of mutual understanding, we together would have the opportunity to move beyond fear."

An international group of neuroscientists has located the hippocampus as the site in the human brain where mapping occurs. It is situated in the limbic system, which is also responsible for emotions, memories, and storytelling. Perhaps the ability to imagine a journey across unknown terrain, or to actually create that terrain as the Tri-Faith Initiative has done, can be a first step in writing a whole new story. "[It] gives us the opportunity to narrate our own stories and histories," said another Tri-Faith board member, Nuzhat Mahmood, of the shared campus project. "The reality is that our respective histories include many examples of cooperation and understanding between our three faiths. We want to tell that story, and write our next chapter together."

Chrysalis Space

Recall a time when you experienced a positive encounter across differences. It may not have ended in agreement but should be one that ended on a note of mutual respect and acceptance—or, at the very least, compassion. Maybe it was an encounter with someone of a different faith or culture, race or gender identity, age or class. Or maybe it was a person with whom you share common identities while holding different values or opinions. If nothing comes to mind as a positive encounter across difference in your own experience, think of a story you might have learned from someone else. You can also use the story of the Tri-Faith Initiative, visiting their website to view the campus.

Try to remember the characteristics of the space you were in when you had that encounter—or, if you are thinking of a story shared with you, imagine the space it took place in. Notice any details of the space that might have supported this encounter. Was it crowded or spacious, outside or inside, bright or low lit, tidy or a little cluttered? Did it include particular visuals, scents, sounds, or tastes? How did it feel to you, and how did that feeling influence your encounter? Name at least five sensory aspects of it.

Now imagine the characteristics, similar to those or different, of a different space, one you might create or find that would allow you to show up as you are while welcoming others who are in some way different from you to show up just as they are. Focusing on the space itself, what would it be like to be truly welcoming to *both* of you? Also ask yourself what you might overlook that is important to others who are different from you. Draw or describe this place, and then ask yourself, is there any place you know and have access to that might offer something similar? Or how might you create such a place?

To write or reflect from a prompt, begin with these words and follow wherever they lead:

"It would be a place . . ."

THRESHOLDING TOGETHER

With a thresholding buddy or a group of thresholders, gather for a meal after each of you has read the reflections on navigating the unknown. Then choose any of the following questions to start your conversation:

- Name one prominent emotion you have been experiencing on your threshold(s). What knowledge does it offer for your navigation of this unknown terrain? How does it advise you to chart or to change your course, considering where you have been and where you are going?
- What images, symbols, words, or phrases are especially meaningful to you in the between? It might be a whole poem or part of one; a photograph; an animal or being; a symbol or object. If you made a collage you are willing to share with the group, bring it to the gathering and talk about what it means, naming anything you learned while making it.
- Bring the map you created to share with the group. What is the terrain you drew and how did you name it? Did you experience any surprises while making your map? What does it tell you about what you might need as you move into the terrain of the unknown awaiting you?
- Share a time when you experienced surprising clarity that served you well in the midst of unknowns. How did you know what you knew, and how did it feel when you trusted it and followed its guidance?
- Tell about a place you have experienced that gives you a cognitive map for relationship across difference. What was it like? What encounters did you experience in it? Are there places you have access to now that could make space for difference in your cognitive maps?

Threshold Skill 6:

PREPARING FOR THE JOURNEY

Often, when packing for a long trip, I begin by laying everything out on my bed. Clothes, shoes, toiletries, passport, journal, camera, other supplies. As a reality check, I put my empty suitcase or backpack on the bed too, noticing the limitations of its size. Then begins the challenge of removing what will not fit in my bag. What will I need in the place I am going? And how can I know if I've never been there before? If you've ever lugged a heavy bag on a long hike across a big city or up a steep mountainside, you know the best answer is not always to err on the side of having too much.

Preparing for any journey is, in part, a matter of having the right clothes and supplies. But even more important may be checking our inner supplies of flexibility, curiosity, balance, and good humor. These four weightless things can do more to prepare us for new adventures than any quick-dry, all-purpose, reversible item of clothing we might purchase for our travels. When we are equipped with these four inner resources, we can get by with a smaller bag because we'll be better able to adapt to unanticipated events and needs with resiliency and creativity.

The same is true on the threshold. We might think we need special equipment or expertise where we are headed—and sometimes, this will indeed be the case. When we're adapting to a new limitation or disability, even the simplest piece of equipment can make things so much easier. But not every change will require this. Before we look for preparations that come from the outside, we might check our inner inventory of what can only be supplied from within. Just a small amount of curiosity and flexibility can help us find and make use of more external resources than we might otherwise be willing and able to access. Similarly, good humor is a leavening agent that can lighten the heaviest load.

While things like curiosity and humor may not apply to caterpillars, a caterpillar has its own internal resources to draw on when its time in the chrysalis begins. Remember, it has eaten its way from that tiny egg to the plump tubular being that splits its last skin. It has busily prepared for its journey by devouring the food it needs to grow. But when it dissolves inside the chrysalis, its intake is over. The only resources it needs now are coded microscopically within its imaginal cells. Its task inside the chrysalis is to trust that coding. To recalibrate its balance. To become so flexible that the old structures of its caterpillar body will disappear. To become so open to the new vibrations of its imaginal cells that it will let them lead to a dramatic reorganization.

How have you been preparing for the changes that lie ahead? Are you packing large bags, hoping to bring along as much as possible to ease your way? Or are you looking for ways to travel light, considering how to reduce the baggage you bring from where you have been? In the early days of personal computers, the first portable computers were big heavy devices mostly made portable by the fact they could be closed like a suitcase and had a handle affixed to the outside. Aptly named "luggables," they were a far cry from the smartphones we slip into our pockets today, offering a good reminder that just because something has a handle and is purported to be portable doesn't mean one would want to travel far with it.

Chrysalis Space

When living through significant change, it is often wise to leave our "luggables" behind. Take a moment and ask yourself, what habits, belongings, and identities might you be better off setting down instead of lugging them along as you cross your threshold? Make a list. If you let go of these, what part of yourself might be encouraged to emerge? How might you build up a greater supply of flexibility, curiosity, balance, and good humor to replace the lug-gables you leave behind?

Revisit the embodied exercise in Letting Go on pages 19–20. Then browse your list above and the one you might have made earlier in response to the questions on page 20. Choose one thing from your lists, and, if you want a writing or reflection prompt, begin with the words below and follow wherever they lead:

"If I leave _____ behind, I might feel . . ."

Changing Needs

If it is difficult to know what we will *not* need, or what we can leave behind, it is equally challenging to know what we *will* need in the unknown that awaits us. Where do we begin to answer that question, and how can we really prepare, not knowing where we are headed?

Surgeon and author Atul Gawande, in his book *Being Mortal*, writes about the many options and decisions affecting quality of life and care as people enter their last years. He notes that one of the big challenges in caring for people near the end of life is that our health care system—and perhaps our larger culture itself—is led by goals of cures and fixes, while at some point everyone will be beyond fix-ing and curing. To support people in their final years (and months and days), he argues, we must ask and be guided by what each per-son defines as well-being when cures and fixes are not possible. Not only will this definition be different from one person to the next, but

Gawande also cites studies showing how often our own personal goals and needs for well-being will shift as the end of our lifespan approaches.

What we consider to be "living well" may be different when we are physically healthy and strong than when, at any age, our circumstances have made us aware of our fragility and the possible shortness of time remaining. My own experience of cancer, as other survivors have told me it has done for them, taught me that the mere appearance of what some call the "c-word" on one's medical chart can rearrange priorities and habits in unexpected ways. A fellow breast cancer survivor recently told me she no longer worries about speaking her truth for fear of hurting others' feelings. It is not that she has turned into a rude person, but that honesty and openness have become more important to her than not "rocking the boat" now that her own boat has been so hazardously tossed about by her cancer diagnosis.

We can ask this question on our collective thresholds too. What do we need for living well today, given the fragility of the earth and predictions of its decline? Might we answer this question differently now that the double "c-word" of climate change has been recorded on the earth's medical chart? What does living well look like now for the earth and for us? Does it rearrange our priorities, personally and collectively? Does it make us any more willing to rock the boat with big changes based on honesty and compassion for the earth's well-being and our own? In these pandemic times, we are all learning lessons about fragility and impermanence. Its daily changes ask us, again and again, what is essential for our well-being now.

When preparing for your journey through change, ask yourself—multiple times as you go—what do you need to experience well-being now? And now? And now? Ask the question with as much curiosity and openness as you can muster, listening carefully for answers that may shift. What you needed before will not necessarily be what you need now or what you will need in the future. The caterpillar knows only its need to eat and grow until its last skin is shed. We too might know only an appetite for what has fed us before until we move more fully into our chrysalis space. Each step of the journey might reveal a new kind of well-being and new needs to support it.

Chrysalis Space

What does well-being look like for you now? Revisiting the map you drew earlier of where you are and where you're going (see "Making a Map," page 123), what might you need for cultivating strength, curiosity, persistence, resilience, and joy while crossing the terrain ahead of you? Imagine yourself in the new terrain your map describes. How might your sense of well-being change and what will that well-being require?

If you want to reflect from a prompt, begin with these words: **"Perhaps what well-being means now . . ."**

Inhabiting Change

One of the benefits of being in a familiar time and place is that it accommodates our habits—all those repeated patterns of thinking and doing that make life a little easier. Habits can be good or bad, of course, and they run much deeper than simply determining if we drink coffee or tea or rise early or late. The origins of the word *habit* are rooted in the conditions and appearances that make us who we are. Early usages of the word denoted one's physical or mental constitution, and present usage often refers to our tendencies or patterns of response, growth, and being. They are a significant part of our identity.

What are the habits that surface when you face change? What responses rise in you instinctively, and are those responses affected by practices you may have cultivated for greeting change?

It is natural to respond with the protective reflexes meant to help us survive. *Fight, flight, freeze, or fawn,* mentioned earlier as reflexive responses to danger, start in the most primitive part of our brain, which is wired to keep us alive. All of these are responses of our autonomic nervous system, which kicks in without our choosing. We may have every intention intellectually to embrace change, but our instinctive "lizard brain" will take over when a possible threat is perceived, becoming a rapid-fire control center that gives fear or anger first say in what is possible and not possible on the threshold.

Fortunately, we can cultivate particular practices or new habits that will make room for different, chosen responses. Simply noticing a response of fight, flight, freeze, or fawn in ourselves nonjudgmentally is a good place to begin. You can explore these reactions on your own or with a somatic therapist, if your response is strong. What is your first reaction to change of any kind and to the specific kind of change your threshold brings? If it causes you to want to strike back, run away, freeze, or appease, how might you pause just long enough to observe and name that, remembering each is a natural response? Or if a change you're experiencing causes you to lose awareness of your body, how might you redirect your attention to wherever you are right now and what you are feeling? Notice anything near you or within you (your breath, the chair you're sitting in, an object, or a bit of light or a repeating sound) that offers support or unthreatening presence or pleasure. Let yourself be curious about what you experience in these sources of support and in yourself. (You might want to revisit the reflection titled "The Body of Love," especially the practice described on page 9.)

Noticing what is happening inside us and immediately around us—and developing habits that help us do this when we experience stress—will give us more choices in how we respond to the fear that naturally arises when encountering the unknown. Learning to pay attention to what we feel, where we feel it, and how and when, allows us to use our own chosen methods for settling it. This might be as simple as humming, one of my personal favorites, or singing or chanting. It could be just a few minutes of slow breathing, especially by taking a deep breath in and exhaling slowly through the mouth with lips pursed to make the exhale even slower. It might be walking or rocking or alternately tapping one hand and then the other on your heart or your knees. Or sitting still in a chair for a few minutes, with awareness of the chair supporting you and the floor supporting the chair and the earth supporting the floor. Even pretending to walk while you are seated can help, pushing down on your feet as if taking five or six steps, then waiting to notice any effect this might have. It could also be as basic as bouncing or jiggling. (*My Grandmother's Hands*, by Resmaa Menakem, is a great resource for understanding the importance of settling our fearful responses and metabolizing trauma in our bodies.)

Embodied spiritual practices, including those listed above, are useful in settling our lizard brain's fight, flight, freeze, or fawn response while stimulating the vagus nerve, which in turn calms the heart and breath. Prayer and meditation as well as yoga, qigong, and tai chi all have a grounding effect that slows us down and can open us to the discomfort uncertainty creates. Whenever I travel, I try to find time and space to practice even five minutes of tai chi each day as a way of connecting to the new ground beneath my feet. It's a practice that helps me find my place in new surroundings and to set down a few new tender roots to support me while I am there.

Another habit that can be helpful is collecting (and when possible, committing to memory) passages, poems, songs, prayers, or quotes that strengthen and calm us. Not only does this stock us with a ready supply of comforting words, but when traveling to someplace unfamiliar, it also offers something to share in cross-cultural encounters with others—especially the songs. When language is a barrier, I have spent a whole evening taking turns singing songs to each other. The music offers a bridge even when we do not know the meaning of the words the other person is singing.

At home, we can make good use of memorized poems or passages as well. When journeying into a new experience, a new role or relationship, or a new understanding, we can bolster our courage by calling up a poem or song committed to memory and reciting it in a challenging moment. The rhythms and rhymes will help settle our bodies, while the words offer wisdom and support. They also remind us that we are not alone but are in the company of others who have ventured into the unknown before us, leaving behind their poems and songs as guidance now helping us to find our way.

"The great thing about poetry," says poet and novelist Guy Johnson, "is that no matter what lonely street you are on, someone has been there before you. And survived." Johnson describes a time when a poem recited by his mother, the writer and human rights activist Maya Angelou, gave him the strength he needed following his ninth spinal surgery. Temporarily paralyzed from his neck down by a car accident years earlier, he had been told on his surgical thresholds that he would likely not walk again. In the middle of this medical journey, Johnson recalled a poem his mother had taught him as a child. The poem, "Invictus," was written by William Ernest Henley, who had survived his own traumatic medical experiences—including the loss of a leg to tuberculosis of the bone and an eye in a riding accident. One day Johnson called his mother from the hospital, asking her to recite "Invictus" to him. She replied:

> *Out of the night that covers me,*
> *Black as the Pit from pole to pole,*

I thank whatever gods may be
For my unconquerable soul.

He listened as she recited the rest of the poem, ending with its last line:

I am the master of my fate:
I am the captain of my soul.

Then he asked her to recite it again together with him. Only after they were done did he tell her that while they were reciting the poem, his doctors had been removing the stitches from his back.

Memorizing songs and poems and other habits of body and mind can help us stay awake and attuned to our own agency as we pause between what we once knew and what awaits us in the future. Because our bodies and minds are designed to be on high alert, full of tension and constriction in the face of the unknown, we can prepare for this journey by becoming practiced in habits that settle both our lizard brain and our body. Using those practices can buy us time in which to cultivate awareness and curiosity toward the unknown. They create space that invites greater flow inside us—the movement and opening for growth.

Chrysalis Space

What practices or habits have you cultivated, or might you cultivate now, to stay present during your fear or anger and other strong feelings in the face of the unknown and to settle your body when experiencing those responses? Take five to ten minutes to engage a familiar practice, or try one mentioned above or described more fully in other reflections (some options are described on pages 19 and 48. Afterwards, scan your body for places of constriction and places of flow. Continue that practice for another few minutes or try a different one, focusing on any part of your body where you still feel constriction. Then turn your attention to another part of your body that feels more open, asking yourself, if this part of my body were to speak, what might it say about the changes I am facing today? Write the answer down or just sit with it, receiving it, absorbing it.

Being Alive

Inhabiting our bodies is a good way to stay present during fear without letting it rule us. It also happens to be an astonishing invitation to experience more joy and vivacity.

Decades ago, when visiting my sister for her wedding in southwestern Colorado, a small group of us spent a hot, sunny afternoon on a tall rocky precipice overlooking a deep, aqua blue lake far below. We'd come in our swimsuits, not just to look but to leap. To launch ourselves from the stony ledge into thin air, where my sister—who had done this before—informed me I would have time to think a whole thought between the time my feet left the cliff and the moment I slipped into the water below.

I was young and knew little about the quivering energy that often accompanies big life transitions like weddings, not only for those getting married but often for others attending the events. Although I was wholly unaware of it then, it seems no coincidence to me now that we chose an activity and location supremely well suited to discharging that threshold energy by flinging our bodies from the solid ground beneath our feet toward the distant, unknown waters below.

My new brother-in-law was the first to jump. His bare feet slapped against the stone, never slowing for a second as he ran up to the rock's edge and catapulted his body forward in a single sailing arc. It was beautiful. His arms and legs swung joyfully through the air, tasting the instant's freedom until, with a distant splash, he slipped out of sight, appearing soon after with a broad, exuberant smile.

I was feeling none of that joy myself, instead anchored to the stony ledge by my fear of heights. Only after my sister and everyone else had jumped, some of them multiple times, did I muster a reluctant resolve just strong enough to cast me from the cliff toward the water below. There was nothing speedy or graceful or carefree about my launch, but oh, what a full-bodied thought I had when my feet left that cliff! My skin was kissed by the wind, my hair brushed back from my face, my hands and feet were giddy with weightlessness. And the thought sailing through me was a sweet, complete song that, for an instant, swept my mind clear of all fear. As the cool water rose up to meet me, I wondered, why had I not done this sooner?

It is tempting to consider the threshold space between where we've been and where we are headed as a gap of danger to be crossed as quickly as possible, steeling ourselves to the experience. But the truth is that as terrifying as this space can be, it is powerfully alive with energy and dynamic vitality.

International peacemaker Danaan Parry used a parable of the trapeze artist as a metaphor for the space that opens when we let go of what we know. Swinging on a trapeze bar, Parry noted, the acrobat holds on to the bar, comforted by how real and reassuring it is in their hands. Their focus is set on a second bar, hopefully just as real, swinging toward them from the other side of the ring, waiting for them to take hold of it. But everything is in motion. The only way to grab the new bar swinging toward them is to let go of the old one first and sail across the open space toward the new bar, for a brief time holding nothing.

Parry was interested in the nature of that space in between. "Is that just a scary, confusing, disorienting nowhere that must be gotten through as fast and as unconsciously as possible?" he asked. He answered emphatically, "No!"

> *What a wasted opportunity that would be. I have a sneaking sus-picion that the transition zone is the only real thing and the bars are illusions we dream up to avoid the void where the real change, the real growth, occurs for us. Whether or not my hunch is true, it remains that the transition zones in our lives are incredibly rich places. They should be honored, even savored. Yes, with all the pain and fear and feelings of being out of control that can (but not necessarily) accompany transitions, they are still the most alive, most growth-filled, passionate, expansive moments in our lives.*

Pausing on the threshold is not always a matter of stillness. It can also be a pause of sweeping, animated motion. An experience of being extraordinarily alive and awake to the world and to oneself. This is an experience that can change our whole orientation toward life long after we've arrived on the other side of our threshold. As feminist play-wright Eve Ensler said in 2005, "Real security is not only being able to tolerate mystery, complexity, ambiguity, but hungering for them and only trusting a situation when they are present."

Chrysalis Space

Think of a time when you took a leap, literally or figuratively, that made you feel more alive, more awake to the moment in a heal-ing and full-spirited way. What helped you take that leap? What thoughts or feelings did you have as you took it? On the threshold you are crossing now, how might you inhabit the space in between in ways that are open to movement and perhaps to joy?

Finding the Way Home

Every journey, in its own way, asks the question, *Where is home, and how do you find your way back to it?*

In Joseph Campbell's teachings about the hero's journey, the hero crosses a threshold twice, first when leaving home and later when returning, and is sometimes so transformed by the journey they are not recognized by those who knew them when they left. But any time we are as deeply changed as that, our sense of home itself is also likely to be transformed.

How do you recognize home when you are not the same as when you left? When you've grown or adapted or experienced changes in understanding or identity so that what was once home no longer fits the way it did before? It may feel less comfortable or even unwelcoming. This can be one of the risks when a person comes out, publicly living their true identity after hiding it before. Whether it is related to sexual orientation, gender identity, or a refusal to silently witness or accept expressions and actions of racism and other oppressions, any shift that newly exposes who you really are might be met by resistance from those who want you to be otherwise. You may become painfully aware of the need for a different home or a new family. When that happens, answering the longing for home in threshold living might point us in a new direction or toward different relationships.

What we are really talking about when we say home is a sense of belonging—that resonance between our inner core and our surroundings. Not everyone has had a home like this. But as writer David Whyte points out in his monologue "On Belonging and Coming Home," even a sense of homelessness can ironically help us find our way back home. "As a human being," Whyte says, "all you have to do is enumerate exactly the way you don't feel at home in the world—to say exactly how you don't belong—and the moment you've uttered the exact dimensionality of your exile, you're already taking the path back to the way, back to the place you should be." Whether we've experienced it or not, the ideal of home is that place or community that welcomes who we are and who we are becoming. It not only accepts us as we are; it encourages and nourishes us. Ecologically speaking, it is a habitat where we flourish and bloom. Which brings us back to the question of what is now required to support our well-being, our flourishing, our blossoming.

In the pause between what is no longer and what is not yet, we might discover our greatest need, like the caterpillar's, is for time and space where we can dissolve our old ways of being. In this stage, home might temporarily be wherever we are able to let go of old structures and wait a while for the new ones to emerge. It may be a home metaphorically made of camouflage and protection, as the chrysalis offers the caterpillar's goo. For us humans, it is also made of the relationships, elements, and interactions that will support and protect our becoming. Inside this space, it will be alive with vibrations and new arrangements in the making. A good home on the threshold is an interconnected ecosystem that builds resilience and supports change.

Resmaa Menakem describes this as an environment that makes room for harmony with others. "Resilience," he says in *My Grandmother's Hands*, "is . . . a flow. It moves through the body, and between multiple bodies when they are harmonized. It is neither built nor developed; it is taken in and expressed as part of a larger relationship with a family, a group, a community or the world at large."

At a recent interfaith conference on undoing racism within communities of faith, a young Black participant asked a question of Okogyeamon, a Black elder and longtime leader in antiracism work who had convened the gathering. The younger participant described his own experience of the particular toll taken on people of color showing up for the work of antiracism. He asked, how do you stay engaged in this work?

Okogyeamon acknowledged the size and importance of the challenge. Then he said that for him, it was a matter of knowing where home is and making sure to spend enough time there to be replenished. He made it clear that he wasn't just talking about a house or a place of retreat where the food and furniture is familiar and the door can be closed to the outside world—although his own home is definitely that for him, as well as many friends and colleagues. He was talking about a set of relationships that are restorative. Where is home for you? he asked the young man. Look for a community that will support and sustain you. For me, he explained, it is a small handful of trusted people who keep me in the game.

Chrysalis Space

Who and what keeps you in the game as you live and work on the threshold? What relationships restore your commitment to transformation—both your own and the world's? How might these relationships help you find the protection and support of home as you live in and with change, crossing your personal and shared thresholds? Some of these relationships may be with longstanding friends or loved ones or mentors; others may be new acquaintances appearing in your life now with just the kind of companionship, guidance, example, support, or inspiration that you need on this threshold. What places or larger communities—including any small group of people or other beings in nature—offer you safe space in which to pause, to restore balance and energy, to experience flow and resiliency on your threshold?

Make a list of anyone or anything that comes to mind as you consider the questions above. What would it mean to regard these as your home on the threshold? How might you make use of the space they open for you to support your transformation, your resilience, your passage into the not yet? If you wish to write or reflect from a prompt, consider what sense of home you might find and need on the far side of your threshold and begin with these words, following wherever they lead:

"The home I need most . . ."

A WIDER HORIZON:
Bootcamp for Fostering Peace

Not long ago, David and I had the honor of witnessing a significant threshold of one of his students who entered the Marines right after graduating from high school and invited David to attend his Marine boot camp graduation in San Diego at the end of the summer.

It was a new experience for me, and I was surprised, as a life-long pacifist, to discover how much I related to the ceremony and the values it celebrated. There was music. Plenty of inspirational words. Both seriousness and humor. And lots of talk about transformation. I marveled that if you took away the marching and the guns, the uniforms and the national flag, generally speaking, it had a fair amount in common with many religious services in which I've taken part. The speakers lifted up the three core values of the Marine Corps that constituted the foundation of the boot camp training that had just ended. These too had a familiar ring. There was honor, the ethics of "an uncompromising code of integrity" and "respect for human dignity." Courage, understood as "inner strength . . . to do what is right" and to "overcome fear." And commitment, explained as a "spirit of selfless determination and dedication." Even as I stood to applaud these values and the marching platoons who had completed a most rigorous and disciplined training in them, I could not help asking what it would mean if we dedicated equal resources to training people in these same values re-oriented toward a nonviolent approach to keeping peace.

I am not, by far, the first person to ask this question. In 1960, then-Senator John F. Kennedy asked it differently in his 2 a.m. campaign speech to 10,000 University of Michigan students waiting on the steps of their student union. His impromptu and sleep-deprived words, in what he described as "the longest short speech I have ever made," became the basis for the Peace Corps, which he signed into existence as president less than a half year later. That day in San Diego, though, I was thinking of something different than the Peace Corps, despite its admirable and important model of service. I was thinking of the rigorous discipline of boot camp training and how it might be reoriented toward honing the character and specific skills needed for nonviolent peacekeeping. This idea, developed differently by Mahatma Gandhi, Martin Luther King Jr., and many others historically and today, has also been expertly explored by West Point Military Academy graduate and US-Iraq war veteran Paul K. Chappell.

In a series of seven books, the first written during his active duty, Chappell argues that our world as a whole is pre-literate in the skills and understandings of peacemaking and peacekeeping. Just as societies worldwide once tolerated slavery and treating women as property, he posits, our own current toleration of war itself will one day be considered an unacceptable error of tragic proportions. He proposes waging peace instead of war by establishing a worldwide literacy program of education and training to re-define our understanding of human nature and human needs and to equip us with the skills needed to de-escalate violence before it erupts in war. Since leaving the military, Chappell has dedicated his life to this vision with a soldier's discipline and commitment. As an international speaker and peace literacy educator, he is committed to redirecting our search for security from its current association with war to what he regards as a more sound and reliable association with peace.

This is a powerful example of chrysalis transformation, first deconstructing the myth that humans are inherently violent and that war is inevitable, then making way for new understandings and realigning them to create surprising new forms. It is an approach that insists we begin by shedding, like a skin too small, the belief that peace is unattainable. It asks us to prepare for the unfamiliar terrain of a peaceful world by being trained in new skills that we can practice, personally and collectively, with the discipline of a soldier. As Chappell notes, one of the first and most important peacemaking skills we can learn, especially in relation to our opponents, is listening.

Chrysalis Space

What skills and literacy do you bring to the global thresholds you are most concerned about today? How are they sustaining you and helping you to survive? How are you sharing them with others and developing them further, possibly in surprising new ways?

It can be easy to get overwhelmed by how much we need to learn to counter our old conditioning and to bring about social change. But the most important learning is how to revisit and re-examine our old understandings and worldview, redirecting them toward different conclusions and outcomes. Every one of us has something to offer in our growing collective understanding of what is at stake today on our shared thresholds. If you have trouble naming your own expertise, remember it might be something you learned serving a different purpose. Paul Chappell was trained as a military soldier and then repurposed that training to make a powerful case for a nonmilitary understanding of peace. Or it might be something you've learned as a marginalized person surviving an oppressive system. Audre Lorde's observation, "The master's tools will never dismantle the master's house," reminds us that much of the wisdom needed to overturn oppressive systems will come from the lived experience of those who have been marginalized and oppressed and from the different ways of thinking and being they have preserved or developed. For those privileged by any oppressive system, the most basic training they will need is in listening to those who have been marginalized and from that listening, learning how to re-examine, reframe, and redirect their own skills and knowledge toward liberation.

What do you already know that you can apply to bring about the changes you desire in the world? And what additional training or learning might give you a greater literacy and more effective skills to prepare you for that new world? If it is a threshold related to peace, have you learned the principles and practices of nonviolence, in communication and action? If it is a threshold related to racism, what do you know about recognizing and responding to the characteristics of white supremacy and the culture of whiteness and how can you model or share that knowledge with others? What more might you learn to help us all thrive in the world as it is now and grow into more anti-racist ways of being? For any threshold, what practices do you have, or might you learn, to calm yourself when experiencing fear? How might you practice them to become a steady presence when anxiety moves through a crowd? This is not a checklist of everything you need to learn right now to build the world you want to live in. We can only start wherever we are and, one day at a time, do and learn what we can. Take a single step to learn or practice one thing today that can support you and others in making the change we desire. And then do that again tomorrow. And the next day. And the day after that.

To write about or reflect on this, begin by surveying what you already know. Then move on to things you wish to learn in the future. You might use these two prompts, either alternating between them or reflecting at length on the first and then, when you're ready, moving on to the second.

"It will be useful that I know . . ."

"What I would also like to learn . . ."

THRESHOLDING TOGETHER

With a thresholding buddy or a group of thresholders, gather for a meal after each of you has read the reflections on preparing for the journey. Then choose any of the following questions to start your conversation:

- Thinking about your threshold, share one habit, belonging, identity, or belief that might be a "luggable," better left behind to lighten your load. What will it mean if you do?
- Describe a practice you use to calm or settle yourself when experiencing strong reflexive responses of fear or anger. What do you experience when you do this? How might it be useful on your threshold?
- Tell the story of a time on a threshold when you took a leap, despite your fears, that made you glad you did.
- Name one relationship, community, or place that offers you safe space in which to pause, to restore balance and energy, to experience flow and resiliency on your threshold, to keep you in the game. Do you expect that to continue as you move through this change? How has your sense of belonging changed already? How might it change in the future?
- Name one global threshold you are concerned about, whether or not you have been actively engaged in addressing it. Share some of your skills or knowledge that might be helpful in that issue and name one skill, practice, or area of knowledge you wish to learn more about.

Threshold Skill 7:

CLAIMING COMPANIONS

Let's be honest. For some of us, it can be hard to ask for help or support, especially when we are feeling vulnerable—which is to say, when we need it most. Not everyone wrestles with this need for self-reliance. Under the stress brought by changing circumstances, relationships, and capabilities, some people instinctively turn *toward* community. This is a significant strength of many nondominant cultures today and historically. But others, of both marginalized and privileged identities, can become guarded *against* community at the very moment they might most benefit from its support. I've heard people say their personal threshold is unique, so no one else could really understand or relate to it. I've also heard others insist they are on a journey they must or should make on their own. I've convinced myself, at times, of that rugged exhortation to pull myself up by my bootstraps.

How curious it is, the currency this phrase has in the Overculture today. The respect it garners within the dominant culture of self-reliance. The aspiration it inspires. The expectations it fosters. And the judgment it projects. Linguistic researchers tell us the phrase "pulling yourself up by the bootstraps" originated in the nineteenth century as an insult. Describing someone trying to do the impossible, something that defies the laws of physics, "pulling yourself up by your bootstraps" was a derisive comment about those with impractical aspirations of self-sufficiency, as delusional as Don Quixote chasing his windmills. No one knows exactly when or how the bootstrapping phrase shifted in meaning after first appearing as an insult in 1835. But by the twen-tieth century, when it showed up in a news headline, "Up by his own bootstraps; a hard route to success!" it had become an expression of praise for persistence and achievement against all odds. I suspect it is no accident that the meaning of this idiom changed during the same century when Ralph Waldo Emerson's writings about self-reliance gained so much attention and favor.

Another century later, as we face so many seemingly impossible tasks on the global thresholds we share, it might be helpful to remem-ber the original meaning of the phrase—that if it's pulling up we need, it is delusional to think any of us can do it alone. Collaborating with others might be exactly what is required to get better leverage and a bigger lift. The seventh threshold skill, claiming our companions, calls us back to this wisdom. When facing difficult obstacles and odds, turning to others is the most sensible, prudent approach to take.

Numerous cultures and religions around the world teach this essential lesson of interdependence as foundational to human thriv-ing. An African proverb states, "*Ubuntu ngumtu ngabanye abantu*"—"A person is a person through other people"—meaning we only become fully human by being in relationship with others. In Taoism, it is the principle of *hsiang sheng*, or "mutual arising," which notes that all beings (and being itself) exist only in relation to everyone and every-thing else. Nothing arises in a vacuum. We are who and what we are because of everything else around us. As Alan Watts once summed it up, "Individuality is inseparable from community." Or, to paraphrase community organizer Sam Grant, without community, individuality is no more than a shadow. We need one another to be fully ourselves, on and off the threshold.

If the caterpillar's story of transformation seems too solitary to support this thresholding skill of mutuality, a closer look, both within and beyond the chrysalis, suggests otherwise. Inside the chrysalis, after the caterpillar's form has dissolved, the cellular realignment that follows is an extraordinary example of interdependence. The vibrating imaginal cells initially cluster with other cells of like vibrations, but even this clustering is not enough to create the new form of the butterfly. As the imaginal clusters take on specialized forms and functions, they are drawn into relationship with one another across their differences. The distinct vibrations begin to align the clusters into an arrangement of both harmony and dissonance, sorting them into an interdependence that might be described as the song of a new organism. Each imaginal cluster links to the others and comes to depend on them for tasks it needs but is not suited to undertake. Only together can they grow into a new organism that will carry them into a new winged way of being.

After emerging from the chrysalis, this interdependence reaches across time and species as the monarchs' multigenerational migration south expands and depends upon an even wider collaboration. Traveling thousands of miles from Canada and the northern US to their wintering site in the mountains of central Mexico, the butterflies reciprocate all along the way with milkweed and other flowering plants, depending on the plants to fuel their migratory flight while pollinating the plants and participating in their propagation.

This takes me back to my visit to the Orfield Sound Lab (see "The Gifts of Stillness" on page 99), and the true gift of that visit that I experienced only after leaving the sound lab and finding myself back in relationship with others. At the time, I had been overwhelmed by the cacophony of a volatile national election season. The vitriol of public speeches, debates, news coverage, and even the personal commentaries of friends and associates were all shutting me down. I had gone to the Orfield Sound Lab on that bright autumn day to retreat from the noise around me and inside me, to be alone, in the quiet, and to rediscover who I was.

The silence of the anechoic chamber was just what I needed. But it was only when I left the Sound Lab that I received the real discovery I'd been seeking.

When my half hour of silence and solitude in the anechoic chamber ended, Steve Orfield opened the door and turned on the lights. I blinked. If my ears had earlids, they would have blinked too. I collected my things and left as quietly and quickly as I could, not wanting my own words or anyone else's to stain the open canvas that had been stretched wide and waiting within me.

I made my way through the building lobby and out into a small parking lot, where I paused on the curb in the warm October sunshine and then crossed the street into a small urban park. It was noon, and the park was alive with the sounds of children enjoying their lunchtime recess. I let the heat and light of the sun drench me. I was like a new shoot in spring breaking through the cold and dark winter soil. My senses woke up, bright and newborn, vibrating at a fresh frequency that stirred my memory as if from far away and long ago.

My whole body reverberated ecstatically with the symphony I had just stepped into. Every sound was crisp and clear. Perhaps the world had been hung with invisible crystals while I was in the anechoic chamber, and now they were clinking together musically in sound and silence both. Wind and car wheels whirred. Chirping birds and a scolding squirrel traded commentary in the trees overhead, where the gold autumn leaves were turning to crimson. I no longer heard my own pulse as I did in the anechoic chamber, but instead noticed the rhythmic beat of a red-and-white jump rope going *thwack, thwack, thwack* as it was turned by two girls in black skirts and orange and blue hijabs at either end, and another girl in a purple hijab hiked up her skirt in one hand and jumped in and out without missing a beat. Two more girls in sneakers and skirts and colorful head coverings played catch nearby.

Across the park, a pack of boys ran up and down the soccer field after a ball. Only the goalies stayed put. The boys' chatter rose and fell in swells of excitement I understood clearly, though their Somali words were not in my vocabulary. They didn't need to be. The leaves cracked beneath my feet. This, I said to myself, tears of gratitude running down my cheeks. This was the singing, shouting, jumping, running, changing world that I love and I live in.

My heart was pounding in my chest with a rhythm of gratitude, in a synchrony of hope. Called back into relationship, I was in the game again—not for the strategic reasons of any electoral campaign, not for any decision I had made in my mind, but because my heart was hitched to a changing world that claimed me with a beat beyond my own.

Chrysalis Space

Who are the companions and what are the relationships and arrangements you need now, in the pause on your threshold—both the kindred spirits, vibrating in accord with your own note and tune, and those causing friction and discord you may need in this passage? As the writer George Saunders says, "the idea is to be . . . really comfortable with contradictory ideas," noting that we might find wisdom in "two contradictory ideas both expressed at their highest level and just let to sit in the same cage sort of vibrating."

Make a list of people, beings, communities, ideas, activities whose vibrations you have recently noticed—because they resonated with your own inner rhythms or because they disturbed you with a sense of dissonance. Try to list without judgment, just noticing whether they awakened feelings of harmony or dissonance in you. Keep the list in front of you for a few moments of reflection. Let yourself hum quietly, slowly shifting notes, experiencing both

the notes that harmonize with the ones before them and also humming some that create friction with the ones preceding them. How
do you experience each? Let yourself make up a tune, comprising
both harmonic and dissonant note shifts. When you're ready, let
the tune come to a close, breathing in silence, welcoming it all.

If you wish to write a reflection, scan your list and, choosing
one or several entries on it, consider where they resonate with you
harmoniously and where they create dissonance. Ask yourself how
each of these might support you on your threshold, beginning with
the prompt below and following wherever it leads:

"In the song that is beginning now . . ."

Witnesses and Fellow Travelers

Traveling, especially in a place where you do not share the language and
culture, can be a lonely experience. But opening our senses and paying
attention to our surroundings with our whole bodies can awaken us to
connections that shatter the isolation of being a foreigner.

Five times a day, while staying in northern India many decades
ago, David and I heard in person for our first time the muezzin's
call to prayer traveling across the water from the thin, white mina-
ret beyond our view. In our home in Minneapolis, until recently, city
regulations prevented the call to prayer from being sounded outside
a mosque. When we first heard it in India, though we did not understand the Arabic words of the adhan, we were surprised by our hearts'
response—opening as if to some familiar knock, swelling as if already
answering with our own unspoken prayer.

Paying attention, with our senses open, is a gateway to the heart,
both vulnerable and replete with possibility, as gateways often are.
When touched by poetry or rhythm, music or dance, color or taste or

texture, our attention can surprise us with relationships and connections we didn't even know we were waiting for.

On a different trip, traveling in Latin America, I once shared a room on the Rio San Juan with a North American woman I'd only met a month earlier. We did not know each other well. That day, our plans had changed unexpectedly when our reservations had fallen through late in the afternoon and our small group had to search for accommodations with few options. Travel itself is often an experience of dwelling with many unknowns, especially when plans unravel and you scramble for shelter or food that you'd thought you knew how to find. The weather was hot; we were all tired. Our spirits were low. Spent and weary, having found basic housing for the night, we retired to our room, swept the mouse droppings from the mattresses, laid out our sleep sacks and hung mosquito netting over them. My roommate was near tears; neither of us spoke. I disappeared into the bathroom, where the walls did not quite meet the ceiling, and I could hear my roommate's sighs just a few feet away.

Under the cold-water-only spray of the shower, I began to sing the alto part of an old, familiar tune: *Do-o-na no-bis pa-a-a-a-cem, pa-cem.* From the other room, separated by a wall that did not meet the ceiling, my roommate joined in with a sweet soprano voice, layering the high notes over mine. Together, we continued for several rounds, singing from our separate rooms, with our distinctive voices, sorting the emotions of our weary, traveling hearts into the harmonies of that old and simple song. *Give us peace. Give us peace.*

"Thank you," she said when I returned to the bedroom after the song was over. "Thank *you*," I answered. No more was said. No more was needed. Lifting the veils of our mosquito netting, we climbed into our separate beds, each drifting off to sleep feeling a little less alone.

No matter how many times I have learned this salvific lesson that I am not alone, when I am frightened, worried, or weary, I tend to forget it. I need practices to remind me that, like every other being, I was born into relationship and belonging. I might have to open a path (or start a song) to claim it. I might have to let down my guard to receive it or participate in it. But I do not have to build it, like some flimsy rope bridge suspended over a gaping canyon. If I listen to my body and its own deepest knowledge, I learn that I am designed for relationship and that I have many ways of participating in it.

As a young adult, during a time of many personal changes, I was living alone and my world was coming apart at the seams. Relationships and work were all challenging me to grow into myself in new ways, and when I looked in the mirror, I sometimes did not know who was looking back. One sunny Sunday, waking to a particularly anxious quaking inside, I called an older friend who lived a few doors down from me and, without sharing any reasons, I said I was having a hard time. Paul didn't need the details. He probably wouldn't have been the best one to receive them anyway. But he understood something basic about my anxiety and need. He invited me to his house and when I arrived, he had a single chaise lawn chair waiting for me in the backyard. He settled me into it with the *New York Times* and a cup of coffee, and then busied himself with yardwork nearby. It was a gentle offering of supportive space that turned out to be just what I needed to sort out my "not-yet-speech-ripe" feelings. Today, looking back, I might even call it chrysalis space, a sheltered place in which to pause and be with my own thoughts with a supportive friend quietly within reach.

Other times, I have found chrysalis space in larger gatherings where I have joined in, experiencing the rhythms of music or poetry, with singing, drumming, or dancing. Even breathing together in a community gathered for silent meditation has often broken down my isolation and nested me in a belonging that supports and encourages my unfolding. The gatherings themselves might have nothing to do with thresholding, but any experience of shared movement or stillness, rhythms or silence, creates a larger, collective body that can reinvigorate and calm us when we participate in it. Like the comfort of a strong embrace, these group experiences can open us up to what we are feeling, letting down our defenses and getting us in touch with our own inner resources as well as the resources of community.

One of many challenges of the Covid-19 pandemic has been to find new ways to access shared group experience. Soon after the stay-at-home orders were issued in places around the world, people began experimenting with this—singing to one another from Italian balconies and American porches, organizing online conversations, celebrations, and dance parties, conducting rituals by phone and online and much more.

Often group experiences and rituals, whether in person or online, are specifically tailored to supporting thresholders. Graduations, weddings, memorial services, and inaugurations are all ceremonies intended to honor and support those crossing a significant threshold as well as those affected by the thresholders' passage. The tears that fall in even in the most celebratory of these ceremonies come from the emotional uncapping that occurs when we join others to witness threshold dynamics. In fact, the gathering of witnesses in many threshold rituals is what makes the rituals powerful. The witnesses' presence says, with or without words, that they are standing by—to honor, encourage, and support the thresholder's shifting of identity and the grief of letting go. (The potency of blessings, often included in these ceremonies and rituals, is addressed in more detail in the final reflection of this book, "Honoring the Journey.")

In the pandemic, we have learned that transformation can be witnessed without large in-person gatherings. In its most basic form, it can happen in conversation with a single person who is willing and able to bless us with their attention. Any conversation, at its core, is less about the words exchanged than it is about relationship. The Latin roots of the word *conversation* mean the "act of living with," "to live with, keep company with," or, literally and appropriately to threshold dwelling, to "turn about with." Our conversational companions can be powerful witnesses—those who verify our journey by observing it without judgment, without seeking to advise or direct. They listen or observe as supportive bystanders offering strength and encouragement, serving as a mirror, offering back from an outer perspective the truth of our journey and its toll as well as its possibilities.

Chrysalis Space

Who are your witnesses, conversational companions, and fellow travelers? Who will keep company with you, live with you through the changes now in play? Who will "turn about" with you, even if the turning is your own and they might only participate by being present as witnesses to your passage, to your transition?

Pausing for a few moments of silence to open your heart and memory, what words, music, or gestures of support from others come back to you? Let yourself experience them again, reminding you that you are not alone. Receive their comfort and encouragement as you remember them now. Record their names or words of support in your journal if you like. Store them within your memory or write them on a piece of paper you can post where you will encounter or easily access them when needed. If you like, you might choose a touchstone to associate with them—a stone or charm or any small object that reminds you of their support—and carry that touchstone with you whenever you are most in need of their presence and strength. Or you may place it or the names or photos of these companions on an altar, creating a gallery of support in your home.

Companions Across Time

When I ask thresholders to name their journeying companions, often the first ones that come to mind are contemporaries, those physically or virtually present in the here and now. But thresholding companions are not limited to this extant pool of possibilities. When we widen our invitation to include those who came before us and those who will follow after, we gain a steadier balance supported across a greater span of history.

Not accidentally, relationships that are pollinated across history and geography and culture can teach us and hold us accountable in important ways. Claiming companions of different times and places can counter both the hubris and the hopelessness that sometimes overbreed when we ignore a longer arc of consciousness.

Peace activist and Quaker Elise Boulding used to talk about the "200-year present" that we all live in. She described this as thinking back to the youngest age you can remember and naming the oldest person who held you and figuring out roughly when that person was born. Then, thinking about the youngest person in your family today and calculating what decade they might live into if they live a long life. Often, these dates will span somewhere around two hundred years, spanning the lives of people who touched us and those whom we will touch.

We need this longer vision on the environmental thresholds of the twenty-first century, whether it comes from Boulding's 200-year present or First Nations' instructions to be responsible to seven generations back and seven generations forward. But stretching our awareness out to past and future generations has benefits on our personal thresholds too, as it calls us into relationship with both our inheritances and our future self or legacy.

We know that trauma is passed on through both DNA and social systems as large as a nation and as intimate as a family. Until we are able and willing to experience the grief and loss and pain of our own lives—and to metabolize these experiences by feeling and processing them—we will likely pass our pain on to others, often unwittingly, now and in the future. As therapist Stephi Wagner incisively put it, "Pain travels through families until someone is ready to feel it." How we cross any threshold makes a pathway that can help or harm those who follow us. Every step we take that clears a path toward our own wholeness makes that healing more available to those who will follow us. An old song from Europe in the voice of the ancestors encourages this discernment:

> Oh, may this be the one who will bring forward
> the good, true and beautiful in our family lineage;
> Oh, may this be the one who will break the harmful
> family patterns or harmful nation patterns.

The power of ancestors—those connected by blood and any other lineage of relationship—can be especially available to us on the threshold, when our consciousness may become more porous and expansive, open to a larger spectrum of being than we might normally acknowledge or experience. Dreams or waking sensations sometimes bring loved ones no longer living vividly near us. One thresholder still mourning the sudden death of her husband a few years earlier said it was her husband himself calling her through and beyond her grief.

In different cultures around the world, certain times of year are regarded as being particularly open to connection between the living and the dead, especially late autumn in the north, on nature's threshold between the season of life and growth and that of frozen ground and bare trees. Samhain, historically celebrated in Celtic culture and with pagan rituals today, Días de los Muertos, and All Souls Day all fall at the end of October, on the northern hemisphere's seasonal cusp between autumn and winter. During these days, old teachings say the veil is especially thin, allowing those still living to more easily encounter loved ones who have died, and those who have died to return in many forms. In the early months of the Covid-19 pandemic and the heightened awareness of mortality it opened, it did not surprise me that my own deceased parents began showing up in the background of my dreams, as if to remind me that the veil was lifted by the pandemic itself. As if to say we are all here together now, the living and the dead.

It is a connection that does not require a specific belief about an afterlife, only an openness to the lingering legacy of those who have died. If they were blood relatives, we might carry traces of them in our DNA—not only in our genetic make-up but also in emotional inheritances long observed and more recently verified by scientific research. If they are ancestors without a blood connection—people with whom we have shared love, experience, common cause, or dreams—we can carry their legacy forward while adding to it with our own efforts and pursuits.

Some of the ancestors we draw upon will be *ancestors of resilience*, their example and life story teaching us how to be resilient ourselves. Others may be *ancestors of brokenness*, including those who were broken by oppressive systems or relationships as well as those so broken out of relationship and connection that they participated in oppressing others. From these we are reminded of the importance of healing in our own lifetime so the brokenness will not be transmitted to the next generation. Finally, there are *ancestors of wholeness*, the largest group, comprising the earth and all beings woven into the interdependent web of life and death that holds and heals us all.

Any of these ancestors can be companions to us when living through big change, and not just as sources of inspiration. We can make use of their legacy by wicking up their wisdom and encouragement, tending to their unhealed wounds, burning off their pain and anger, turning away from their violence and oppression of others, or letting ourselves be guided or encouraged by their resiliency. Calling up the power of our ancestors awakens us to our own choices for tapping into and channeling the forces of history in potentially new directions. And strengthening our connection to the ancestors of wholeness, or the wider web of life, opens us to the greatest and most healing ancestral power of all.

Chrysalis Space

Who are your ancestors, both the broken and the resilient? Who has gone before you, clearing a path that you may or may not wish to follow? Who will come after you, and what will your path offer them?

Imagine yourself crossing a river, wading in up to your waist and feeling the tug of the current. Your feet search for boulders and high ground that will allow you to safely forge the waters. Looking up to the shore ahead of you and the one behind you, who do you notice there and what does their presence mean to you as you take your next steps? Consider naming them and choosing one to write a letter to, describing your threshold and what their presence means to you.

Guides and Wise Ones

Years ago, David and I were hiking on a mountainside in the Julian Alps. After hours traversing a steep incline, the path we were on disappeared beneath a swath of loose rocks about twenty feet wide. The field of scree, likely the remnants of an earlier avalanche, originated far above, beyond our view, and continued about twenty-five feet below us before disappearing over a precipice. There was no going around it. If we were to continue hiking, we would have to go across it.

David, in his typical style, sized up the situation and moved quickly across the rubble. In seven rapid strides, he easily reached the other side where the path continued, and turned to wait for me. Pausing behind him, I made the mistake of watching. I saw the loose rocks shift beneath his feet with each bold step. I watched, wide-eyed, as the rocks clattered down the mountainside and tumbled out of sight over the edge. I heard them landing with a distant percussion far below.

Slowly, I followed. But I lingered too long on the scree and began slipping down with the loose stones, sending more of them tumbling over the edge. The more I slipped, the harder it was to muster the courage to take another step, until finally, in the middle of the loose rocks and sliding slowly down toward the precipice, I stopped walking altogether. Terrified, I looked first toward the rocks disappearing over the edge below me and then toward David standing on the solid ground, now four to five feet above me. I could not move. I was frozen by fear, even as the rocks beneath my feet were slowly sliding downward and I was sliding with them.

"Keep moving!" David said calmly but firmly, his voice finally jolting me from my paralysis and pulling me forward like a lifeline until I reached the other side, several yards below him but safely above the mountain's drop off, and collapsed in a heap of tears and relief.

Has this ever happened to you, perhaps on the shifting ground of a threshold you're crossing now or have crossed in the past? It's a classic freeze response created by fear and unpersuaded by all evidence that not moving is itself a danger. It is very different from the threshold skill of attentive pausing. When we become paralyzed by fear, we need something or someone to shake us awake from fear's lockdown and break us free of the grip of emotions that harden and stop flowing. When a friend of mine suddenly died in her home some years ago and her partner and I followed the ambulance to the hospital, we were ushered into the hospital chapel to wait for word from the medics working to revive her. This doesn't look good, her partner mumbled to me in the chapel, and then stood rigid as a silent statue, staring without expression at a small work of stained glass at the end of the room. Finally, after what seemed like an eternity, I reached into their frozen state, gently touching their elbow, softly speaking their name. After a few minutes, I convinced them to sit down, and having moved to a chair, the iceberg of shock began to thaw and their tears could finally come.

Who are the companions or guides that might be calling out to you on your threshold, urging you to keep moving (or maybe inviting you to sit down and cry), tossing you a lifeline of strength, courage, and, more than anything, a compassionate connection that might unfreeze you or gently encourage you into and across your shifting terrain? They might be people you know personally, or they can be wise ones from any time or place. Poets and teachers whose words offer a through-line you can follow. They might even point you in a new direction you had not noticed before. Rumi advised in a poem, "Don't insist on going where you think you want to go; ask the way to the spring."

Just as we rely on GPS for navigation, we might name the guidance of wise ones as one part of our TPS, or "Threshold Positioning System." TPS can alert us to signs to look for, turnoffs we might otherwise miss, bridges closed for construction, or, as the Rumi poem suggests, even nearby springs and other resources we will need along the way but would not know where to find.

Our TPS will sometimes speak to us in words, but also in gestures, symbols, images, or even place markers left behind by those who passed before us. In the Arctic, the ancient stone stackings known as inuksuit can mark a good place to hunt seals, an entrance to a shelter, or the direction to a safe harbor—each providing information critical to survival in the harsh climate and long sunless winters. Is his book *Inuksuit: Silent Messengers of the Arctic,* Canadian ethnographer Norman Hallendy writes that the word inuksuk (the singular form of inuksuit) means "that which acts in the capacity of a human." From a distance, an inuksuk sculpture can resemble human form, with stony shoulders beneath a stony head, as if the one who built it, possibly centuries earlier, is still standing watch there, offering guidance, advice, and companionship—a reminder of the companionship shared between people and the land itself. "Look at the hills, the sea, the inuksuit everywhere," said one Inuit elder, describing a landscape that could falsely appear to a visitor's eye as uninhabited. "We are all made of the same stuff. We all possess a spirit, only the way we are arranged temporarily separates us."

Inuksuit will be most plentiful in places where people have been required to wait, according to Osuitok, another Inuit elder. Traveling ancestors might have built them to pass the time, or to share a message—maybe marking a migratory route where hunting will be fruitful at a certain time of year or marking a narrows where safe passage can be made, but only at high or low tide. It is in these waiting places that some of the most exquisite and beautiful structures called inuksuapik can be found, standing out from all others because of their extraordinary shape and the color and textures of their stones.

Thresholds are replete with waiting, which is why we have such a wealth of poetry and art, myth and music, legend and image created in the midst of change. All of these resources offer messages from the ones who have been there before us. They can companion us and call us out of our frozen state, reminding us that the isolation we may feel is only a temporary arrangement, helping us to keep moving.

Chrysalis Space

Who are the messengers encouraging you on your threshold, and what are the messages they give you? Perhaps they are calling you on, despite your fears; giving you comfort, encouragement or guidance; offering important information for survival; or extending to you simple companionship and the reminder that you are not alone. Pause in the silence, attentive to their supportive presence. Make a list of the messages they share. Keep the list close at hand, carry it in your pocket, or post it where you can read it often. Consider placing it next to a stack of stones as a reminder of the wisdom that accompanies you, even across time.

A WIDER HORIZON:
The Priority and Power of Belonging

In the early months of the Covid-19 pandemic, as stay-at-home orders were issued and many activities came to a halt or moved online, we were continually asking, what are the essential services that must continue even as others must be shut down or limited? As the virus spread with alarming speed, we were required to quickly prioritize our individual and societal needs—for protection from the virus and for other threats to survival. Some of the trickiest dilemmas of this triage weighed health considerations against economic ones, especially for people in poverty who not only lacked a financial safety net but also often carried higher risk factors for contracting the virus in its most serious forms. Complexities also surfaced around the harder to measure but very real social need to be together in groups balanced against the spread of infection, especially in large gatherings.

These are the kinds of questions that prompted psychologist Abraham Maslow in 1943 to propose what is known as Maslow's hierarchy, often regarded in the dominant culture as explaining in a somewhat sequential fashion what is most essential for human survival. The hierarchy is a pyramid resting on a wide foundation of what Maslow named as physiological survival needs, including food, shelter, and sleep. He postulated that humans must first meet these needs before then moving on to fulfill others, in this order: safety; love and belonging; esteem; and self-actualization.

But Maslow's pyramid is challenged by the pandemic's demand that we all participate in protecting one another's safety as inextricably linked to our own. As a model based on the Overculture's value of self-reliance, the pyramid suggests that human nature begins from an individualistic posture, competing for the resources we need for physiological survival before we move on to the needs more frequently nested with those of others. In this understanding of human needs, it is only when fed and clothed, sheltered and well slept and safe, do we move on to meet our social needs for love and belonging. As such, not only does it defer our need for belonging, but it also shapes our understanding of human nature by denying the way we are wired for relationship and community as a basic characteristic of our humanity.

All of this turns in new directions as research by clinical psychologist Deb Pace has revealed that Maslow's work was greatly influenced by his encounters with the Blackfoot Nation and their understanding of actualization. Significantly, and disturbingly, he not only failed to credit Blackfoot culture; he also removed the Blackfoot concept of actualization from its community context, dramatically altering the importance of belonging in the model.

Many cultures today and historically have regarded belonging as a basic human need and a priority for well-being. And Maslow himself, late in life, wondered whether the pyramid needed to be revised. What might become possible if our dominant culture recognized and named the danger of the myth of self-reliance, so foundational to patriarchy and systemic racism, and how it denies all of us the sense of belonging we need as fundamentally as food or water?

Like the caterpillar turning upside down to suspend its chrysalis and prepare for transformation, these questions disrupt the pyramid thinking of the Overculture and invite a different perspective—a more dynamic understanding based on relationship and exchange rather than a static hierarchy. "Needs are not hierarchical," notes psychologist Pamela Rutledge in her article "Social Networks: What Maslow Misses."

> *Life is messier than that. Needs are, like most other things in nature, an interactive, dynamic system, but they are anchored in our ability to make social connections. Maslow's model needs rewiring so it matches our brains. Belongingness is the driving force of human behavior, not a third-tier activity. The system of human needs from bottom to top . . . are dependent on our ability to connect with others. Belonging to a community provides the sense of security and agency that makes our brains happy and helps keep us safe.*

In a pandemic and post-pandemic world, we come inescapably face to face with the interdependence of human survival. We humans do not only need one another for our belonging and social well-being. In a time of viral danger, it is abundantly clear that safety itself is a collective project—as it is for climate change and so many other threats. We need to work together to redefine our understanding of survival's demands. To learn that the interdependency of needs and power cannot be statically stacked in a hierarchical pyramid but might be better depicted as a dynamic ecology in which multiple needs, rising and falling, are interwoven by relationship, collaboration, and cooperation.

Many people lived with this worldview for a long time, but what might it mean for all of us to make this shift in thinking? It will require a lot of imagination, for sure, but also some recovered memory. To fully make use of the pandemic chaos and disorder—the goo in the chrysalis of the 2020s—we might need to rediscover and extend nonhierarchical ways of distributing and sharing power that existed long before our time and are currently be applied today beyond the hierarchical thinking of the Overculture.

The people of Cherán, Mexico, in the past decade, have demonstrated the power available in reclaiming their belonging to one another. An Indigenous community of 16,000 people about 200 miles west of Mexico City, Cherán has faced significant threshold challenges and threats related to the environment, gun violence, systemic oppression, and dehumanization. According to author Rubén Martinez, the town's name is a *Purépecha* word meaning "a place of fear," originally said to acknowledge the dangers of its rocky, mountainous landscape. Its more recent history gives the name added meaning as a place where people came together to overcome fear as a threat to their survival.

In the early 2000s, illegal loggers began clearing the mountain forests surrounding Cherán. By 2008, several strong-arm cartels, shored up by corrupt Cherán politicians and police, expanded the logging at an alarming and violent rate, earning them the name *rapamontes*, or forest rapists. For four years, 200 or more trucks of stolen lumber passed through Cherán's streets every day, each guarded by bandits armed with AK-47s aimed at the villagers. Extortion, kidnapping, and murders created a zone of fear that quieted resistance while at least 70 percent of the trees in the area's forests were felled and removed. Those who stood up to the loggers and cartels frequently disappeared.

Finally, some of the town's women began gathering surreptitiously to discuss other options. On April 15, 2011, fifteen women led an uprising against the cartels, blockading the loggers' pickups as they drove through town. Armed with sticks, rocks, and firecrackers, the women kidnapped five of the loggers and held them hostage in an old stone chapel, securing them with the women's cotton shawls. While the church bells rang out, alerting the rest of the townspeople to join the effort, the women barricaded the entrances to the town with burned out trucks and successfully turned away Cherán's corrupt president and police when they arrived to free and defend the loggers.

No one knows the future of this effort. But as I write this ten years past the uprising, the *Los Angeles Times* and the BBC have both reported that Cherán remains free of cartels, illegal loggers, and its corrupt leaders. It has recovered many old Indigenous practices and barred entrance to the community by politicians, political parties, and state police and is now governed by a twelve-person council that rotates into and out of power. The town has replanted over three-quarters of the surrounding deforested land, established one of the largest rainwater collection systems in Latin America, and developed a sustainable economy managed by the community. In recent years, the community has experienced almost no violent crime, despite its location in one of the most murder-prone regions of Mexico. The path to these achievements has been based almost entirely on claiming companions around a common hearth.

During and after the standoff with the loggers, the people of Cherán lit bonfires, or *fogatas*, on every corner of the community, providing security for people to gather, watch over their neighborhood, and share information with each other. But *LA Times* reporter Michael Snyder observed that these 189 fogatas, which burned for nine months, soon "doubled as public kitchens, to become the basic unit of Cherán's emergent political order: a hearth rather than a crucible, to forge a new society." The fires became a way of recovering what the town proudly calls "Our Strength," a slogan that now appears in *Purépecha* throughout Cherán.

Almost a decade after the uprising, Snyder reported that just one fogata still burned, lit by ten women every Thursday and Sunday night. But the valuing of companions in times of danger and of peace continued as local residents gathered for nourishment, support, and planning through their times of change.

Nearer to my own home, I am inspired by the activists who have tended the intersection in Minneapolis where George Floyd was murdered in May of 2020, launching uprisings against systemic racism and violence against Black people, Indigenous people, and people of color in the Twin Cities and worldwide. A year after George Floyd's murder, even as car traffic returned to the street where he was coldly killed by a white police officer, the extended sacred shrine built by the community over time remains. With murals and painted messages, plantings and night-lit candles, multiple metal sculptures of justice-demanding fists, and gathering areas for music and mourning and for sharing provisions and visioning, the activists tending the intersection are continually asking themselves and one another: what does justice require, and what must we create and demand for ourselves and others to thrive?

On the thresholds of our own time, how will we companion one another today? What new diagram of needs might inform our efforts to live with and support one another now, in our longing to build a world where all of us can thrive?

Chrysalis Space

What would you name as the basic human needs for survival and well-being? Try to brainstorm what they might be without placing them in a hierarchy. If you want, look up Maslow's pyramid and write out its categories on small pieces of paper and throw them into the air, letting them tumble down reassembled with the needs you just named. What new arrangement will you make with these? What ecology of relationship and interdependence might emerge if you began with the need for belonging and worked outward from there? Draw a collage or diagram of those needs if you like, possibly highlighting the most important ones while acknowledging their interdependence, their influence on one another and their movement.

Choose one community you belong to as you have experienced the pandemic, ongoing uprisings against systemic racial violence and oppression, or another shared threshold. It might be your family or friends, neighborhood, faith or vocational community, or an organization working on a cause. Does this community support the diagram of human needs you just made above? If so, how does that inform the group's choices on this shared threshold? If not, how might a different perspective on human needs, well-being, and belonging change what is happening or what is possible on that threshold?

THRESHOLDING TOGETHER

With a thresholding buddy or a group of thresholders, gather for a meal after each of you has read the reflections on claiming companions. Then choose any of the following questions to start your conversation:

- Name someone who is different from you, in any significant way, whose presence is important on your threshold. Explain why.
- Name a witness who has supported you in the changes you are living through now. How has their presence encouraged, advised, or guided you?
- When you imagine yourself mid-stream, headed toward the far side of these changes, who is on the opposite bank awaiting your arrival? Who is behind you, cheering you on?
- Tell about a time when you were stuck on the threshold of change, not fruitfully pausing but immobilized and shut down, and some message caused you to move on. What was the message and how did you receive it and from whom?
- Share your own list of survival needs and how they might be arranged in an ecology of well-being. What might this mean for the shared thresholds you are on with others today?

NOT YET

Here,

Here,
where already
you have left behind,
by choice or by force,
what you knew
what you cherished
what you maybe took
for granted.

Here,
where not yet
do you know
where you're headed,
what it will take
what it will give
how it will change you.

Here,
    on the threshold,
        you balance
        on a comma
    between the no longer
and the not yet.

Now,
may you pause,
breathing in,
breathing out,
on the cusp
in between.

Notice
where fullness gives way
to emptying,
as the full moon
each month
sloughs
in its waning
and makes way
for new waxing.

Now,
letting go
of attachments
and assumptions,
may you release
what you've clutched
in your fear,
making room
for the stranger
knocking,
who is always you.

Now,
may you discover
what you've carried within
    all along
but not known, named or
        needed—
ancestors' whisperings,
newborn powers,
the hope of the young,
the resilience of Earth and
    her beings.

Now,
they are crucial.
Clear a path
to their wellspring.
Walk it often.
Keep it open.

Now,
may you listen,
one ear turned inward
to your heart
and the body's knowing.
One ear turned outward
to the suffering—
and joy—
that will teach us.

Now,
look around you,
at the others
waiting with you
on the curl of this comma.
You will need them.
They will need you.

Together,
we will round this bend,
cross over
into the not yet,
where,
having let go,
we might finally learn—
a new way
is possible
Now,
Here,

Threshold Skill 8:
MOVING ON

As necessary as pausing is on the threshold, when the time is right, we must move on, even when we still might not know exactly where we're headed. Now we are entering a new stage of threshold living—entering new ground not yet known or possibly not even named, except as what is "not yet."

The threshold skill of moving on requires breaking out of old habits of thinking, being, and doing—particularly the habit of needing to know and control where we are going. Instead, we are asked to turn our attention to *how* we are going and *how* we might make room for unknowns by cultivating curiosity and increasing our capacity for dwelling with and in uncertainty. This recalls Keats' notion of "negative capability," a phrase he used to praise the creative literary genius of Shakespeare and others "capable of being in uncertainties, mysteries, doubts, without any irritable reaching after fact and reason."

Mastering the capacity to move on despite uncertainty is a lesson we can learn from migrating species such as the whooping crane. In the mid-1900s, when the number of whooping cranes fell to forty-seven, all in the same flock, a small group of imaginative conservationists and ultralight pilots in North America banded together in a project called *Operation Migration*. Their goal was to increase the birds' odds of survival by establishing a second migratory flock. Each summer for over ten years, the ultralight pilots carefully costumed as giant human-sized birds to avoid taming the new flock and taught a new clutch of crane fledglings in Wisconsin to fly behind the ultralights as their leader. Each fall, the pilots then led their fledglings south to a nature preserve in Florida, where the birds joined a growing number of adult whoopers from previous years. And each spring the growing flock in Florida would make their return migration back to Wisconsin on their own.

Among many things that fascinate me about this project is what the ultralight pilots learned early on from the young fledglings about starting the fall migration each year. Like their wild-born counterparts, the young whoopers first learned to fly in circles, always returning to their starting point at the end of each day's flight. Over time, the circles widened as the cranes' strength and abilities grew, but at the end of the day, the birds returned to the place they knew. It is a pattern familiar to many thresholders—venturing out toward the unknowns ahead of us, but then, if we're able to, turning back to the ground of what we know whenever we tire or desire familiarity.

At a certain point, though, for both fledgling and thresholder, the circle must be broken, and the *Operation Migration* pilots discovered this could be harder than they had imagined. The first time they continued flying southward without arcing back to their starting point, the birds flying with them became restless. When the flock had to pass over a freeway below, the sound of the rushing traffic beneath them was so unsettling that first one bird and then another peeled away from the group and turned back toward home on their own.

The habit of circling back, apparently, needed to be broken slowly. The first day the pilots did not circle back had to be a short one, and any noisy barrier below had to be crossed early in the day and at the highest possible position in the sky to avoid startling the fledglings out of formation. On our own threshold journeys, whether personal or shared, if we don't use similar care and attention, we too can get caught in circular habits that keep us from moving on.

It is not that circling back itself is bad. At any time when we become overwhelmed by change, we might need to return to something familiar, if we can, to quiet our fears or muster new confidence. Then the next time we can make a bigger circle or go a little farther, even land in unknown terrain. It is a rhythm and pace that can vary widely. Each of us must discover our own threshold process and timing for moving on externally and internally. Monarchs do not form their wings until they are in the chrysalis and every semblance of the caterpillar has long since been dissolved. Other butterflies begin to form wings inside their caterpillar skins, tucked out of sight and folded inside, without function in the moment, but waiting there fully formed and ready with the power of not yet. Knowing when to move on is about paying attention to your own circumstances and needs, finding the right timing for you.

Chrysalis Space

What is the unknown potential folded out of sight in the "not yet" of your thresholds? Is it ready to emerge, allowing you to move on? Have you been moving in circular patterns that keep returning you to where you were before? Are you ready now to break those patterns and to touch down on new ground at the end of the day? What is the shortest distance you might travel to practice landing on unfamiliar land?

To reflect on this, you might use an exercise that will require one plain white sheet of 8½ x 11" paper, a half sheet of unlined, preferably colored paper, and either tape or glue. Using the half sheet first, turn the paper vertically and write, free association-style, about some circular pattern of thinking or doing that you are experiencing on your threshold. Fill up only one side of the paper. Describe one or more habits you feel stuck in, possibly beginning with the prompt: **"What makes it hard to move on is . . ."**

Then fold and score this written sheet vertically in half, tearing it along the fold from top to bottom and going right through your words. Tape or glue the two halves on opposite sides of the larger unlined sheet of paper positioned horizontally, making an open gap between the writing on either side. Scanning the words on either side of the gap, circle or underline any that resonate with you, for any reason. They can be words you like or ones that you don't, but they should raise some curiosity, interest, or response in you.

Now ask yourself, what would it mean to break your circular thinking open, as you just have by tearing it in two? What might it feel like to break through your old ways of thinking or being and to open unfamiliar ground as you move on? What new movement on your threshold might be possible then? Imagine any new possibilities that might appear as you do. Write a new passage in the gap between the two torn halves of your previous reflection, using as many or as few of the words you underlined or circled as you like, possibly with different meanings. Begin with the prompt:

"Moving on, I might discover . . ."

Seeking Safety

The temptation to circle back to familiar ground often stems, understandably, from a desire for safety. But defining safety, and how to find it, will vary for each one of us. It can cover a range as wide as the alphabet, from abstinence to zip guns and a full dictionary of options in between. Even the protective, camouflaged shell of the chrysalis doesn't seem safe to the caterpillar whose immune system attacks the first imaginal cells as a threat.

By definition, the threshold is a place where defenses come down and doors open to something new. That encounter necessarily brings some amount of risk and discomfort. This requires distinguishing between safety and its cousin comfort, on the one hand, and support and what we might call nurture, on the other. Clarissa Pinkola Estés writes, "The difference between comfort and nurture is this: if you have a plant that is sick because you keep it in a dark closet, and you say soothing words to it, that is comfort. If you take the plant out of the closet and put it in the sun, give it something to drink, and talk to it, that is nurture."

In antiracism work, these distinctions become important when navigating demands for "safe space." For people of color and biracial and Indigenous people, a need for safe space may arise from constant exposure to the relentless, sometimes life-threatening realities of systemic racism. It must be honored as such. But for white people, insistence on having "safe space" is more often a resistance to discomfort. We need to know the difference between being unsafe and being uncomfortable and to acknowledge that growth is unlikely without discomfort. And we also might ask if anyone benefits from feeling unsafe. Can we shift to building the trust that makes "brave space" possible? Maybe this kind of brave space, important in antiracism work and on any threshold, is the same as chrysalis space, an environment that will hold us while we break down old ways of being and live in the gooey chaos long enough for something new to emerge. It is a daring space that makes room for transformative emergence.

A good measure of whether you are finding the support you need on a threshold is whether you are nurtured in ways that allow you to grow through and into your changes instead of shrinking back from them. "God is always revising our boundaries outward," writes the Quaker writer Douglas Steere. Are the people in your life supporting your growth into new and larger boundaries, or are they begging you to stay the same or get smaller and less powerful?

Even changes that diminish our physical size or strength can offer us the opportunity to grow in other ways. Some people with terminal diagnoses and long litanies of loss will shine brighter even as their physical presence and strength diminishes. A member of the thresholds group one year who was dying of cancer showed what it could look like to move on with courage and curiosity, even on the final threshold of life's biggest unknowns. She attended just one session before her pain and illness prevented her from returning, but in that single appearance, she showed up fully, enlarging her own circle of companions even as her own death approached and, in the last chapter of her life, becoming a teacher and guide for others. Describing her threshold to the group as the final one we will all cross over, she said plainly, "I'm on the same threshold that we're all on, really—waiting for the bus that will come for every one of us at the end of life. It's just that I'm already at the bus stop, and I can see the bus coming."

Is this safety? In a threshold way, I would suggest it is—moving on with eyes and heart open, claiming companions for support and nurturance, making room for growth even when the road is uncomfortable and the destination unknown.

Chrysalis Space

Has your spirit grown smaller or taller on your threshold? What might nurture your growth in this time of change, helping you to show up and expand your boundaries or live larger, even in the midst of loss?

How have you defined safety on your threshold? How is it related to comfort, nurture, or support? Would anything change if you sought support instead of safety? What might "brave space" look like for you on your threshold, and how might you begin to find, create, or support it?

Think of a time when you grew in a way you valued because you mustered the courage to show up or move on even when it did not feel comfortable or safe. What did you learn in that experience, and how might that guide you now? If you are writing, you might begin with the prompt below and follow wherever it leads:

"The brave space I need now . . ."

Going with the Flow

Sometimes moving on is less about propelling ourselves forward and more a matter of not resisting the movement change unleashes around us.

In Chinese philosophy this is known as accessing the power of wu. *Wu* literally means no or nothing, but it might be better understood as the great potency of what is not yet. Think of it as the power of the seed before it is planted, the prospects of a day before dawn, the promise of nighttime before dusk. It is embedded in the tiny eggs that will hatch as caterpillars, and within the caterpillar, it is in each imaginal disc coded to become a unique part of the butterfly yet to be. Thresholds are packed through with the power of wu, but our fierce resistance to change—or our rigid expectations and efforts to control who and how we will be on the far side of change—can make that power inaccessible to us. Wu expresses an often hidden potential best tapped by a posture of waiting without insisting we must know what we're waiting for.

My friend Chris tells the story of a director she worked with as a young actor who stopped rehearsal one day to comment on Chris's role in a particular scene. She couldn't imagine what attracted the director's attention to her. She had no lines in the scene and was just supposed to be sitting still while the others on the stage carried the play forward. Yes, the director said, you're sitting still just as the scene tells you to, but I've never seen anyone use so many muscles to sit still! The director then taught her how to "use no more muscles than you need" to sit and be still, to relax and be present to the action developing on the stage around her.

In yoga, some teachers tell us to stand with our bones so well balanced that our bodies can be at rest, muscles draped over our skeletons like a set of clothes on a chair. Properly positioned with feet planted, knees slightly flexed, and weight distributed between left and right and heel and toe, one can stand for a long time without tiring. "Don't push the river," says the Chinese proverb, reminding us not to create effort where it is not only unnecessary but also ineffective. "What's easy is sustainable," advises adrienne maree brown in *Emergent Strategy*. "Birds coast when they can."

Living on the threshold naturally puts our muscles on high alert, prepared for action, for fight or flight or fawn. Even the fourth option, freeze, which betrays no motion, is not a restful state but one of tension that, like my friend Chris on stage, uses a lot of muscles to hold still. Intentionally or unconsciously, we become engaged in the fight before we need to, losing our ability to creatively adapt.

When my mom was diagnosed with ALS, there was no treatment for the terminal disease and very little medical intervention available to ameliorate its appalling losses of mobility, speech, and even the ability to eat. Even so, I can't tell you how many well-meaning loved ones encouraged my mom to "fight the good fight" in her "battle" with that horrific illness. Fortunately, her care team in the ALS clinic gave us a different approach. Rather than resisting it, they taught us to move with it, not giving in to it any sooner than necessary but trying wherever we could to anticipate its losses and equip my mom to adapt to them as readily and creatively as possible. With so little energy left, they told her, why not use the energy you have to adjust to the losses rather than trying hard to deny or defy them?

This is the concept of wu wei in Chinese philosophy, *wu* meaning not yet or, simply, not and *wei* meaning being, doing, or making. Translated literally as "not doing" or "not trying," it can be easily misunderstood as doing nothing. A passage of the *Tao Te Ching* describing wu wei says: "The Tao never does anything, yet through it all things are done." And "The Master does nothing, yet ... leaves nothing undone." It can look like inaction, or a posture of submission or even acquiescence, because it refuses the quick kneejerk responses we come to expect in certain situations. In reality, it is the deepest kind of action that moves from an awareness of inner and outer conditions and the relationship between them. It can be best understood as not forcing. It is a protester going limp upon arrest. It is a whitewater paddler aligning their raft with the current, reading it and riding it instead of muscling against it. It is my mother adapting to her loss of strength, mobility, and speech with new equipment, techniques, or assistance. A person practicing wu wei declines the ego's first response to resist unwanted change and instead moves in "harmonious action" with their surroundings. They creatively participate with their circumstances and with others, rechanneling the forces at play in a new direction and discovering a larger set of options in response to what is known and unknown.

This holds true on the global level as well. A wu wei approach to international issues avoids impulsive defensiveness, instead considering how to make use of existing energy or movement in relationship. In the early 1950s, as Cold War tensions were building worldwide, President Dwight Eisenhower called a meeting of his Joint Chiefs of Staff to discuss China's recent threats to attack several islands in the Taiwan strait and to decide whether to drop an atomic bomb on China. Not long before, the Quakers' American Friends Service Committee had called attention to the famine spreading in China with a plea to Americans to mail small sacks of potatoes to China with notes quoting a biblical passage that said, "If thine enemy hungers, feed them." Having learned of the campaign, Eisenhower asked an aide to investigate how many sacks had been delivered in China, and the aide returned with the answer: 40,000. Hearing this, the president reportedly said, "If 40,000 Americans think we should be feeding the Chinese, what are we doing thinking about bombing them?"

Just as our bodies react to threats with responses of fight, flight, fawn, or freeze, our organizations and larger systems often do the same—with knee-jerk retaliation, blow for blow; or backing away from conflict; or attempting to appease the perceived aggressor; or locking down in "the way things are." The habits created by these responses convince us that the patterns they create are who we are, as individuals or as a shared culture. But they are born of a narrow mindset tightly focused on the smallest definition of survival and not by our capacity for relationship and compassion. They dismiss our participation in a greater web of being and a longer arc of time.

Wu wei offers an alternative that is equally natural to who we are as beings deeply connected to others. It begins by grounding us in our surroundings and our interdependence with others and then expands our awareness to the larger fields of energy that we share. When we have experienced ourselves as part of that larger web of life, we start to notice rhythms that neither begin nor end with us. We become aware of energy moving around us like the currents of wind and water, inviting us to align ourselves with that movement while remaining centered in and guided by our own identity and integrity. That is the power of wu wei.

Chrysalis Space

How many muscles are you using in response to your threshold? Sitting comfortably in a chair, take a few deep breaths in and out through your nose and scan your body for any places of tightness, knotted tension, or alerted stiffness. Begin at the top of your head and work your way down, noticing the muscles in your forehead, your jaw, your neck, and shoulders. Taking a deep breath and rolling your shoulders back and down, continue scanning through your arms to your hands and fingers. What is happening there? Then move your awareness through your torso, noticing how fully your lungs inflate and empty with each breath. How are your hips aligned and settled in the chair? Trace the muscles in your legs down through your feet to the floor below. Open your awareness to any sensations of the floor beneath your feet and the chair beneath your bottom, and the earth beneath it all, asking your body how it is responding to this support and what it is doing with it.

When a butterfly emerges from the chrysalis, it hangs upside down to let gravity help pump fluids from its abdomen into its wings. How might you too make use of gravity, steady and reliable, that holds you, now and always?

If you've noticed any pockets of tension or tightness in your scan, especially those that feel more prominent in response to your thresholds, with your next out breath, let yourself hum a little. Notice how it feels in your body and your bones. With your lips closed and your the teeth of your upper and lower jaw not touching, keep humming for a few minutes, making a tune or wandering randomly from note to note, observing where in your body you feel the high notes and the low ones. Close your eyes if you like; move or sway a little. Intentionally open any channels that might send the vibrations into any part of your body experiencing tension. Then consider how you might return to this state of attentive connection as you move into the currents of change, participating fully in both the known support that holds you and the unknowns toward which you are headed.

Yes, and . . .

Gift giving—and receiving—is a significant practice of relationship, and especially so in many Indigenous cultures where gift economies extend the reach of gift exchanges beyond simple reciprocation. A gift economy is an ecological model of exchange in which the gift keeps moving, circulating and spreading its energy across a growing number and range of givers and receivers. Like a seed on the wind, the gift scatters and settles, takes root and then blooms, bears fruit, and lifts off as seed once again. In a gift economy, the gift changes hands repeatedly and sometimes changes form too. If a gift (such as food) is consumed, it can keep moving by being shared with others as it's eaten or passed on as a new gift generated by gratitude and offered to the original giver or anyone else. The important thing is not to hoard, deny, or discard it, any of which will cause the gift to cease being a gift. In a gift economy, knowing how to generously receive is as important as giving. One follows the other inseparably as two sides of the same coin flipped in the air; even when the coin lands, the other side is still there waiting for the next toss.

On the threshold, where so many gifts come our way, including a good number disguised as losses, it can be helpful to receive them in the relational spirit of a gift economy. One of the best ways I know to understand that is to learn from improv theater. Improvisational performers step onto the stage without a script, depending largely on a foundational practice called "Yes, and . . ." In this practice, the actors are all there to support one another. Each person's task is to make the others look good, which happens when the story keeps moving in a compelling way. Every time an actor speaks a line or performs an action, it is considered to be a gift to another actor. The second actor receives the gift by responding "Yes," and building on it with another action or spoken line, often beginning with the word "and." More experienced improv artists leave out the words "Yes, and . . ." while speaking or acting in that spirit. But those of us who try this as novices are often surprised by how difficult it is to fully receive a gift we hadn't seen coming, and to add to it rather than rebuffing it with a "Yes, but . . ." spoken or implied.

The first time I experienced this practice, I was in a writer's residency with twelve writers convened from around the country. One night, we were joined by an improv artist who taught us about keeping the gift moving. Two of our group members agreed to try it, and our improv teacher told one of the volunteers to begin by searching for something on the ground, and the other to approach, saying, "I see you are looking for something." They were to continue by making it up from there. So, the first person replied, "Yes, and it's my contact lens." The second person then got down on his knees and said, "Yes, and I've lost my car keys too. I'll join you. We can look together."

We onlookers thought they were doing great. But our teacher pointed out that the second actor had never fully accepted the first gift given to him. Although he said "yes," and even got down on his knees with her, he redirected the story away from her contact lens toward a search for his car keys. It was more of a "yes, but" response, our teacher said, apparently much more common in real life than "yes, and."

On any threshold, both the ones we have chosen and the ones we never wanted to cross, we are given circumstances unanticipated and unwanted. I know I often turn them away by answering, "Yes, but." How might I instead receive them fully and find a way to pass them on as gifts for others or gifts for my own future self? This is not a denial of the very real losses involved on the threshold and the need to grieve those losses. It is, rather, a chance to consider how we receive the losses and how we might keep the larger story moving.

This can be more easily said than done, especially when we get attached to a particular part of our threshold story. Something that helped me practice "Yes, and" in my own cancer journey was a blessing I learned from John O'Donohue's *To Bless the Space Between Us* that I had memorized during my recovery. "May you find in yourself a courageous hospitality," it said, "toward what is difficult, painful, and unknown." Make room for it, all of it, the blessing said to me, asking me to ponder several questions: about what I might learn from my illness and what part of myself might emerge as I recovered. As I let this blessing shift my relationship with my illness, I began to discover some of the gifts that awaited me there.

Asking those questions can reveal a lot on the threshold, including a number of options for moving on that we might not otherwise have considered had we not welcomed the unwanted aspects of our passage, saying, "Yes, and. . . ."

Chrysalis Space

What might it mean to have courageous hospitality toward the events and changes your threshold is bringing? If you listen to the changes that await you in the "not yet," what do they want you to know? If they could speak truthfully but benevolently, with concern for your best interest, what might they say to you? How might you receive what they say as a gift, say "Yes," and continue with the word "and"?

Write down several circumstances related to your threshold that you wish were otherwise. Choose one and imagine you are in an improv skit, responding to it as a gift, beginning with the phrase, "Yes, and. . . ." Continue writing the scene out, wherever it leads you.

Tapping into Joy

Like letting go, the threshold skill of moving on can arouse fear, grief, or even anger over the uncertainties of the "not yet," but it can also bring deep joy. When we step into the present moment without attachments to what we've known before and what we've expected or desired for the future, we are opening the way for many emotions, including joy. This is not a false happiness that denies our losses and the difficult feelings they stir. Rather, it is an insistence that we not deny joy just because we are experiencing loss. William Blake's familiar words are worth taking to heart:

Joy & Woe are woven fine
A Clothing for the soul divine
Under every grief & pine
Runs a joy with silken twine.

Not far from where I live is a sacred site known by the Dakota people today, whose ancestors originally dwelled in this land, as a *bdote*, meaning a place where the waters meet. There, at the confluence of the Minnesota and Mississippi Rivers, is the river valley honored in many Dakota creation stories as the center of the earth and the origin of the Dakota people. It is also, tragically and horrifically, the historic site of a concentration camp, where in the bitter winter of 1862–63, the US army based at nearby Fort Snelling held captive 1,700 Dakota women, children, and elders. The people had been forced to walk 150 miles to their imprisonment, and during that winter hundreds died of illness or exposure on the very site of their people's genesis.

Today the place is marked with interpretative plaques explaining the sacred creation stories as well as a historical account of captivity and oppression. Sorrowfully commemorating their ancestors' forced march and confinement, a group of Dakota people in the area regularly convenes to cover the same ground, ending at this site. The 150-mile walk takes six days and is not a protest but a ceremony for healing, honoring the ancestors' suffering, strength, and resilience. It includes many stops, not only for rest and food, but also for pounding wooden stakes into the ground along the way and at the final site, each with the name of an ancestor on a red and yellow cloth tied to it. The ancestors' names are spoken as the memorials are placed along the route, recognizing their presence among those walking. The healing power of the walk, participants say, comes from the grief that rises. But also, at the end of the march, from the presence of Dakota children joining in at the bdote, where their youthful energy and laughter, their running feet and unchecked joy restore the living energy of the site's creation story and remind the elders of the larger woven cloth of life.

The thresholds skill of moving on into the "not yet" is about resisting the temptation to get stuck, not only in one stage of our thresholding passage or story but also in one emotion or another. We are making room for a variety of feelings—grief and joy, despair and hope, fear and courage—to co-exist with each other and to move through us without attachment. We experience and name each one, asking what it has to tell us and to teach us. And then we send it on, so that we too might keep moving.

Of course, this opens us up to difficult emotions we might prefer to keep at bay. But it also makes way for tremendous joy and hope, for a wakeful state of being that is delightfully alive, singing what writer Wallace Stegner called "the unbroken doublesong of love and lamentation." Those who are able to do this often express surprise that even an unwanted passage, like a challenging diagnosis or the loss of a loved one, can bring great joy and connection to the present moment—and also to community and nature, to self and others, and to the past and the future.

I think of it as a state described by conservationist John Muir as a connection beyond all the limitations and mortality of individuality. In *My First Summer in the Sierra,* he wrote,

We are now in the mountains and they are in us, kindling enthusiasm, making every nerve quiver, filling every pore and cell of us. Our flesh-and-bone tabernacle seems transparent as glass to the beauty about us, as if truly an inseparable part of it, thrilling with the air and trees, streams and rocks, in the waves of the sun,—a part of all nature, neither old nor young, sick nor well, but immortal. Just now I can hardly conceive of any bodily condition dependent on food or breath any more than the ground or the sky. How glorious a conversion, so complete and wholesome it is.

On our shared thresholds of social and environmental change, it can be easy to get stuck in emotions of despair, fear, or anger—or guilt over not doing enough. These feelings are appropriate—and necessary—as we witness the violence, oppression, and ecological destruction we are seeking to change. We do not want to ban these feelings or shut them down. We just want to keep them moving, which makes room for other feelings as well. Social change (and personal change, as well) takes time, and we will never last for the long haul if we don't find joy in the journey too. We burn out quickly when our environmental work does not include the pleasure and healing of communing with nature. We wear out and wear down in our antiracism efforts if we never experience glimpses of the Beloved Community we seek to make real. We get used up in our collaborations to dismantle patriarchy if we are not nurtured by new models of working together as alternatives to the power hoarding of hierarchies.

"To really transform our society," writes adrienne maree brown, "we will need to make justice one of the most pleasurable experiences we can have." Not only is it wise to welcome joy when it comes, we also need to create opportunities to share it. DJ activist and scholar Lynnée Denise calls this "misery resistance," rooted in some of the longstanding practices of Black communities, where dancing and singing bring people together while offering the body a way to metabolize pain. It can also be found in some communities organizing for change—and any thresholding group, perhaps one you have formed—intentionally sharing meals as pleasurable time for bonding, growing closer, and feeding more than a physical hunger. On personal thresholds as well as shared ones, we need the strength that comes from joy and pleasure in order to tap our deeper reserves of resilience.

I have been grateful to learn one form of "misery resistance" from Marcus Young, a Minneapolis-based artist activist and the founder of a participatory radical street dance practice called "Don't You Feel It Too?" (DYFIT). Promoting both inner liberation and social healing, DYFIT creates dance events in public places, in which each participant uses earbuds to move to their own chosen music while sharing space with others dancing around them. Dancers gather before they start dancing to connect with each other; they synchronize again at the close of their session by bowing down and then sprawling out on the ground for what could be interpreted as the peaceful yoga pose of Savasana or a protest die-in but is more basically a radically embodied way of claiming space in the public realm. In between the beginning and ending of each session, the dancers all move around one another, each to their own music. If passersby stop and ask the dancers what they are doing, they answer with just five words: *Don't you feel it too?*

The power of this practice results in joy for participants and observers alike. It was developed as an experiment during the 2008 Republican national convention held in Saint Paul, where anarchists from near and far were regularly facing off with police outside the convention hall. As tensions rose, Marcus Young and his cohort of dancers wanted to be present on the scene as part of a public protest without contributing to or getting caught up in a possible clash between factions. They began listening to their own music, each one of them, to diffuse their own stress and dancing to it as an expression of vulnerability. In an interview with *Minnesota Monthly*, Young said they wanted "to create a bit of mystery, to practice joy and exuberance, to work out the anxiety we felt in our bodies." What they discovered over four days of showing up and dancing was that not only did *they* feel better, but their movement and unexpected joy gave them access to the center of the gathering and their dancing began to create a buffer zone, a middle ground where the tensions of the situation were given space to diffuse.

Movement—of bodies and emotions—keeps us awake and alive, even joyful, when change is in the air. Decades ago, as I rounded the bend in a challenging time in my personal life, my therapist suggested I make a soundtrack for going forward. I compiled a set of songs that I titled "Victory Dance," which I played whenever I could, sometimes dancing to it as a way of shaking out the emotional deposits pocketed in my body. Now, in our thresholding groups, we sometimes take a break for qigong or a simple practice of literally shaking things out, bouncing or jiggling to keep our feelings—and ourselves—moving on.

Chrysalis Space

What are the primary feelings you have experienced on your thresholds? Are there any emotions that might be stuck in an "on" position? Are there other emotions you have not felt at all? Let yourself be curious about the emotions you are feeling and not feeling without judgement. Are some emotions irrelevant on your threshold, or are you shutting them down before they can offer you their wisdom? How might you keep your feelings moving, making room for new ones as you do?

Consider especially your experience of joy on the threshold. When and how have you felt it? Has it been allowed to reside in partnership with grief or despair, with fear or anger? If you have not felt it, can you imagine any part of your experience where it might be hiding? How might you offer joy a wider welcome?

To write about this, first take a short stroll or roll around the block or around your house. Then listen to a favorite piece of music, if possible, letting yourself dance or move to it in any style that invites your heart to sing along. Then, begin writing with this prompt and follow wherever it leads:

"If I let my heart sing now . . ."

A WIDER HORIZON:
Rethinking Onward and Upward

One of the common thresholding phrases that can create a lot of trouble is the saying, "onward and upward." Intended as a wish for success and progress, it might seem positive enough until we stop to ask what we mean by success and what we mean by progress. What do you consider to be an "upward" move? Does it include taking a job that pays less or wields less power, influence, or status, sometimes a necessary threshold move for any number of reasons? Is it progress or success to turn in your car and take mass transit instead, whether it is because of aging or disability or to spare the planet additional gas emissions? Do we consider it an "upward" move to leave a longstanding relationship, even when we know it may bring, for the short term or longer, loneliness, grief, financial insecurity, and the need to gain new skills we might not want to learn? Each of us has our own definition of success, but many of them are shaped by the Overculture's understandings of achievement and status. How much we earn, what we own, and how much independence we have are all frequent signifiers of success in the dominant culture. So when we move "downward" in earnings or possessions or independence, even people who say these signifiers aren't important might experience it is a less positive direction.

I definitely did not feel like a success, as our young family's breadwinner, when I left the job that was making my spirit shrivel up and then moved us across the state to start over in a new community, with no guarantee of income or stability. In retrospect it was the right move, but by every common measurement of success and progress, at the time it did not look so great. Years later, we would again experience "downward" mobility when David needed to leave his job, at that point providing our primary income, without having another lined up. That too was the right move, but not exactly an "upward" one. In each case, we had to reframe what success and progress meant as we moved into significant uncertainty and financial loss. Similarly, when aging or disability makes it impossible to live independently at home, the move into assisted living is often seen as a "downward" one rather than a step of progress or success. My friend Sheila, an artist living with Parkinson's disease, was one exception. When she left her much-loved home, while acknowledging the losses involved in that move, she noted how much easier it would be for her to continue painting if she were assisted with other tasks of daily living.

Our understandings of success and progress also matter on our shared thresholds. What if progress is not about going faster or farther, but might be better achieved by going slow or staying put? What if upward mobility means sharing more and owning less? What if growth of a business or an organization is not measured by a higher budget or larger sales, service, attendance, or production numbers but rather by deeper satisfaction or the greater well-being of employees, customers, and the larger community? What if success is rewarded with less autonomy and isolation and greater connection to others, including those who are struggling? None of these is a new idea, and thankfully many people and organizations are living them out in the world today. But each of them is a significant upending of the messages and practices of the Overculture and assumptions about progress and success that rise from them.

Of course, this does not negate the need for equity in earnings and opportunity. Our systems still need to pay more to those whose work has been undervalued because of who they are or because of the work they do. But challenging the mythical promise of upward mobility can be important for all of us. When more people begin questioning those messages in a serious and open-ended way, we will begin to create a chrysalis space inviting exciting and unnerving social change. The upheavals of the Covid-19 pandemic, for example, have catalyzed questions about topics as far-reaching as social safety nets, work-life balance, gas consumption, and collective responsibility for personal and social well-being.

Every year since 1997, the Aspen Institute has named some twenty people between the age of thirty and forty-five as Henry Crown Fellows. Chosen for their outstanding successes and entrepreneurial accomplishments in any sector, each is poised on a threshold of achievement, considering how they might leverage their success to become leaders of broader impact, supporting social change and seeking to improve the world. For two years, the cohort meets several times each year for seminars, mentoring, and networking intended to encourage their growth as leaders.

In 2011, journalist and author Anand Giridharadas was named a Henry Crown Fellow, an honor he received as a mark of achievement as well as an extraordinary opportunity. Four years later, when invited to present the keynote address at the Institute's extended gathering of fellows, Giridharadas boldly used the opportunity to question the Institute's and his own notions of success, provocatively challenging the systems—and thinking—that created the prosperity and privilege of that success by increasing disparity in the wider population. He asked what I might call a "caterpillar's questions." These are questions articulated from a new upside-down perspective; resulting, if pursued, in dissolving old ways of being, and starting whole new vibrations that might lead to something quite surprising.

Giridharadas noted that "The dominant ethic worldwide among the winners of our age in business, government and nonprofit sectors" is a consensus that those winners "must be challenged to do more good, but never, ever tell them to do less harm." He said:

> We talk a lot here, about giving more. We don't talk about taking less. We talk a lot here about what we should be doing more of, we don't talk about what we should be doing less of.

On the shared threshold of growing economic disparity, we might be advocating a livable minimum wage or we might be speaking truth to power, as Giridharadas did from a position of privilege and as many more do every day from a position of disadvantage. But any effort to shift the inequities and bring about a more just distribution of the world's abundance will require significant challenges to the Overculture's understandings of merit, power, success, and progress. We will need a willingness to enter brave space, where old assumptions can dissolve before new understandings are fully formed. We will need curiosity, an ability to go with the flow, to say "Yes, and," and to take risks and discover new ways of moving on in a story still being written.

Chrysalis Space

How do you define success, progress, or positive change? Take a few minutes to jot down any associations you have with each of these. Do any of these associations influence your willingness or reluctance to become involved in the issue of income disparity or another shared threshold today? Choose one cause or issue related to a shared threshold you are currently not engaged in. What would true progress on that issue look like? Does that align with your own definitions of success and progress, or do they contradict one another? What new definitions of success and progress might be helpful on your personal or shared thresholds?

Reviewing the associations with progress you jotted down a few minutes ago, experiment with a different perspective on success or progress. Choose a different definition or understanding of success or progress and write about what it might look like on your threshold(s), beginning with these words and following wherever they lead:

"It could be another kind of progress (or success) . . ."

THRESHOLDING TOGETHER

With a thresholding buddy or a group of thresholders, gather for a meal after each of you has read the reflections on moving on. Then choose any of the following questions to start your conversation. Consider pausing between each person's time talking to jiggle, jump, or dance for a few minutes to wake up your bodies and a little joy held there.

- Describe one circular pattern or habit of thinking or doing that makes it hard to move on toward the uncertain future. Can you think of a way to interrupt that pattern?
- What would brave space look like on your threshold? How might it differ from safe space? What might you need to cultivate brave space for yourself and others?
- What do you do that offers a way to practice wu wei? It could be a martial art, yoga, or tai chi. Or maybe it is taking a deep breath or closing your eyes briefly, or taking a short walk or roll to clear away your assumptions and better attune you to the energy, movement, or relationships you might align yourself with. Describe your own practice and one time it has made a difference for you.
- Tell about a time when you said, "Yes, but. . . ." What would it have looked like to say "Yes, and" instead, and what might have happened if you did?
- Describe a time when you did something to shake up your emotions and experienced joy or another welcome emotion in the midst of your change. What songs might you put in your soundtrack for change?
- How do you define success, progress, or positive change, and does that influence your ability or reluctance to move on? Do these definitions affect your involvement or lack of involvement in a shared threshold we are on now?

Threshold Skill 9:

IMAGINING A WAY

One of the best ways I know to get things moving is to engage my imagination. The facts of my situation, and the logic and reason I use to arrange them, will only take me to edge of what I know. Even using my five senses will only extend as far as the range of my sight, hearing, taste, smell, and touch. But imagination has the ability to reach farther by accessing the deeper well of the unconscious and creatively rearranging what I've known before. The uniquely human capacity to imagine is a valuable threshold skill that can open a way into and through the unknowns of the not yet.

When we cling to what we know, it is easy to forget about the massive storehouse of knowledge hidden within each of us, a vast library filed away behind a door aptly labeled "the unconscious." It is there, in the back stacks of our mind, that our experiences first get shelved, and cognitive scientists tell us that as little as one percent of that material gets transferred to our conscious mind. Like a "closed stack" library where patrons submit requests for materials to be retrieved by librarians, our unconscious stores an expansive collection of knowledge entirely out of sight. Some of it is also out of reach of language itself, collected and shelved as preverbal feelings, sensory experiences, and images that constitute the knowledge we call intuition. Dream worker and author Jeremy Taylor called this knowledge "not-yet-speech-ripe," using an old Anglo-Saxon term for the unconscious.

Fortunately, accessing the treasures of the unconscious does not require mastering the Dewey decimal system or turning to a librarian. Rather, we can be assisted by the colorful cast of characters appearing in our dreams at night, or by any piece of music, poetry, or art that speaks to us. We only need to pay attention to anything flinging open the doors to the unconscious and beckoning us in to wander among the hidden stacks, often without knowing what we are looking for.

Imagination, dreams, ritual, and the arts are all tools for accessing this larger pool of memory, knowledge, and awareness. In the dominant culture today, these intuitive ways of knowing are often disparaged as less reliable and useful than science and historical fact. But any scientist worth their white coat knows that exploration begins with a dance between curiosity and imagination. Especially when facing an unknown future, we need to access a larger body of knowledge—and our imaginations, creativity, and dreams all extend our awareness to do just that.

Wang Maohua, a tai chi master in Beijing, once gave me an important lesson that changed my understanding of tai chi and now also guides me on the threshold. He began our time together by asking me to show him the tai chi I practiced at home. But soon after I launched through several forms, he stopped me. I was pushing myself through the moves, he observed.

"Try to focus your attention on the space above your head and below your feet," he advised instead. "Extend your awareness to the space beyond your fingers." He led me in a meditative journey through my body, awakening me first to the space within my body and then beyond it. And he told me to stop pushing my body. "Instead," he said, "let your body move by a gentle intention into the space around it, where your awareness is already waiting to meet it."

We can borrow this practice of "gentle intention" on the threshold, casting our awareness across the gap of the unknown. By imagining ourselves on the far side of our threshold, we are actually stretching our attention beyond the limits of our senses. Gentle intention will open our awareness, allowing us to perceive beneath the surface of things. It is a way of open-ended wondering and imagining about the "not yet" we are moving toward. Then, having imagined ourselves on the far side of the threshold we are crossing, we look up to find our own self waiting there, encouraging us on, and welcoming us as we arrive in a place where we have never been before.

Chrysalis Space

How do you access the closed stacks of your unconscious? Do you regularly use your imagination? Do you record and recall your dreams, mining them for meaning and wisdom? Maybe you engage your hands in creative work, with or without words, that draws up unconscious knowledge from the well of your intuition; or maybe you make music or move your body in dance or physical exercise until you are awash in endorphins or afloat on the theta brain waves that increase creativity.

Whatever your favorite method is, for the next two weeks, do it more often. (If you don't have a favorite method, choose a new one—something simple—and do it as often as possible in the next two weeks.) Each time you do this practice, pause afterwards to notice: how and where did your awareness expand and what did it feel like when it did? What did it tell you, possibly without words or with a not-yet-speech-ripe understanding? Try to record just one image, word or phrase, feeling, sound, gesture, taste, smell, texture, or shape that might help you recall it on another day.

After two weeks, review the notes you've made. What message might your unconscious be sending you? What deeper knowledge is tapping on your shoulder, rising up through your imagination, your creative activities, and your dreams, waiting for you to notice? Choose a favorite creative activity, such as writing, painting, dancing, or music, and use it to give expression to the knowledge within that you are noticing now.

The Power of Stories

One of the most imaginative ways humans have of creating chrysalis space for change is our power to tell stories. Inside the stories we create and share, identities are formed and transformed, possibilities are defined, imagined, and explored, and surprising new plotlines are continually revealed. Stories are busy workshops building and rebuilding the frames in which we perceive the world and ourselves. They shape our understanding of reality, and in this way, they shape us.

"All that we are is story," wrote writer Richard Wagamese, who regarded the human capacity for story as more than individual authorship. For him, stories are a tool for connecting with others and together creating a better world. The task of every one of us, he said, is to create the best possible story with others, and then share these stories freely and frequently. As we do, he said, we will enlarge our own story and understanding, discover our greater kinship and participate in changing the world's story too.

This was not a theoretical proposition for Wagamese. He knew the power of story firsthand. After a childhood of neglect, abuse, and painful separation from his family and his Ojibwe roots and culture, his storytelling, spoken and on the page, opened a path back into relationship with his own identity, family, and heritage. Not surprisingly, his stories often did the same for his listeners and readers. Being unafraid to speak honestly of tragedy with compassion and humor, he let his stories enlarge the human heart and reveal a greater kinship spanning culture, geography, and even time. He was a mesmerizing storyteller, sometimes beginning by calling in his ancestors and often weaving his own stories together with traditional Ojibwe tales. Remembering the first time he spoke an Ojibwe word after being reunited with his birth family as a young adult, he wrote in *One Native Life*, "When I said [the word] aloud, I felt like I'd really, truly spoken for the first time in my life." The word he spoke was the Ojibwe word meaning "come in."

Each of us, on the threshold, is invited to discover our own true language, to "come in" and be at home with who and where we are in the midst of change, and to live into a story of larger possibilities and kinship. This means letting our stories grow with us or finding new stories that make space for who we are becoming. When a monarch emerges from the chrysalis in its new form, the wings are folded and small, while the abdomen is swollen and too heavy for flight. In the first moments free of the chrysalis, it is imperative that the butterfly suspend itself with room for its wings to expand as it pumps fluids into them. If the wings lack space to unfold in this way, they will forever be unable to fly.

As humans, when we move through change personally and collectively, some of the stories that supported us before might not be spacious enough for the transformation now underway. So we want to keep asking: Are the stories shaping our worldview expansive enough for the changes we are experiencing now? Will they accommodate and support the unfolding that our future well-being depends on? If not, how might we revise them, add to them, or imagine a whole new story that begins today?

Chrysalis Space

What is a story you tell yourself about who you have been and a story about who you are now— stories that bring you to a threshold today? Are these stories big enough for who you are becoming? Do they offer healing? Do they enlarge your understanding of kinship? What new plot twists are possible? How might you open the next chapter of your life, the one beginning now, in a way that allows for more possibilities, greater kinship, new directions, and a healthy involvement of your imagination?

To write about this from a prompt, start with the words below and follow wherever they lead:

"Starting now, this could be a story . . ."

Winging It

One morning in May, I sat at the open, east-facing window where I meditate, enjoying the spring fragrance of lilacs and apple trees in bloom outside. The air was full of birdsong, and a few robins were swooping down to the dewy grass to claim a meal of earthworms. In front of the window, several long strands of a spider's gossamer were shining in the sunlight, stretched across the yard from the lilac bush to a fat spruce tree some thirty feet away. I marveled, first that the threads remained unbroken by the day's gentle wind. Then, pausing to consider, I wondered how the spiders that had spun the strands across such a distance did it in the first place.

Known as ballooning or kiting, a spider's wingless travel across wide open spaces is an act of faith and risk. Typically practiced by smaller spiders or spiderlings, ballooning begins with a climb to the highest point it can reach. There the spider rises up on its legs, points its abdomen skyward and releases several silken threads into the air. Some of the threads cross one another, forming a triangular balloon or parachute that catches the wind and carries the spider away, while it unreels a shining filament connected to its launch point. A lucky lift will transport the spider to a safe landing where it can attach the other end of the gossamer now stretched like a vapor trail across a surprisingly large gap. But not every launch is lucky. Many spiders that start this journey never make it to the end. A few, lifted into the jet stream, have been found hundreds of miles away in the middle of large bodies of water. Still others, participating in mass ballooning events, have escaped floods by kiting in such great numbers their landing on dry ground creates a silken covering as white as a new fallen snow.

In the thresholding phase of Not Yet, we inevitably face large gaps of unknown distance. How can we cross them without wings? What capacity do we have to spin a silken line into the unknown? Can we, as William Stafford once said in his poem "Any Time," "weave a parachute of all things broken" and depend on that parachute to carry us across?

It occurred to me that day in May, looking out of my window, that just as the spider's spinnerets release their gossamer strands into the wind, one of the thresholder's tasks is to release multiple dreams and creative launchings to discover which ones will take hold. Better not to question at the outset whether those dreams will reach the other side or be strong enough to carry us with them. Our task is to send the strands out, as many as possible, on the chance that some will make a small parachute and, if we wait, given a little wind, that parachute might just carry us where we long to go.

There are lots of ways to do this. It might be creating a collage of words or images. Or brainstorming, alone or with others, generating as many ideas as possible without critiquing which are feasible or desirable. For instance, one thresholder discouraged by the direction his workplace was taking, decided to retire earlier than he had planned and suddenly faced a blank slate of many years. To consider how he might use that time, he began by brainstorming volunteer opportunities instead of a new job because that allowed him to cast his net much wider.

As adults, we sometimes pinch off our dreams before anyone but us sees them, or sometimes even before we have seen and claimed them ourselves. But the threshold is a good time and place for profligate dreaming. Releasing as many silk threads as possible—each spun of what could be—and then waiting to discover what happens, what might catch, where any lift might come. This is not the methodical spinning of a web, designed to catch and hold prey. This is a wild act of imagination, faith, and risk, casting out multiple strands of possibilities, hoping a few will join together making a kite that will fly and carry us.

Chrysalis Space

Without altering the givens of your threshold, what wild dreams do you have about how you might receive those givens? The word "maybe" can be useful to get your spinning started. Or the words "what if." Use either of these to begin ten to twenty sentences about a threshold you are on. Don't hold back. Don't test them for soundness before writing them down. Just fling them out like gossamer in the wind and notice which ones shine, which ones reach out across the gap you are facing, which ones line up with others in a way that might carry you, wingless as you stand, given a little lift from the wind. Choose one that especially attracts your attention, whether it seems possible or not, and write more about that, beginning with the sentence you already wrote and following wherever it leads.

Stretching and Strengthening

If we're going to talk about kiting as a threshold skill, it is worth noting two truths: a kite can be hard to get off the ground; and when we do, holding on to the string is imperative.

In the kiting-as-imagination metaphor, the necessary running start in creative thinking is something many of us as adults have not done for a very long time. We might be out of shape. We might need some practice, stretching, and strengthening to reawaken the creativity that came so naturally to us as children. Like the superhero capes and make-believe games we packed away with other childhood belongings, our larger supply of creativity might have been left behind as we assumed the roles and responsibilities of adulthood. Fortunately, it only takes a few simple steps to begin recovering it.

First, forget about the notion that creativity is all in our heads. Imagination is fully embodied and every bit as circulatory as our blood. Creativity benefits from movement, flow, and a continual exchange of input and output. It is most vibrant when our bodies and minds, ideas and feelings are unrestricted and relating freely to one another. Just as tension constricts blood flow through our muscles, it will also cut off the free flow of thoughts and feelings in our awareness. So the first step in stretching our imagination is to relax and let go. Inhabit the larger field of creative energy present in your whole body. If this feels challenging, do some yoga or tai chi, dance to a favorite song, or hum while sitting still or moving. You can also return to the exercise after "Shedding Old Skins" in the first Threshold skill, Letting Go (page 28).

Remember, this is about stretching, not straining, just as the practice of tai chi stretches our human experience between earth and sky but not to a breaking point. Chungliang Al Huang, a professional dancer as well as a tai chi teacher, points out that the extension in tai chi is not done in a straight line, where opposing extremes pull in a tug of war. Rather, he says, tai chi movements are rounded explorations of opposite directions that curve and fold back on themselves with the curling energy of *yin-yang*—opposites in motion and in relationship with each other. This kind of stretching leads to greater energy and wholeness rather than stress and eventual fracture.

Next, having relaxed our bodies and minds, it's time to release the inner critic. I have a particularly strong inner critic that I've come to think of as a muscle-bound bouncer named Will, who is often posted at the door of my consciousness. My imagination, whom I've named Maggie, is a sprite of a character wearing red shoes and a skirt of many colors, quick to dance and dart around Will's guarded position. But Maggie doesn't always manage to get past Will. Will can be very effective at guarding the door.

You might think I'd want to get rid of Will, but what I've realized is that sometimes I need Will's support and muscular protection. So when I'm trying to encourage my imagination to come forward, I have learned to send Will out on a long errand, maybe even an extended vacation. Maggie is a threshold dancer; she needs to be able to come and go with ease and joy for extended periods of time, and that requires dismissing the bouncer and leaving the door unguarded for a while.

Then, even with the door wide open, I might still need to practice stretching my creative muscles. Warm them up. Strengthen them in training. Robert Grudin, in his book *The Grace of Great Things, Creativity and Imagination,* offers several activities for strengthening our imaginations. I especially like these two: Daydream about yourself in a different identity, living somewhere else or in a different time, and make up a children's story that creates a whole new reality with different beings, habits, rules, and possibilities. If you can, create the story in the moment, telling it as you make it up—which will also be an improv practice of "Yes, and" in which your own imagination plays both parts. Other activities I highly recommend include doodling, dancing, singing, or playing with colors—with paints or crayons, fabric or paper, or taking to the streets with a box of sidewalk chalk.

The more we exercise our imagination, the more readily our creative powers will spring into action when we need them. Like messengers trained to be quick on their feet and familiar with the material in our unconscious, a well-exercised imagination will call up a wealth of images and intuitions, memories, and feelings that we can then put in new arrangements, like kites ready to fly in the slightest breeze.

This brings us to that other important thing about kites: holding onto the string. You need to keep your feet on the ground when your imagination takes flight. "A kite ... cannot fly unless strung to the ground," Grudin points out. "It has no power without ties to the 'real' world conceived by us as accurately as possible. But its relationship to the world ought to be dynamic rather than subordinate. The strength of imagination lies precisely in its friction with a sense of reality that is equally strong." Imagination is sometimes wrongfully posed as the opposite of reality. Perhaps its real power is more accurately an extension of reality, an exploration of all that lies beyond the limits of our knowledge and our senses. That, to me, sounds a lot like the frontiers of threshold living.

Chrysalis Space

How fit is your imagination? Have you been using it frequently? When did you last let it stretch its legs, run about just for fun, or take off on a flight of fancy? Consider how you might engage your imagination for this next leg of your journey. And if your imagination is a little out of shape, don't worry. It will come back, likely faster than you might think, with a little time and attention.

For the next ten days, set aside some daily time, even just ten to fifteen minutes, beginning with relaxation and letting go, and then playfully moving into daydreaming, doodling, dancing, or any other creative activity that appeals to you. After five to fifteen minutes of creative play, stop. This is not meant to go on long. Consider what you've made or done. Notice how it felt. Ask yourself what your imagination has to say to you, as an experience or an expression. How will you respond? And what ties your imagination to the realities of your threshold in ways that give your creativity more power, not less?

Keyhole Views

We humans are drawn to wholeness, and our imaginations often help us get there. How many times have you been in the middle of a movie, a play, or a book, and long before the last act or chapter, you begin guessing how it will end? Good storytellers leave multiple clues as their tales unfold, some pointing to the ending that eventually will come and others subtly leading us astray so we can experience the pleasure of surprise when a different ending is revealed. These clues draw us into a story in the same way that ancient ruins, only half standing, attract us as we observe what is there and add to it, imagining the broken, waist-high walls that remain as a full dwelling with doors and windows and children peering through them; or looking at a roofless, bombed-out church and seeing in the mind's eye elaborate stained glass panes and soaring rafters overhead, maybe even hearing the faint strains of choral harmonies and prayer.

The human brain is wired to complete what it encounters. We like to participate in creation and completion. Give me three notes, C, E, and G, and my western-trained ear will add another C, high or low, to finish the phrase. Point my eyes to the night skies, and I will cluster the stars into constellations that I then see not just as points of light but as a dipper, a swan, a horse, or a warrior. Give me enough time gazing at those stars, and I will weave stories that bring the dipper, the swan, the horse, and the warrior into relationship with each other. Our human brains reach for connections, patterns, and narratives whenever we listen, wherever we look, or however we turn our attention toward the world around us.

The challenge comes when we study the pieces before us and experience the limits of our senses, experience, and memory. How do we perceive a wholeness we have never personally encountered? How to conjure or believe we might find wholeness on the far side of a threshold that has tallied up so many losses? Or, in our work for justice and equity, how do we create the Beloved Community evoked by Martin Luther King Jr. but never fully realized in his time or our own? Imagination is crucial.

If we require a wholeness already made for us, we are bound to be disappointed by the world's broken fragments and many barriers. We might experience our threshold as a closed door that permits no view of where we are headed. But creative thresholders sometimes describe a moment, a small event, or even a single comment along the way that offered them a keyhole view of a new possibility—just enough of a glimpse to open the door of their imagination, allowing them to project themselves as being whole on the other side.

My friend Barbara had felt a call to ministry as a young woman, but because her Christian denomination did not ordain people who were openly gay, she had assumed the door to ministry was firmly closed to her as a lesbian. Then one day, Janet, an ordained woman in Barbara's denomination, asked Barbara why she wasn't in seminary. Barbara confided that she was in a relationship with a woman, expecting the minister to commiserate with her about that closed door. Instead, Janet smiled broadly, and said, "Wonderful! What's her name? Let's have a party to celebrate!" Her surprisingly exuberant acceptance gave Barbara what she later described to me as a keyhole view of a church that would wholeheartedly welcome her as a leader without reservations or conditions. It was a glimpse, a momentary experience of acceptance from others and herself, that worked like a key, unlocking a door inside Barbara's own imagination. It allowed her to experience, for even that brief moment, being a minister celebrated for who she was. She enrolled in seminary, was ordained (in her own denomination, which later came to welcome gay and lesbian clergy) and went on to serve internationally and in the US in creative and challenging ministries. It was a turn of events and fulfillment of vocation Barbara had been unable to foresee before that comment and the keyhole view it opened to her.

Keyhole views give us new eyes or new ways of perceiving ourselves and our circumstances. As they unlock our imaginations, we become empowered, freed of old tyrannies that have ruled too long. It might be the tyranny of internalized messages about who we are and what we can or cannot do. Or it could be the subjugation of our true identity and gifts by a world that continually turns us away because of our gender, race, class, age, abilities, religion, or orientation. It might be trauma, from our personal experiences or those of our ancestors, binding us with fear in ways that keep us living too small. Any of these, and other forms of confinement, can be broken open when so much is in flux. The question is, will we take advantage of this fluid state to be true to who we really are?

In Nicaragua in the 1960s, when Ernesto Cardenal arrived on the Solentiname archipelago, he was a Catholic priest assigned to establish a church for the community of impoverished islanders. But he brought more than the Christian sacraments. He brought paints and brushes, paper and pencils, and it was these art supplies and the invitation to create with them that the campesinos later credited with awakening a new way of being, personally and collectively. As they learned to paint and write poetry, many of them came to support or join the Sandinista revolution. They helped overthrow a corrupt, multigenerational dictatorship that had depended upon a population asleep and disengaged, unable to imagine a different life.

"Before Ernesto came ... before the poetry and the painting," Numbia Arcia said when interviewed after the revolution, "our lives were *asleep*. That's what campesino life had always been—una vida dormida. [The poetry and painting] helped us wake up."

Around the world, in revolutions within nations and personal lives, the connection between imagination and transformation is evident and powerful. A little imagination goes a long way in encouraging new ways of being, offering assurance that a different reality is already there, waiting to be inhabited.

Chrysalis Space

What constrictions are you currently holding—messages about who you are and who you might become that fail to make room for the fullness of your spirit or identity or longings? When you consider the changes occurring in your life now, what keeps you smaller or more fragmented than you wish to be?

Now ask yourself what keyhole views of self-acceptance and a greater wholeness have you been given? They might be single events, brief comments, or glimpses so fleeting you may have dismissed them. You will know them as keyhole views if they momentarily caused your heart to open, your breath to quicken, and your spirit to soar. Try to recall one such experience and let yourself savor it, taking your time with it. If nothing comes to mind, imagine one—a small incident that would make your heart sing by helping you imagine yourself in the future, accepted and whole for who you are now or who you are meant to be.

Notice what your body and spirit feel when you linger with this experience of acceptance and wholeness, either remembered or imagined. Imagine that feeling spreading throughout your body and your being. Breathing slowly, with each in breath, store this feeling in your muscles, your blood, and your bones. With each breath out, rid yourself of any messages that deny the balm and wholeness of this feeling. After five minutes, ask yourself, if I carry this wholeness with me, what new ways of being and seeing might be possible as I live through this change?

A WIDER HORIZON:
Monumental Changes

Imagination and creative work of any kind are critical in bringing about monumental change in the world. If we cannot imagine it, it will not be possible to bring it about. What Audre Lorde said of poetry is true of other forms of imaginative work: "Poetry is the way we help give names to the nameless so it can be thought. The farthest external horizons of our hopes and fears are cobbled by our poems, carved from the rock experiences of our daily lives."

In the twenty-first century, conflicts have erupted across the United States over the names and faces of the public imagination as presented in statues commemorating confederate leaders, proponents of slavery, and Spanish conquerors. The controversy is not new. Almost fifty years ago, the American Indian Movement requested the removal of an obelisk in Santa Fe Plaza commemorating "fallen heroes" who died fighting the Indigenous people of that land. Instead of removing it, legislators opted to add another interpretive plaque. The plaque said the language of commemoration carved into the obelisk (which included the word "savage") was of a different time and did not reflect current beliefs. One year later, an anonymous editor using a chisel removed that most offensive word from the obelisk, but as of this writing, the obelisk with the rest of its message remains.

Since then, the significance of our public monuments has been underscored by an increase in both the number of statues being removed and the tension and violence related to their removal. After the 2017 Charlottesville killing of a peaceful activist by a white supremacist violently denouncing the removal of a confederate statue, many cities, especially in the south, took action, some quietly in the middle of the night, to remove monuments honoring confederates and prominent slaveholders or celebrating slavery, white supremacy, and the conquest of Indigenous people.

The significance of these removals as threshold events is clear, affecting both what we honor from our shared past and what we imagine for our shared future. They also play a key role in how we navigate this time in-between. Less than ten years ago, neuroscientists revealed that a key brain function required for accurate navigation is a person's ability to distinguish permanent landmarks from those that move or will not last, proving unreliable for wayfinding. How true, especially in threshold times. If we continue to navigate in the present using landmarks honoring so-called "fallen heroes" whose atrocities we mourn and whose values we reject, how will we imagine and find our way toward the values we hold and a future we desire? What new landmarks and names might prove more dependable for orienting ourselves toward justice, equity, and mutual respect?

In Auburn, New York, a bronze statue of Harriet Tubman was unveiled in 2018 in front of the new Equal Rights Heritage Center. Shirley Chisholm, the nation's first Black woman congressperson, will soon be honored with a statue in Brooklyn's Prospect Park, as well as a new 400-acre park of her own in Jamaica Bay. In Minneapolis, the city's largest lake was recently retitled, shedding the name of a southern legislator and major proponent of slavery and recovering the lake's original Dakota name, Bde Mka Ska, meaning Lake of the

White Earth. Farther west, San Francisco removed a sculpture titled "Early Days" depicting a Spanish priest with a defeated American Indian at his feet. Soon after, the city renamed its international airport terminal to memorialize assassinated gay rights leader Harvey Milk.

Do these new names and statues matter? Does it make a difference to change the landmarks and lexicon of our maps, printed or electronic, as well as the ones in our brains? Author Rebecca Solnit suggests it does. "They are crucial parts of the built environment," she says in a 2017 *Guardian* article, "ones that tell us who matters, who decides, who will be remembered. They furnish our imaginations. They also shape the sense of the past that we call on when we decide what future to choose and who to value and listen to in the present. When we decide who 'we' is." Diversifying the names and monuments of our landscape does not change history, but it does influence how truthfully we remember it and how richly we imagine our options going forward.

The landmarks we topple and raise and name today will determine the guideposts orienting our imaginations toward tomorrow. On this cusp between the no longer and the not yet, it definitely matters.

Chrysalis Space

List some of the significant landmarks in your community that you depend on to know where you are and where you are going. They might include monuments or memorials or the names of streets, bridges, lakes, rivers, plazas, hills, and neighborhoods. Notice who and what those names honor and who and what may be missing or underrepresented.

Sketch a rough map of your own, renaming different places and adding monuments that might better orient you toward the future you desire. Consider some of the shared thresholds we are on and imagine any landmarks and names that could provide more reliable direction and inspire a more equitable future. Imagine what it would be like to live in a place named in that way.

THRESHOLDING TOGETHER

With a thresholding buddy or a group of thresholders, gather for a meal after each of you has read the reflections on imagining a way. Then choose any of the following questions to start your conversation:

- If you cast your awareness out beyond the reach of your senses, what knowledge about the changes you are living through might you find? Share a dream you have had recently that told you something about your threshold you had not realized before.
- Share one wild wish that does not deny the realities of your threshold but still seems impossible or ridiculous. Is there part of that dream that you might keep in mind or adjust to make it possible?
- What is a creative activity that helps you exercise your imagination? If your imagination is out of shape, describe a time when it was more active and what made it so. If it is in good shape, share what you do to keep it so. How might you keep your imagination actively engaged on your threshold now?
- Recall a time when an experience or something someone said or did gave you a keyhole view of something you longed to believe could happen. Describe how it felt and share what that meant to you, then and now.
- Share your map of new landmarks or newly named places. What might it mean to navigate by them?

Threshold Skill 10:

WIDENING WHAT WE TRUST

One of the reasons wholeness can be evasive on the threshold is that we sometimes think of wholeness as how we experienced it before without imagining it as large enough to span the changes we are going through. This makes it hard to find trustworthy ground for the journey. If wholeness is limited to what we knew before our passage began, the losses we accrue as we move through change will likely leave us feeling incomplete. But if we can take a larger view, like a camera zooming out to include both sides of the threshold in its frame, we begin to understand that who we were before and who we are becoming *both* contribute to a more ample—and whole—identity across time. From this more expansive perspective, we learn that the caterpillar and butterfly share equal belonging in an identity large enough to encompass their metamorphosis. Doing the same with our own transformation will widen what we trust, practicing the last of the ten threshold skills listed here.

One sunny March morning, on the chilly cusp between winter and spring, I was visiting the southern shore of Lake Superior with my friend Tom. We scaled a tall bank of crusted snow and gingerly walked onto the frozen lake, stunned by a dazzling display of ice and light that surrounded us. On an earlier day, the lake had frozen smooth only to be shattered by wild, muscular waves crashing up from beneath. Large anvils of ice, broken from the surface, had been tipped upright and frozen into place by winter's frigid grip, making a vast and clear mosaic, an expansive field of shards arranged by nature's hand, shimmering like icy sparks set free and ignited by the low and shifting sunlight.

Awestruck, we stood still, taking it all in along with the March sunshine, which was barely but undeniably gaining warmth as the earth tilted toward spring and its promised thaw. Suddenly, a loud crack shattered the silence and bellowed through the lake beneath our feet. We startled with two opposite responses of alarm. I jumped straight up into the air and came down hard, landing with my full weight on two booted feet, as if foolishly making my best effort to break the ice beneath me. Fortunately, it held. Next to me, Tom spread out horizontally and flat, his arms and legs extended across the ice like a Da Vinci drawing, wisely distributing his body weight across the ice to reduce the chance of falling through.

A threshold can feel like a field of ice—slippery, potentially dazzling, and at times marked by dangerous cracks and thin spots. But we can make it more reliable by spreading our whole self across it as Tom did that day, distributing the length and weight of our being across a wider base that includes where we have been and where we are going.

This happened when I showed up in my forties for my first day of seminary classes. I felt every bit as tremulous as I had when starting a new school in seventh grade. I carried within me that same awkward eleven-year-old with the long braids and the fresh scab on her chin from falling off her bike the day before. Also with me that day, as I looked around the seminary room at my classmates, young and old, was the young teen who had won a sermon contest in the church of her childhood, which would not let her deliver it because they did not ordain women. And the aspiring clarinet student who a few years later, to the horror of her conductor, botched her solo in Ravel's "Bolero" in concert with a semi-professional symphony. I had so many failures and vulnerabilities with me as I re-entered my role as a student. Looking back now, I understand that it would have helped me to expand my identity in that vulnerable moment to include my past successes too—and my hopes of discovering some emerging part of myself, long dormant, that had prompted me to return to school in the first place. Stretching my identity across a wider range of being, I could have looked around the room at classmates who seemed so much more confident than me and known that I belonged too, that I was just where I needed to be.

It's a lesson well explained by eleven-year-old Rachel in Sandra Cisneros' short story, "Eleven."

> *What they don't understand about birthdays and what they never tell you is that when you're eleven, you're also ten, and nine, and eight, and seven, and six, and five, and four, and three, and two, and one. And when you wake up on your eleventh birthday you expect to feel eleven, but . . . you don't feel eleven at all. You feel like you're still ten. And you are—underneath the year that makes you eleven. . . . Because the way you grow old is kind of like an onion or like the rings inside a tree trunk or like my little wooden dolls that fit one inside the other, each year inside the next one. That's how being eleven years old is.*

Like a tree trunk, we add new layers of being as we live through the years and the conditions they bring. Each year, the trunk is marked by another concentric circle, wrapped around what came before. Time adds to what began in the seed, and the tree becomes wider and stronger, neither leaving behind nor limited by what it has lived through. The years wrap around the heart of the tree, protecting it, supporting it, nourishing it. Even the narrow rings, formed in harsh conditions when growth was not possible, represent another circle of support around the tree's core, supporting an even larger crown of branches and leaves above.

In our thresholding, not only does our current identity include the years we have already lived through; it also includes the future we are living toward. Just as the acorn carries within it all the potential—crown and roots and trunk—of a large oak tree to come, so too, our own future growth is folded within us. Being fully in the present moment, we can find strength in expanding our wholeness to include past and future, roots and crown and seed together, in an ever-growing identity reaching toward the light.

Chrysalis Space

Imagine yourself as a tree, each period of your life adding another ring—some of them marking significant growth, others showing almost no growth at all when difficult circumstances required all your resources just to survive. Draw a set of circles representing a cross section of your life's trunk. Place some circles close together as periods of survival; others farther apart to mark those times when conditions supported your rapid growth. Name the stages represented by your circles. Was it the era of grief, of new relationship, of illness, or learning, or strength?

Choose one or more of the stages to write about. Describe whether it was a time of new growth or perhaps one of difficulty (or both at once), and what made it so, holding each stage in relationship to the heart at its core. Remember, in a human life, some of the periods with the most challenging conditions can also be times of great growth. How might those years have prepared you for the years to come? How have they produced the dreams you are now planting in the future? If you want a prompt for your writing about each stage or ring, begin with the prompt below and follow wherever it leads:

"Here is where I . . ."

Trusting the Other

Stretching our trust wider will not be easy. In fact, it might be getting even harder in the twenty-first century, with its growing polarization. As environmental and political thresholds spread stories of scarcity and fear, we are witnessing greater polarization between nations, races, political factions, religions, and much more, and this antagonism is both a hallmark and breeder of mistrust. "It drains our reservoirs of trust," says peace activist John Paul Lederach in an interview with Krista Tippett, "and it pulls [you] back into only trusting, in the narrowest sense, people who already are, and believe, very much like you." Whether we are tending to personal thresholds or global ones, it is worth noting that the climate we live in is one of diminished trust. Of course, we have good reason *not* to trust the falsehoods and malice gaining volume today. But when we become convinced to trust only what and whom we already know and where we have already been, it becomes especially challenging to cross any threshold into the new and unfamiliar.

What and whom do you trust in the midst of change and how do you determine what is trustworthy? Is it limited to the familiar? Does it include people who are different from you, or is it narrowing down, excluding those labeled as "other" for any reason? Does your trust include the different parts of your own changing identity, or do you also consider some parts of the person you are becoming as an unwanted "other"? This is especially common on thresholds defined by significant losses—diminished strength or health or income, the death or departure of a loved one, or the loss of home or employment or capacity. Well beyond the challenges of the losses themselves, the stigma of labels such as unemployed, homeless, widowed, divorced, disabled, or mentally ill often stirs a wild mix of emotions when newly affixed to us. What can be trusted when the very circumstances we have backed away from when they happen to others now occur in our own lives? Not only will this make it almost impossible to trust the changes we are experiencing, but it will also make it difficult to trust ourselves—and the person we are becoming.

This happens on shared thresholds too. When communities, organizations, institutions, nations, or societies are undergoing significant change, the fear aroused often labels whole groups of people as the untrustworthy "other." Frequently, the power this label wields is related to some part of ourselves that we regard as unwanted or untrusted and then project on others. But the practice of widening our faith helps us look beneath the labels that create divisions between us and within us as we discover a deeper trust that leads us back into relationship—with others and ourselves.

Stretching our trust across the gaps of difference is not a new call. It's as old as the teachings of all world religions and as common as folktales about the enchanted prince turned into a frog awaiting the kiss of a princess to reverse the spell and return him to human form. In *The Living Labyrinth*, Jeremy Taylor says the archetypes present in these frog tales are reminders that "In order to be healthy and whole, each person must recognize the superior, hidden worth of the most lowly and despised elements of both psyche and society." Wholeness, on the threshold and elsewhere, comes from accepting ourselves as we are so we can grow into the person we want to be. The same is true of our societies and our aspirations to make them more just. If we want to end the oppression of one segment of society, we cannot disregard and despise other populations, or we'll simply replace one oppressive system with another. Taylor writes, "Each one of us must learn to trust, and eventually 'kiss and marry,' the part of ourselves that is most 'enchanted' (i.e. unconscious) and seemingly most repulsive, underdeveloped and frog-like."

The threshold skill of widening what we trust begins with self-acceptance—of who we are and where we are in the current circumstances of our life. It is not a commitment to stay there. It is just an important, early stage in growing into our full self, waiting to be revealed as we make use of the dynamics of the threshold to become the person we wish to be.

Each of us is nested in time and place; in relationships, communities, and traditions; in identities, roles, and responsibilities that shape and guide us. In the best of circumstances, any of these can be chrysalis spaces that protect and nurture us through big changes. Unfortunately, when living on the threshold, it can be hard to experience a deeper belonging to ourselves. What held and claimed us before we began our journey may no longer fit or support who we are becoming. We are challenged to cast the net wider.

I met Miriam in the hospital where she was recovering from surgery and I was serving as a chaplain. She was agitated and her nurses asked me to visit but warned that she might not welcome my presence. I could feel her anger in the room when I entered, and she was quick to tell me its many causes. The uselessness of her doctors. The hopelessness of her condition. The friendlessness of her home life. The failure of her faith community to support her as a woman. The betrayal she felt almost everywhere she turned. I imagined it would take very little for her to add me to that list, so I mostly listened. When I finally spoke, I asked her two questions. How long had she been separated from her own people, and how and where might she rejoin them? Then I gave her a rock and read her a poem about finding strength and healing and companionship in the earth's mountains and rocks.

The poem and my questions opened a long pause. She began to cry. As Miriam remembered her own belonging in nature, she also began to recall the human relationships she had forgotten that embraced her just as she was. Her anger slowly dissipated. Her body begin to relax as she rediscovered and reclaimed, in a wider awareness, a sense of trust she had lost.

The beautiful thing about the natural world is that its interdependence excludes no one. Each of us has a part to play in it, both giving and receiving. Whether we are winged or weighted, gravity cradles us all. In naming what we trust when experiencing great change, we can begin with gravity. Then move on to places, natural or human-made. Then try the more changeable conditions of sun and rain, wind and stillness, night and day. Eventually, this will bring you around to people and other beings, and the countless relationships that can offer belonging and foster trust even through the challenges of change.

Chrysalis Space

Sit quietly in a chair for a few minutes of deep breathing. Notice how the chair supports you and how the floor supports the chair. Consider the building that supports the floor and the earth that supports the building. Open your awareness to the reliable force of gravity that holds all of this in place, usually without our notice.

Where do you feel a sense of belonging that you trust? Begin large, perhaps with nature as a whole; then get more specific. Consider the places, relationships, communities, or traditions that welcome and support you, even as you change. Are there others you have not claimed before, where you feel a growing sense of new belonging now? How might you become more centered in any of these, old or new, as you move across your thresholds? What would it mean to trust—and love—the parts of yourself you would rather not claim, especially aspects of your identity emerging as you cross your threshold?

Trusting What Does Not Hold Still

Claiming our place in nature's web of life is more than a connection between species, ecosystems, and places. It also enfolds us in time that is seasonal and cyclical, reminding us that we are part of movement that does not end, constantly transforming, turning, and returning. Every loss on nature's thresholds is nested in larger, repeating cycles of birth, death, and rebirth. Every winter is followed by spring. The heated summer day turns over to night's cooling, and the sun we long for when suffering a fearful and wakeful night will not fail to rise come morning. A drop of water thawed from a frozen lake will be lifted up as mist, transformed to cloud, and then fall down again as rain. Even as the particulars of nature's cycles shift under environmental stress, the largest daily and seasonal cycles will continue as long as the earth revolves around the sun. From nature we learn to trust change itself and time's unfolding, not passively but participating in its continuous emergence. It teaches us to trust motion itself, letting ourselves move with it and often in shifting directions.

Movement across a threshold rarely follows a straight line from start to finish, which can be more hopeful than it sounds. You might think it would be easier if the crossing were a one-time unidirectional passage connecting a definitive beginning and ending, like a bridge to be forgotten or even burned as soon as our feet touch ground on the other side. But most thresholds are neither that succinct nor that concrete. They might have begun long before we noticed and will probably extend well after we stop thinking about them. They are connective, not just between here and there, and then and now and yet to come, but also between this and that, and you and me, and one and all. Thresholds are abundantly relational, expansive, and multidimensional, which is why they offer so many opportunities to change our lives and the world we live in, and not just in relation to the specifics of our threshold.

Chinese teachings name five elements or moving forces—fire, water, wood, metal, and earth—that are *mutually arising,* interconnected by a continual relationship of cause and effect that is not just sequential but simultaneous. Each element feeds or supports one other element: Wood feeds Fire; Fire (as ash) creates Earth; Earth produces Metal; Metal holds Water; and Water makes Wood grow. Each element is also restrained by a different element: Fire melts Metal; Metal cuts Wood; Wood (as roots) breaks up Earth; Earth absorbs Water; Water douses Fire. Trying to permanently hold on to any single element is futile and against the laws of nature, which are continually interactive. Participating in the flow of energy and influences between elements allows us, instead, to tap into the dynamic power of relational transformation. Imagine it as a rushing river flowing around rocks and logs and banks. Just as an experienced kayaker learns to read, navigate, and work with the swells and currents of a whitewater river, with practice, thresholders can enter the flow of change and experience a rich, adventuresome, and fruitful ride. When a church member once asked me how I was managing a period of great change in our congregation, I replied that it was going to be a wild ride. To which he replied, with a wide grin, "Without a wild ride, how would we ever get to 'wheeeeee!'?"

As a child, I had a hard time learning to ride a bicycle. The training wheels helped while they were low to the ground and kept my bicycle evenly balanced. But when my father raised them up, a little at a time, I kept relying on them. I pedaled along, eventually at a ridiculous angle, one training wheel groaning beneath my weight while the other spun uselessly in the air, and me viewing the world at a slant that was far from poetic. I was nowhere close to learning how to ride with just two wheels on the ground.

Then our neighbor Nancy took both training wheels off and told me riding a bike was all about trusting the motion. Balance comes from movement, she said, explaining that I just hadn't gotten enough speed to feel it. Her theory was that I needed a slow-motion way to trust the movement itself. She taught me to wobble. To jiggle my handlebars, back and forth and back and forth, making just enough motion to stay upright even at the slowest pace. Under her instruction, I wiggled and wobbled, gradually pedaling faster as I did, until my forward momentum finally took over, showing me that motion itself really can be trusted.

With all the metaphorical wobbling we can experience on the threshold, can we learn to trust it as a new experience of balance? Might wobbling be a slow-motion way to experience a new mode of moving into and through our times of change?

Chrysalis Space

What is wobbling on your threshold and how might you learn to make use of that movement? Are you able to wobble metaphorically until your forward momentum picks up? What small experiments in trusting movement and change might you try?

Think of a time, on this threshold or any other, when you have wobbled a bit while growing into new skills or abilities that later became easier. Maybe it was a time when you broke your silence and spoke up in a trembling voice for yourself or others, in a small or large way. Maybe you were experimenting with new skills you needed—recovering your mobility after a fall, trusting a new relationship after losing an old one, navigating a new city after a move, or socializing after becoming sober. Choose one time when you wobbled your way into a new capability. Take yourself back to that experience. How did you muster the courage to wobble, and what did it feel like when you did?

Take a few deep breaths, sitting with that experience of wobbling. Then recall a time when you did that same thing without wobbling. Notice what it felt like to trust yourself when doing it. Or imagine what it might feel like when you do it in the future. Take a few more breaths, staying with that experience of trust. How might you pocket that confidence and draw from it, as you wobble on your threshold today?

Correlating and Connecting

Learning to trust a life in motion raises the question of how we know where we are and where we are headed. Even if you aren't fully in control of where you are going, as we usually are not on the threshold, you will still need trustworthy tools to know where you are at any given time.

The migrating monarch gives us a good example. Every autumn, the monarchs in the northern and northeastern United States head off to a destination thousands of miles away they have never before visited. They are at least two or three generations removed from their predecessors that left Mexico flying north almost a half year earlier. How do they know where to go? What guides them to the same trees on the same mountaintops in Mexico where their great-grandparents wintered the year before and earlier generations before that? No one has yet discovered how the destination is mapped in the monarchs' DNA. But we do know the butterflies follow that inner map by correlating the angle and movement of the sun with their own circadian clock. Their compound eyes see ultraviolet and polarized light waves, and fine hairs on their head measure the wind. All of this information feeds into a positioning system in motion, constantly recalculating with every wing beat and gust of wind to deliver the monarch to just the right spot in Mexico where it can weather the winter with a million other monarchs who have arrived there using the same navigational system.

We humans, of course, have a plethora of navigational tools at our disposal, but we also have the ability to doubt and dispute them. Our inquiring minds—and the steady stream of sometimes conflicting information they collect—can make it hard to know which directions to follow. Especially on the threshold, when so much is in flux, we might not even know which way is up and which way is down.

In the 1920s and 1930s, the photographer Alfred Stieglitz took over 200 photos of clouds and presented them in a series he called "Equivalents." Most of the clouds were framed by nothing but sky and some offered no orientation of up or down. Without any context, their meaning could not be pinned down. Viewers were invited to interpret them according to the emotions they experienced when looking at the photographs, matching each image with an inner emotional equivalent. A century later, we may be more accustomed to this kind of invitation from abstract artists, but Stieglitz was one of the first to explicitly issue it, and his "Equivalents" series was clear about naming the relationship between our inner and outer landscapes—another reminder to pay attention to our dreams. Learning to correlate the information we get from both is key to centering ourselves, knowing where we are, and knowing where to place our faith on the threshold.

"Faith is the most centered act of the human mind," said twentieth-century theologian Paul Tillich in *Dynamics of Faith*. To be sure that what we have faith in is worthy of our trust, he said, we might ask ourselves whether it leads to a loss of our center, or if it grounds us more deeply in a context growing ever larger.

Chrysalis Space

How do your inner ways of knowing respond to the images and information from the outside world trying to guide you on your threshold? Do your dreams, intuitions, and gut feelings align with outside advice and guidance? Do they resist or rebel? Try to answer without judgement. Are you giving them an equal say? How might you correlate these inner and outer sources of guidance to discover a larger way of knowing, a more trustworthy context for your faith? Do they lead to the greater well-being of yourself and others in a circle growing ever larger?

Think of some advice, instruction, or information you've received from an outside source related to your threshold—something you either relate to or resist. Write it down in a sentence or two, as if spoken by another person as the start of a conversation. Then give your inner voice a chance to respond, speaking from a particular part of your body that is making itself known (maybe the knot in your stomach, the lump in your throat, the pain in your neck, the song in your heart, or the bounce in your step). Write a dialogue between these two voices, inner and outer. What do you learn?

ON A WIDER HORIZON:
Living into a Larger Body

As humans, our natural response to what we fear is to think small. When threatened or frightened, our brains will consider fewer options. Our muscles tense up, our blood flow is reduced, our vision narrows. This funnels and focuses our energy and actions on what is most critical for our survival. But what if our collective survival ultimately depends on a wider view, a greater flow and shared thinking that includes many options?

For many species, survival is only possible with collective action and relationship within and beyond the species. From the wolf pack to the beehive, from the tree grove to the ant colony, from the buffalo herd to the whale pod, and for humans too, collaboration is the only way to stay alive and thrive.

In the heart of the Chocoyero Canyon, a short distance from Managua, a flock of over 700 pacific parakeets nests in a sheer face of hardened lava rising some 300 feet from the canyon floor. I once hiked in with a few fellow travelers late in the afternoon to see the flock returning, as they do each day, before dusk. To one side, a ribbon of water laced through a crack, creating a long and narrow waterfall. The rest of the wall was pocked with hundreds of holes apparently perfect for a roosting parakeet.

As the sun set that day, we watched the parakeets appear in a cloud of green cresting over the lip of the canyon, swooping down and gracefully turning, folding back over itself like a viridescent sheet flapping in the breeze. Some birds, already settled in the wall, poked their heads from their nesting holes; others moved in and out of the undulating cloud overhead. With binoculars, we could see the birds' rounded yellow beaks and white-rimmed eyes, their tails pointed straight back, and the subtle outlines of their deep-green wings. But the real sight was not in the particulars. It was the emerald wave moving across the sky and through the canyon, beautifully synchronized, a wash of color in a class all its own. A rare shade and patina, it was a green I had only known previously by that single day each spring when the velvety blush of new growth appears across the treetops. There it was in the Chocoyero Canyon, a flock of new leaves in flight.

Hypnotized by the birds, we watched them settle into the wall like buds retreating back into their branches. I felt my body settling with the birds, until a sudden shrill shriek sounded across the canyon in a cacophony of panic. A single black vulture appeared over the top of the waterfall, and instantly, a green veil of parakeets peeled away from the cliff face in a chaos of wings miraculously marshalled. In the diminishing daylight, the flock rose from the canyon in a thick and shadowy cloud of fear and then, on some invisible cue, abruptly dispersed as if propelled by an explosion, birds scattered like buckshot in every direction across the darkening sky. It was a strategy of confusion that left the vulture behind, a circling silhouette without a single catch. Only when the vulture left did the parakeets come back together, forming their flock again before settling back into their nests.

As any skein of swans or murmuration of starlings reminds us, survival is often a shared effort. Each bird in a flock is in constant communication with up to six birds around it, and each of those with another six around them. In overlapping circles of seven, they build a larger body of movement and awareness that keeps them awake and alive.

At our best, we humans do this too. With the connectivity of the internet and the collective imagination of online communities and those formed face-to-face, the fruits and power of collaboration are being acclaimed and recovered by a growing number of thresholders. They are also supporting a host of social movements emerging on our shared thresholds and powerfully participating in shaping our shared future. The Occupy movement, Black Lives Matter, MeToo, Indivisible, the Poor People's Campaign, and Moral Mondays are just a few recent collectives known by their hashtags as well as their dramatic impact on events still unfolding as I write and joined by new ones as you read this.

Whether you call it hive mind or collaborative ideation or simply brainstorming with others, you have probably at some point experienced the joy of collective creativity in contexts that might be personal, professional, or political, or all three together. Ideas bounce from one person to the next, gaining momentum with a generative abundance. On our multiple global thresholds, our ability to create, encourage, and participate in this collaboration will be absolutely necessary in bringing about a future that is different—more equitable, sustainable, and peaceable—than what we have known before. It might seem we are a long way away from that. But like a tree that produces more seeds in the year following a drought, or the imaginal cells that multiply in the chrysalis faster than the caterpillar's immune system can attack them, threshold living often produces an extraordinary abundance of possibilities if we are willing to trust the wider view and expanded kinship that creates and reveals them.

Writer and organizer adrienne maree brown notices this abundance in nature—and our frequent hesitation to join it. "We live in a system that thrives when conditions are abundant and diverse, in a universe that holds contradictions and multitudes," she writes, "and we often reject that chaotic fertile reality too soon as if we can't tolerate the scale of our own collective brilliance." If we can let ourselves join the chaos and participate in it, we might begin to discover bold new ways of living and being on the far side of our thresholds. On a personal threshold of a lost loved one or lost independence, this might mean the discovery of a trustworthy web of relationships that will support and nurture us in the future. On a shared threshold related to ending racism, sexism, or classism, it might be a vision or brief experience of the Beloved Community—the aspirational society Martin Luther King Jr. helped us imagine and work toward as one governed by love of humanity, where all are supported and protected and none are excluded or oppressed.

The late civil rights activist and congressman John Lewis recalled how his own experiences during the civil rights movement in the 1960s helped him gain the wider view and expanded faith that he needed to face the dangers and daunting challenges of his activism then and his decades of public service that followed. In an interview with Krista Tippett, he said:

> *If you visualize it, if you can even have faith that it's there, for you it is already there. . . . During the early days of the movement, I*

believed that the only true and real integration for that sense of the
Beloved Community existed within the movement itself. Because
in the final analysis, we did become a circle of trust, a band of
brothers and sisters. So it didn't matter whether we were black
or white. It didn't matter . . . whether you were a Northerner or
Southerner. We were one.

When have you cultivated, or perhaps been surprised by, an experience of oneness with others that crossed lines of difference, creating a wider circle of trust?

The migrating monarch is designed for collaboration, not just across multiple generations and its own transmogrifications but also with other monarchs and other species. For the millions of monarchs that winter in Mexico, their survival in the cool mountaintops is made possible by clustering together on the trees to share warmth as the temperatures drop. Then as they migrate north, fueling their travel with nectar, they move into service as pollinators, helping more than 200 types of flowers to propagate along the way. Everywhere you look, you find interdependence woven into nature's design. Why would we humans not participate too?

Throughout history, people have flocked together during times of crisis to support survival across differences in class, religion, race, gender, and even species. Author Rebecca Solnit has noted this with her research of major disasters that occurred in the last century, showing that when crisis hits, people work together for the common good. In her book *A Paradise Built in Hell*, she wrote:

Imagine a society where money plays little or no role, where people
rescue each other and then care for each other, where food is given
away, where life is mostly out of doors in public, where the old
divides between people seem to have fallen away, and the fate that

faces them, no matter how grim, is far less so for being shared, where much [that was] once considered impossible, both good and bad, is now possible or present, and where the moment is so pressing that old complaints and worries fall away, where people feel important, purposeful, at the center of the world.

This, she notes, was a common experience following the 1906 San Francisco earthquake. She has found similar behavior in other disasters as well, both natural and human-made—a pattern of people creating what could be called small paradises amid horrific chaos and loss. When the old order is disrupted by large-scale disaster, Solnit points out that people are free to respond from the heart, unbridled by the divisions and oppressive systems of the way things were. This widespread cooperation often does not last, she says, but still it matters. "Like a lightning flash, it illuminates ordinary life, and like lightning it sometimes shatters the old forms."

On the threshold that Covid-19 has placed us on, we have experienced the shattering of many old forms. Of particular challenge has been the requirement that we help one another by maintaining a safe distance and, often, by staying at home. Our very definitions of what constitutes assistance and collective action must be reimagined and rewritten as we mark off six feet between us or isolate at home. Within the first months of the pandemic, people began practicing this with and without technology. Some took on individual efforts such as sewing masks or shopping for loved ones and neighbors with compromised immune systems. Others formed new mutual aid efforts or adapted old ones to new needs, using technology to inventory and match needs and assets. In countless ways, personally and collectively, many soon began asking, can we make these efforts more than a brief flash of lightning? How might we build from them a different order in which needs and resources are more widely and equitably shared?

If we are prepared, individually and together, to make use of the times when old forms are shattered, perhaps we might create new forms that *are* lasting. Listening to ourselves and one another in the chaos of chrysalis space, will we let the DNA of our collaborative coding reshape and rearrange us? Our ability to grow into the larger body of community may allow us to emerge from our current crises better aligned with one another for the migrations needed for survival.

Chrysalis Space

What is a larger body of relationship and community in your life that has been newly illuminated on the pandemic threshold of this time? How might you grow and live into this larger body in the future, shattering old forms and arrangements? What new possibilities have been pollenated on this threshold, and how will you cultivate them? Is there a flock forming where you might experience the expanded, shared awareness that could both protect and guide you as you live with and through change?

Draw a simple curved v-line representing a bird in flight in the middle of your page and write your name or initials near it. Then draw six more birds around you and name them too, either as specific people or named by their particular roles supporting or engaging you in any global threshold. These might be people you know personally or others whose work or leadership on that global issue have inspired or informed your participation. They might already be in your circle of relationship, or they could be people you wish to include in that circle in the future. Draw more birds connected to your six birds and their circle of awareness, or others on the rim of your awareness. Think big: creatively and expansively. Include people from the past and future. Include people who might not be engaged in that particular global threshold but who support your engagement in any way. Keep drawing more, without naming them, until you have a small flock filling your page.

Sit back and look at the flock you have drawn for a while. Closing your eyes, imagine the sound of their wings around you. Imagine the beauty and grace of the movement you are part of, flying in their midst. What new possibilities might arise for you and others, supported by a flock like that?

THRESHOLDING TOGETHER

Below are several suggestions for sharing your final reflections on widening what we trust with a thresholding buddy or group. If you will be meeting one more time after this gathering, as recommended in the appendices, use the conversation starters below as usual and save the book's closing reflections on "Honoring the Journey" to read before your final meeting. If this meeting will be your last as a pair or a group, read through to the end of the book before you meet, including the next chapter on blessing and the epilogue. Let the monarchs' migration story told there reside in your thoughts and heart for a while. Then come back to this section and plan your final sharing with your thresholding buddy or group.

Whenever you have your last gathering to discuss this book, you might want to plan a special meal or treat to honor the work you have done. Included below are suggestions for conversation starters on widening what we trust, as well as a few other activities. You will probably think of others. If this will be your last time together, though, save plenty of time after your discussion for everyone to report back to the group on their threshold and then to bless each other, as described in the sample final meeting agenda in appendix B. I strongly encourage you not to skip this step of offering one another a blessing. It is a powerful closing and an important way to carry the fruits of your thresholding group forward as you continue crossing your thresholds.

With a thresholding buddy or group of thresholders, after each of you has read the reflections on widening what we trust, choose any of the following questions to start your conversation:

- If you were a tree, name one year in your life that stands out as a thin or fat ring and describe why it was a time of new growth or one of difficulty or drought.

- Describe an experience you have had making peace with yourself that might be described as kissing your inner frog. Is there another frog in your identity waiting to be kissed now?

- Talk about a time when you wobbled while growing into new skills or abilities that later became easier. How did you muster the courage to wobble, and what did it feel like when you did?

- Describe a piece of threshold advice you have received that struck you as either spot on or dead wrong. How did you know that? What did you do in response? Is it playing out to be an accurate assessment?

- Share your drawing of the flock you are flying in or name one or more of the people in that flock, especially anyone who surprised you when they showed up in your drawing. How might this flock help you to make lasting change out of the chaos of the pandemic or another shared threshold?

HONORING THE JOURNEY

"Everything flowers, from within, of self-blessing;" wrote the poet Galway Kinnell, "though sometimes it is necessary / to reteach a thing its loveliness."

Blessing, like thresholding, is a matter of relationship. If there is self-blessing that comes from our own flowering, much of it will depend on others—like the passing butterflies and bees—to pollinate its future. The blessings we receive from others are not a given but come by grace and attraction. They are the fruits of kinship and connection, awakening a larger wholeness experienced between us, one to another; within us, as we embrace our whole selves; and beyond us, as we find our belonging in the larger world and universe. These blessings can reteach us our loveliness, rejoin us to our true self, and restore us to our own power.

My friend Kay told me about a blessing she received as a child from her father. Having lost her vision in one eye as an infant, she learned at the age of ten that she would soon lose her sight in the other eye as well. It was frightening news delivered by her doctors on a September day, marking a threshold of immeasurable loss and sizable fear. Not two hours later, though, Kay recalls a gesture of blessing that helped her regain her balance and her confidence. She was sitting at the kitchen table, still reeling from the news, when her father handed her a basket of ripe pears. *Close your eyes,* he told her gently, *and pick the best one.* Reaching into the basket, eyes closed, she carefully felt them all and chose one, to hear her father's immediate delight. *That's right,* he exclaimed. *That's right. You're going to be all right.*

Blessings confer a promise of safe passage on the threshold, where risks and dangers, fears and worries are most plentiful. This is why many common thresholds are marked by ceremonies, rituals, pronouncements, and rites of passage, each conveying their blessing. More often than not, blessings move through the world in commonplace exchanges without fanfare or festivities. A few flowers picked from the garden and delivered to a neighbor in a vase. A few words spoken to a child after a fall and skinned knees. A requested pronoun used when being introduced by a friend. A basket of ripe pears tested and tasted on a day of hard news.

Thankfully, there is no end to the variety and form of blessings we can offer and receive. On any scale, from the grandest to the most minute, at the core of every blessing is the simple and sacred experience of being seen. Being acknowledged and accepted, honored and loved for who we really are.

In the group of thresholders I facilitate each year, the most moving activity comes at the end of our last meeting. After two months of sharing the struggles and triumphs of their thresholds, on that last day, one by one, they report back to the circle, often very candidly, describing where they are and how they are on their threshold. After we have heard a report from everyone, each participant in turn, with the others listening on, faces the person on their left, addresses them by name, and with a few short but heartfelt sentences, blesses the person on the particulars of their threshold. It is a powerful experience of being witnessed, accepted, and loved, right there in the gooey state of change. The acts of camouflage that typically conceal our vulnerability are compassionately broken open, and each blessing in its own words and way encourages the one receiving it to emerge in their own time and in their own new form.

The next day, in worship, the group gathers at the front of the sanctuary (or, during the pandemic, online), where they are again blessed, this time by the congregation. Without knowing the particulars of the changes underway for the thresholders standing before them, several hundred people rise to honor them—along with any others in the congregation on their own thresholds—speaking these words:

For all those pausing on a threshold, about to step into the
unknown, we are present with you.

Although we may not know the particulars of the threshold, which
is uniquely yours, we offer you:

our hands for steadiness on your path,
our compassionate ears to hear your hopes and fears,
and our open hearts to share the joys and sorrows of your passage,
spoken and unspoken.

As you move toward the uncertainty of all that is unfolding,
we remind you of the Love that holds you, certain and true.

May your heart remain open to grieve what you are leaving
and to receive the gifts that will come your way in this crossing.

May your own inner light guide you
and may you learn to trust it, even when it does not shine far
down the road.
If your light begins to flicker and fade, we will offer sparks to
re-ignite it.

May you be blessed by courage to keep moving into the life that
awaits you.
May you be blessed by compassion, especially for yourself.

May this passage bring you new discoveries and renewed faith
and offer you a gateway to ancient wisdom and healing wholeness.

May you always remember the pledge of this community,
extending hand and heart, open to you in all that is to come.

It is a charged moment, for those speaking the blessing and those receiving it. The room vibrates with the grief of letting go and the invitation to make ourselves available to something new, unknown and unnamed. Then the thresholders recess through the congregation, passing over a symbolic threshold and moving down the center aisle, through a sea of witnesses parted to make way for their safe passage. Alive with the energy of change and promise, each of us in the room is blessed by the assurance that we need not go alone.

I have marveled that the butterfly, that great exemplar of transformation and thresholder extraordinaire, emergences from the chrysalis to neither blessing nor applause. But I have also wondered, when I think about the monarch's migration in its miracle of multitudes and miles, whether it might actually be blessed in its southern arrival. Imagine the sound of a million wings, thin as a whisper, fluttering their muffled rhythm; and the sight of their descent in Mexico in late October, flashes of orange and black wafting over cemeteries where feasts and flowers are spread out on the graves for Días de los Muertos. For some of the people below keeping a joyful vigil, the monarchs appear as the winged souls of their departed loved ones floating overhead. So the monarchs are seen; and so, perhaps, they are blessed.

Every day we learn more about the invisible connections that stitch our world together. On the threshold, dwelling in the space between, we learn new ways of perceiving—seeing, listening, hearing, feeling—and knowing that together reveal a larger wholeness. We are blessed by the rhythms of relationship and belonging. We join in a song that began long before us and will continue long after we are gone.

Chrysalis Space

What words of blessing would you be grateful to receive while you are living on the threshold? What might "awaken future wholeness," as John O'Donohue says blessings do?

A blessing will not alter your circumstances, but it can foster a different approach to those circumstances. Ask yourself what words or wishes might describe the brave space you need to participate in the changes ahead instead of defending yourself against them. Consider writing your own blessing that will honor the vulnerability of your threshold and embrace you in a protective circle of love and care.

If you prefer to use a blessing already written, use the one in this reflection or a blessing from another source, but put it on paper in your own handwriting or record in your own voice. If you write your own blessing, it might begin with the words **"May you . . ."** or **"May I . . . ,"** depending on whatever seems right to you and addressing the specific hopes and concerns you have on your threshold. It doesn't need to be poetic, but try to make it concrete or embodied, expressing whatever you most need to receive as blessing.

Having created or chosen a blessing and written or recorded it, keep it somewhere you will run across it often. You might carry a copy of it with you, something you can pull out to read when you have time, or keep a recording of it on your phone to open whenever you want to. Memorize it so you can recite it whenever you want to, wherever you are. Add to it or revise it as time goes by, letting it be a blessing that travels with you across time.

EPILOGUE

Taking Wing

You know this story, learned it long ago, or maybe just read it at the beginning of this book. But listen as I tell it again, from the outside—here on these closing pages, launching their own beginning.

Every inside story is nested in another,
    and another,
        and another.

Each of us is cupped in the larger stories that hold and shape us, that allure and guide us, every seed and egg designed to open out and out.

In a multigenerational miracle, the migrating monarch is designed from the inside out to be a thresholder, genetically coded not only for metamorphosis from caterpillar to butterfly but also for migration across land and time. It takes two to three generations for the monarch to make the trip from Mexico each spring to the Great Lakes and northeastern North America, and one more generation to return south again at summer's end. Every fall, when the northern chrysalises break open, a "super generation" of monarchs emerges specially equipped for the long flight to Mexico within its own lifespan. Awakened by shortening daylight and allured by a mountainous pine forest it has never visited, this monarch will cross a threshold spanning thousands of miles that required several generations to travel in the opposite direction.

Imagine opening freshly formed wings new to flight and lifting off on a journey of a thousand miles without guidance of map or memory. With wings made by listening to the humming inside the chrysalis, the monarch now turns its senses outward. Correlating the position of the sun with its own circadian clock within, it begins the long journey south. Day after day, it rides the air currents, sometimes a mile above the land. Every night it settles down in another foreign place.

High in the mountaintops west of Mexico City, a dozen forests of ancient oyamel fir trees await the monarchs' arrival. Moving across the continent, the fluttering orange shards of sunlight funnel into waves all heading in a shared direction. The enchanted air blooms orange as if a sunset puzzle has been broken apart, its featherweight pieces thrown into the air. Wingbeat joining wingbeat, the gentle murmur of migration grows. A million wings are thrumming, throbbing like a muffled heartbeat collected across time. Loaning their visibility to ancestors of all kinds, the monarchs arrive in Mexico in time for the Days of the Dead. They dance and dart over the cemeteries, wordlessly announcing the return of departed souls.

Still, the journey is not yet finished. Guided by genetic mapping dormant for generations, the amber waves move on across the sky, finally landing in the mountainous forests, draping a many-winged persimmon garment over the towering pines. Soon each trunk and branch is newly clothed in a finely-fitted wing-scaled gown made of monarchs. For months, the butterflies will rest and recover there, sharing a waning warmth by clustering together in the winter sun.

What begins inside summons its complements outside as far and wide as the sky overhead. Each white egg on the underside of a milkweed leaf shines like a grounded star, sister to the ancient points of light hovering out of sight above the monarch's daytime winged migration.

What begins inside cannot be held there long. All life growing and outgrowing, leaving skins behind when they become too small, letting go and unfolding—like these four wings, freshly formed and emerging orange and black from a chrysalis cracked open.

What begins inside is beckoned outward and beyond, each winged flight pollinating a world in waiting.

Will you answer the call, let go of the old, unfold something new, cross over
 from the no longer
  to the not yet?

Here, now. Opening out and out.
 None of us alone, and the journey just begun.

What may look like a period is not a sentence that has ended
 but another possibility beginning,

Here,
 Now,
  Between,
   Again,
    Begin.

ACKNOWLEDGMENTS

This book has been long in the making. I am deeply grateful not only for those who were explicitly involved in reading and commenting on early drafts, but also the many more who cheered me on day after day, year after year, helping me to believe in the project anew after each barrier, setback, or diversion, of which there were many.

First and foremost, I thank my soulmate David who showed up for me through thick and thin and never once let on if ever he doubted I would finish or that it would be worth the effort when I did. If every writer had someone like David at their side, we would have more books in the world, especially the kind that take a long time to write.

In addition, I thank the corps of other treasured ones who similarly supported me on a less daily basis as conversation partners, readers, co-conspirators in mystery and confusion, and encouragers extraordinaire: Naomi Cohn, Callie Fuchs, Beth Gaede, Cat Hammond, Susan Huehn, Pam Kowal, Nicole LeCapitaine, Barb Lund, Kristin Maier, Dottie Mathews, Krista Scarvie, Lisa Schlingerman, Dean Seal, Anne Supplee, Kate Tucker, and Chris Kleisen Wehrman. And my three sisters, Sandy Hering, Susan Hering, and Nan Treul, who all my life have lent me confidence when mine is low.

Yet more thanks to friends and colleagues who, in conversation or in your reading of the manuscript, broadened my understandings or helped me recognize my stumblings in words or the limits of my point of view. The manuscript is far better for your patient teachings; any erroneous passages or understandings are only mine to own. Thank you to Ricky DeFoe, Eleazar Fernandez, Julica Hermann de la Fuente, Okogyeamon, Lucinda Pepper, and Ahmed Anzaldúa.

For expert editing, I especially thank Andrea Lee and Skinner House Books' Mary Benard and Larisa Hohenboken. In particular, this book would not be here now were it not for Mary Benard convincing me not to give up on it as the world's changes surpassed all my expectations and repeatedly brought new challenges.

I cannot forget the colleagues, members, and friends of Unity Church-Unitarian, where each year the thresholding groups were formed and blessed. As a community, you have incubated countless dreams and creative ventures over time. This book is but one of many fruits that emerge from the fertile ground provided there for planting and harvest. Which brings to mind my deep appreciation for other organizations that have supported my work on this book and beyond: Wisdom Ways Center for Spirituality, the Collegeville Institute, Write On! Door County, and the many congregations and organizations that have invited me to lead thresholding programs and conversations on living through change. Your response and engagement have kept me at this project long after I might otherwise have given up.

APPENDICES

FORMING A
THRESHOLDING GROUP

Sharing the Journey

The many unknowns present on the threshold mean we will do better with more eyes, ears, hands, hearts, and minds engaged with the questions we are living. It is not that anyone else has the answers you most need. But they may very well have questions that can guide you toward answers that you carry unseen inside you.

The book's structure is designed to encourage readers to work with the material both individually and together. The questions and embodied practices offered at the end of each reflection are meant to be used as writing prompts or meditations, in movement or stillness, in words or any other form of expression that helps you access your deepest truths. After spending time alone with these reflections, you will get more out of them by sharing with others, and you may want to enlist a thresholding buddy or group to do this work together. It can be both more enjoyable and more fruitful in the company of others. You might consider it a form of "imaginal clustering" in which you and others share the way that change is shaking your own life. As you do, you will discover harmonic notes and dissonant ones. Both will be helpful as you listen and feel your way toward a new arrangement of self and world.

Below are some practical tips for using this book with a group of companions.

Logistics

To facilitate sharing in pairs or groups, at the end of each chapter covering one of the ten thresholding skills, the "Thresholding Together" section offers specific questions and prompts for starting conversations with others. These conversations can take many forms:

- pairing up with a single thresholding buddy
- gathering a group of three to eight people committed to meeting periodically or regularly
- a hybrid model, with a core group of three to six people that, after the first meeting establishing a covenant and practices, will welcome a few guest participants to each future meeting. The guests are invited for their interest in the topic of that meeting and their willingness to engage the conversation and process with openness, compassion, and a commitment to the group's covenant. Key to this hybrid model is the commitment of the core group to their chosen practices and covenant, so that the trust they establish with each other will hold when extended to newcomers.

A thresholds group can be formed among friends and family, within a congregation, a neighborhood, or any affinity group. The size can range greatly, but remember that the higher the number involved, the less time each person will have to share. Also, as groups get larger, they will function better with one person serving as a facilitator (either the same person each time or assigned on a rotating basis).

As you form your group, consider how you want to use the material in the book. If your group makes a commitment to meet twelve times, for instance, whether weekly, biweekly, or monthly, the outline of sessions might follow the arc of the book something like this, with group members reading the corresponding portion of the book before each meeting:

Session 1: Introduction and Beginning Here, naming each person's threshold(s), and considering the threshold practice of listening

Session 2: Letting Go

Session 3: Grieving

Session 4: Practicing Equanimity

Session 5: Taking Part in Stillness

Session 6: Navigating the Unknown

Session 7: Preparing for the Journey

Session 8: Claiming Companions

Session 9: Moving On

Session 10: Imagining a Way

Session 11: Widening What We Trust

Session 12: Blessing the Journey

You can meet in person or online, in the same location each time or rotating several locations, with a meal to share or only food for thought. Choose the frequency of your meetings considering how much time you want to allow, not only for reading but for engaging the reflections in each section. You'll find your own way to do this. But as you do, I suggest a few considerations below that are worth taking seriously as you get started and continue.

Group Covenant

One of the first and most important acts in forming a thresholding group is to articulate the agreement you make with one another. What are you committing to one another, both in the frequency and focus of your gatherings and in how you will be with one another? Trust is all-important in shared thresholding because when the ground beneath your feet feels untrustworthy, you'll want to know what you can depend on when you are with your companions. A covenant is a basic tool for building and maintaining trust. It can be a living covenant, meant to be revisited and adapted as you go, but it should be explicit so that everyone knows what is expected of them and what they can expect of the others. After having agreed to a covenant as a group, it will be easier to hold one another accountable to the behavior and practices you value because you've made a shared and explicit commitment to do so.

I've used a few different covenants in form, but their substance is similar. I like this simple one based on the Four-Fold Way named by Angeles Arrien and adapted for this purpose. The four agreements named by Arrien, plus two more that I have added for thresholding groups, are:

- Show up.
- Pay attention.
- Tell the truth.
- Be open.
- Be kind.
- Honor confidentiality.

At the beginning of any new thresholding group, we revisit the covenant both to remind us of our commitment and to invite the possibility of revising it. It might need to grow as you do, either individually or as a group. In the first meeting, we take turns reading the covenant and the explanation of each part of it out loud together. After each part is read, we pause for comments and questions. In future meetings we might just read the quick version, or refer to it, unless there are newcomers, in which case we want to be clear and explicit about the covenant we are asking them to join.

Show up. Make a commitment to the group and keep it, as best you can. Make the gatherings a priority and attend with your whole self, vulnerable and open. There are lots of ways we have of showing up in body without bringing our hearts and minds along. This is a commitment to do what you can to be fully present. It is also a basic request for common courtesy. If you are unable to participate, let others know in advance. Also, regard one another as equals. When you are together, those who speak more frequently or easily may need to step back, while others may need to step up and speak more often. Honor the vulnerability—and strengths—present in each person and on every threshold.

Pay attention. Listen to others without judgment, assumptions, or a need to analyze or fix. Instead, cultivate curiosity. Offer observations and open-ended questions, without expecting answers. Pay attention to what others say and how they say it; also, notice what they do not say and what they share in gestures, posture, tone, emotions, and other expressions. (See the reflection on listening in the introduction for thoughts about how to listen.) As you learn to pay attention to one another, practice extending the same generosity when listening to your own heart's truths.

Tell the truth. Your truth. Use I statements, not assuming that others' experience or perceptions will be the same as yours and not speaking on behalf of others. Be honest with yourself and let that guide your honesty in what you share with others. If you are sharing an observation about another thresholder, be especially careful to own it as your perception and to let the other person determine what the meaning of your observation is. This doesn't mean sharing every truth of yours; see *Be kind*, below.

Be open. Don't be invested in particular outcomes, for yourself or others. Let go of the need to persuade, convince, or control. Let your thresholding group be chrysalis space where you and others will have room to change and grow.

Be kind. To others and yourself. Leave your judgments of others and your inner critic of yourself behind. Life on the threshold is hard and vulnerable. Treat yourself and others with the tender support you would offer a newborn. On the threshold, there is always a part of us that is just now being born.

Honor confidentiality. Let the stories shared in your gatherings rest with the group. If you need to share the truth contained in a story with someone outside of the group, do it without connection to the identity of the one who told it. Also, don't assume that the story shared in your group time is something the person will want to revisit with you when you next cross paths. Let them determine when and how they share the next chapter of their threshold with you.

First Meeting

Your first meeting will lay important groundwork for the gatherings to come. Take enough time to do it well. It will be helpful to ask people to read the book's introduction and the chapter titled "Beginning Here" before coming to the first meeting.

You might want to begin your first gathering with a meal as a way of building community, but only if you save time for what follows. If you eat first, I suggest ending the meal before you start the meeting to help everyone focus. Also, add breaks in your schedule, planned or added as needed, to stay in your bodies. Basic qigong and body mudras can be especially useful to metabolize any strong emotions that might surface.

Sample Agenda:
First Meeting

Opening reading: The poem "Here" in this book works well for this, or substitute one of your own choosing about living with change. Light a chalice or a candle to signify the beginning of your "time outside of time."

Introductions: Invite everyone's voice into the gathering by asking each person to share something brief and low risk. If the group doesn't know one another, have everyone start with their name and pronouns, then go on to name which weather pattern describes their inner state on that day: *stormy, drought, partly sunny, deep freeze, sweltering heat. . . .* Encourage just the sharing of the weather condition with no more than a single sentence of explanation.

Discussion of group meetings, frequency, location, duration, etc.: It helps to have some of this agreed upon before the first meeting, or at least proposed. This can also include naming any roles you might want for each meeting, such as facilitator, treat provider, clean up, timekeeper, etc. It should also include your agreement and expectations about how you will use the book's reflections and activities, and with what pacing. (Will each meeting focus on a new thresholding skill? If so, will everyone be expected to read and engage with the related reflections ahead of time? Or maybe you will use your time together to read one reflection out loud or do one of the activities or writing prompts together. The choices are yours, but you'll want to be clear with one another.)

Covenant: Bring a draft covenant for the group to read and adopt or adapt. Use the one included above or something similar of your own design. End by asking everyone's agreement before continuing.

Listening: Read the Brenda Ueland passage on listening included in the appendices. Talk about what kind of listening you will practice with one another.

Naming your thresholds: Take turns, with each person sharing their primary threshold briefly and without interruption. Five minutes is usually a good amount of time. If you have a large group, you may want to have a timekeeper to make sure you save enough time for all to speak. Describe the threshold(s) you are most personally impacted by now. Be specific. Be honest. As you describe your threshold, try to answer the following questions:

- Name something you are leaving behind and something (including the unknown) you are moving toward on this threshold.
- What is a question you are carrying with you regarding this threshold?
- What is a hope related to the threshold?
- What is a fear?
- Name any particular kinds of listening, support, or feedback you do or do not want from the group.

    Note: This sharing, while brief, can be emotional. Have tissues on hand. Honor any tears that might come. Remind one another that tears are often a sign that truth is being spoken or heard and that trust is forming.

    After each person speaks, take a few moments for everyone listening to write on a small piece of paper a brief open-ended question to be given to that person. Include your name on the paper and the name of the person it is for. The questions should not point toward any expected answer, nor anticipate a quick answer of any kind. Try for nonjudgmental questions the person might consider over time, possibly opening a different view of their threshold. Give the papers with the questions to the person they are intended for, but each person should wait to read them later.

Gratitudes and hopes: Go around the circle again, each person naming a gratitude and/or a hope for the group's future time together.

Optional closing reading and extinguishing candle or chalice: Before you part ways, make sure to name your next meeting date and time and what you will all read and do before then.

Future Meetings

For future meetings, it will be helpful to develop a rhythm for the group—but note that a recognizable rhythm does not have to be a rut. The sample agenda below is just a framework for what you might want to include. Be sure to break things up with movement, bio breaks, or stretching to help everyone stay present with the group and their own bodies. And as you get to know one another and your group process better, enjoy the rapport you have developed by trying something new. Get creative. Take a risk. Sing a song together or do some drumming. Dance to some music, do some yoga or qigong or an improv game. Have fun. Let the chrysalis space you have created together make way for something new.

Sample Agenda:
Regular Meetings

Opening reading: A passage from the book or a poem or passage of your own choosing about living with change, or the specific thresholding skill you are focusing on in the meeting. Light a chalice or a candle to signify the beginning of your "time outside of time."

Check-in or introductions: Invite everyone's voice into the gathering by asking each person to share something brief and low risk. If you have new participants, have everyone share their name and pronouns and then something simple describing their inner state as you begin, like *what color do you feel like today?* Or *what age are you inside today?* Encourage brief answers without lengthy added explanation.

Details about group meetings, frequency, location, duration, etc.: Have a quick check-in about the timing and location of the next meeting.

Covenant: Review the covenant you've agreed on—as a quick summary if no one is new, or by reading the explanations if you have first-time participants. Invite any suggested changes. End by asking everyone's agreement before continuing.

Entering the topic: Invite each person to read aloud a brief passage, a single sentence or no more than a paragraph, from the assigned reflections—something that was particularly meaningful to them. This can be done in the form of lectio divina, letting the passages be heard one after another without comment, or with brief exchanges about the meaning of those passages.

Thresholding Together: Use the questions provided in the "Thresholding" Together section as conversation starters. Choose one of the questions listed and invite anyone to comment or ask each person to choose whichever question they wish to speak to in their turn. As you do this, let each person speak without interruption. Then allow some time after they're done speaking for conversation or questions before moving on to the next person, remembering that the response to anyone's sharing is not about analyzing or fixing but rather about listening deeply enough to offer observations, clarifying questions, or sharing how their story affects you. If the group is large or imbalanced in how much time some members speak compared to others, you might want to divide the group time up evenly and name a timekeeper as a gentle way of encouraging equal sharing for everyone.

Gratitudes and hopes: Go around the circle, with each person naming a gratitude and/or a takeaway from the conversation.

Optional closing reading and extinguishing candle or chalice: Before you part ways, make sure to name your next meeting date and time and what you are all reading and doing before then.

Final Meeting

For your final meeting, consider honoring the work you have done as a group by having a special treat or a meal to celebrate. (If you share a whole meal, you might want to do that after the agenda below and your blessing of each other.) Follow the simplified agenda below to close by blessing one another on your thresholds. Try not to skip this powerful bridge into the "not yet."

Sample Agenda:
Final Meeting and Blessing

Opening reading: Read a passage or poem from the book or elsewhere about living with change. Light a chalice or a candle to signify the beginning of your "time outside of time."

Check-in or Introductions: Invite everyone's voice into the gathering by asking each person to share something brief and low-risk.

Covenant: If needed, review the covenant you've agreed on as a quick summary.

Revisiting your thresholds: Take turns, with each person sharing briefly and without interruption, where they are on the threshold(s) they named at the beginning of the group. Sometimes people will join a thresholding group naming one threshold and end it naming another they identified in the course of their time together. What has changed in your circumstances and your response to them? What have you learned?

As you update the group on your thresholding process, you might answer the following questions:

- Name something you have learned about your threshold or yourself since your group first met.
- What is something you might now understand or experience differently because of the thresholding work you have done, separately and together?
- What is a new question that has surfaced as you have done this thresholding work?

- Is there a commitment you want to make to yourself or to others as you continue your thresholding journey?

    As each person shares, listen especially attentively to the person on your left for any specifics you might include in a blessing you will give them in the closing activity that follows.

Blessing one another: Go around the circle again, in a clockwise direction, with each person offering a blessing to the person on their left as described below. After you've been blessed, turn to the person on your left and bless them in a similar fashion.

One at a time, turn to the person on your left, looking into their eyes while speaking their name with compassion. Say a simple blessing that honors the journey they've been on and the passage yet to be made, mentioning something you have heard them name as a part of their threshold experience. Or, if you want to use a simple blessing already written, say their name and the words below, modified as you like.

(Name of person),
May you find courage.
May your trust grow.
May you have all that you need to cross this threshold,
to remember your own wisdom, and
to find your way home.

Closing reading and extinguishing candle or chalice: You can end by reading together the group blessing in "Honoring the Journey," noting that you are all both offering and receiving this blessing as you do.

Your group might be done meeting, but your connection does not have to end. You may want to check in with one another by email or other means as your thresholding continues. Or you might even decide to keep meeting on your own chosen pacing in the future. Some groups have had annual check-ins to learn where each person's thresholding has taken them. This may be more desirable or important for some than for others, so it can be helpful to frame any continued connection as an option, not an expectation.

RESOURCES

Angeles Arrien. *The Four-Fold Way: Walking the Paths of the Warrior, Teacher, Healer and Visionary.* New York: HarperCollins, 1993.

William Bridges. *Transitions: Making Sense of Life's Changes.* Cambridge, MA: Da Capo Press, 2004.

adrienne maree brown. *Emergent Strategy: Shaping Change, Changing Worlds.* Chico, CA: AK Press, 2017.

Christine Caldwell. *Getting Our Bodies Back: Recovery, Healing, and Transformation through Body-Centered Psychotherapy.* Boston: Shambala, 1996.

Pema Chödrön. *Comfortable with Uncertainty: 108 Teachings on Cultivating Fearlessness and Compassion.* Boston: Shambhala, 2002.

Pema Chödrön. *When Things Fall Apart: Heart Advice for Difficult Times.* Boulder, CO: Shambhala, 1997.

Susan David. *Emotional Agility: Get Unstuck, Embrace Change, and Thrive in Work and Life.* New York: Random House, 2016.

Frans de Waal. *The Age of Empathy: Nature's Lessons for a Kinder Society.* New York: Harmony Books, 2009.

Clarissa Pinkola Estés. *Women Who Run with the Wolves: Myths and Stories of the Wild Woman Archetype.* New York: Ballentine Books, 1996.

Edwin H. Friedman. *What Are You Going to Do with Your Life?: Unpublished Writings and Diaries.* New York: Seabury Books, 2009.

Atul Gawande. *Being Mortal: Medicine and What Matters in the End.* New York: Henry Holt and Company, 2014.

Miriam Greenspan. *Healing Through the Dark Emotions: The Wisdom of Grief, Fear, and Despair.* Boston: Shambala, 2003.

Richard Strozzi Heckler. *The Anatomy of Change: A Way to Move Through Life's Transitions.* Berkeley, CA: North Atlantic Books, 1993.

Karen Hering. *Writing to Wake the Soul: Opening the Sacred Conversation Within.* New York: Atria Books/Beyond Words, 2013.

Sherre Hirsch. *Thresholds: How to Thrive Through Life's Transitions to Live Fearlessly and Regret-free.* New York: Harmony Books, 2015.

Jamie Holmes. *Nonsense: the Power of Not Knowing.* New York: Crown Publishers, 2015.

Chungliang Al Huang and Jerry Lynch. *Mentoring: the Tao of Giving and Receiving Wisdom.* New York: HarperCollins, 1995.

Elizabeth Lesser. *Broken Open: How Difficult Times Can Help Us Grow.* New York: Villard, 2005.

Resmaa Menakem. *My Grandmother's Hands: Racialized Trauma and the Pathway to Healing Our Hearts and Bodies.* Las Vegas: Central Recovery Press, 2017.

John O'Donohue. *To Bless the Space Between Us: A Book of Blessings.* New York: Doubleday, 2008.

Rebecca Solnit. *A Paradise Built in Hell: The Extraordinary Communities that Arise in Disaster.* New York: Penguin, 2009.

Rebecca Solnit. *Hope in the Dark: Untold Histories, Wild Possibilities.* Chicago: Haymarket Books, 2016.

Jeremy Taylor. *Dream Work: Techniques for Discovering the Creative Power in Dreams.* Ramsey, NJ: Paulist Press, 1983.

Jeremy Taylor. *The Living Labyrinth: Exploring Universal Themes in Myths, Dreams, and the Symbolism of Waking Life.* Mahwah, NJ: Paulist Press, 1998.

Victor Turner. *The Ritual Process: Structure and Anti-Structure.* Chicago: Aldine Publishing House, 1969.

Bessel Van der Kolk. *The Body Keeps the Score: Brain, Mind, and Body in the Healing of Trauma.* New York: Penguin, 2015.

Richard Wagamese. *One Native Life.* British Columbia, CA: Douglas and McIntyre, 2008.

Alan Watts. *Tao: The Watercourse Way.* New York: Pantheon Books, 1995.

Arthur Zajonc. *Meditation as Contemplative Inquiry: When Knowing Becomes Love.* Great Barrington, MA: Lindisfarne Books, 2009.

TRUSTING CHANGE

Finding Our Way Through Personal
and Global Transformation

Karen Hering

Skinner House Books
Boston

www.skinnerhouse.org

Printed in the United States

Cover design and illustrations by Alyssa Alarcón Santo
Text design by Tim Holtz
Author photo by Martha Tilton

print ISBN: 978-1-55896-884-4
eBook ISBN: 978-1-55896-885-1

6 5 4 3 2 1
26 25 24 23 22

Cataloging-in-Publication data on file with the Library of Congress

CONTENTS

For all of us sharing this chrysalis time